THE ROLE OF THE
FEDERAL GOVERNMENT
IN EDUCATION

THE ROLE OF THE
FEDERAL GOVERNMENT
IN EDUCATION

SIDNEY W. TIEDT
SAN JOSE STATE COLLEGE

BRIAR CLIFF COLLEGE
LIBRARY
SIOUX CITY, IOWA

NEW YORK
OXFORD UNIVERSITY PRESS
1966

LB
2825
.T54

Copyright © 1966 by Oxford University Press, Inc.
Library of Congress Catalogue Card Number: 66-14479

PRINTED IN THE UNITED STATES OF AMERICA

To Miles C. Romney, friend and adviser

73888

To the Reader:

The role of the federal government in education has long been discussed and studied. There has been, however, a lack of material focusing directly on this issue, material that provides an introduction to the problem as well as a résumé of the history of federal aid to education and the current arguments of both proponents and opponents of federal involvement in education.

Many articles have appeared in periodicals; statements have been published by interested groups; the *Congressional Record* for the past hundred years has carried accounts of the struggles related to federal aid to education. It has proved difficult and discouraging, however, for the student to assemble such scattered sources of information in his efforts to gain a clear picture of the complicated problem under study. There has been a need for the consolidation of the provocative, informative material required for an adequate presentation of the question.

This book has been written in an effort to gather in one volume a concise analysis of the historical background of the role of the federal government in education, representative arguments for and against the government's greater involvement in educational concerns, a presentation of the questions revolving around aid to private schools, and a discussion of the present and future aspects of this complex problem.

An analysis of federal aid to education is an imposing task, for it is necessary to search out government documents, original statements by individuals and organizations, and testimony before congressional committees. Such a task would have been impossible without the co-operation of the many individuals who supplied copies of documents and statements and who granted permission for the reprinting of their papers. I should particularly like to thank the following persons: Senator Wayne E. Morse of Oregon, Senator Thomas Kuchel of California, Representative Edith Green of Oregon, and John W. Barrett, Legislative Information Specialist, Division of Federal Relations of the National Education Association.

Special thanks go also to Iris Tiedt, my wife and co-worker, whose assistance and encouragement have been invaluable.

S. W. T.

February 1966
San Jose, California

TABLE OF CONTENTS

Nothing is more stirring than the recognition of great public purpose. Every great age is marked by innovation and daring—by the ability to meet unprecedented problems with intelligent solutions. In a time of turbulence and change, it is more true than ever that knowledge is power; for only by true understanding and steadfast judgment are we able to master the challenge of history.

JOHN FITZGERALD KENNEDY

THE ROLE OF THE
FEDERAL GOVERNMENT
IN EDUCATION

I

AN INTRODUCTION TO THE PROBLEM

> Schools reflect the society they serve.
> Many of the failures we ascribe to con-
> temporary education are in fact fail-
> ures of our society as a whole.
>
> HENRY S. COMMAGER

What is the problem that we are to examine? The problem, in its utter simplicity and vast complexity, is that of determining the role of the federal government in education. "To what degree should the federal government be involved in education?"—this is the question that has aroused controversy resulting in widespread debate.

As we begin the study of this problem we shall briefly examine the national significance of education, the dimensions of the present study, and the focus of this book.

The National Significance of Education

Few persons would deny the importance of education to our society, for it is clear that without a highly developed system of education the United States could never have assumed the position of world leadership which it presently holds. Leaders of our nation, representing national opinion, have repeatedly stressed the vital nature of education. Thomas Jefferson, one of the great spokesmen for education, stated: "The commonwealth requires the education of her people as the safeguard of order and liberty."

Perhaps the most ardent supporter of education for all the people in the United States was the late President John F. Kennedy, who stressed the necessity of developing education on a national scale. He challenged the American people thus: "Democracy demands more of us than any other system in education, character, self-restraint, self-discipline. How are we going to get the best education in the world?" In order to achieve the best possible education for all children, he further stated: "Our twin goals must be: A new standard of excellence in education—and the availability of such excellence to all who are willing and able to pursue it."

It is clearly the consensus that education is vitally significant to the American way of life, since it is essential for individual fulfillment, the good of society, and the defense of the nation.

The great significance of education is further illustrated by the amount of money spent on it in the United States each year, which is exceeded only by that spent on the military expenditures. Figure 1 (pp. 6–7) indicates the tremendous and continuous growth of education through the expenditures made annually, which have increased from virtually nothing to the almost incomprehensible sum of $32 billion spent on all levels of education in 1963. Steadily sweeping upward, these expenditures represented 5.5 per cent of the 1963 gross national product.

Figure 2 (pp. 8–9) analyzes the amounts spent on public school education at the elementary and secondary levels. A total of $19.5 billion was spent in 1963 compared to little more than $1 billion in 1920.* This phenomenal increase is reflected also in the amount spent per pupil in average daily attendance, which was only $64 in 1920, but $547 in 1963. During this same period, it is interesting to note that average daily attendance more than doubled.

To illustrate further the magnitude of the educational enterprise, we can note that more than 55 million Americans are students, teachers, or school administrators occupied full-time with the business of education. Figures reported by the U.S. Office of Education and the National Education Association indicate that in the year 1964–65 there existed a total of 128,290 institutions which were attended by 52.9 million students—35.4 million elementary, 12.7 million secondary, and 4.8 million in higher

---

* Figures for 1965 indicate that public elementary and secondary education expenditures are continuing to rise with a reported total of $22.5 billion.

education. A total of 2.2 million teachers worked in these institutions (65, p. 70).

There is little to indicate any tendency for the magnitude of education to decrease. The U.S. Office of Education released the following estimates for education in 1973–74 (73):

Fifty-four million students enrolled in public and private elementary and secondary schools in fall of 1973. This is 7.1 per cent more than in 1963.

Eight million students seeking degrees in colleges and universities, nearly double the 4.5 million enrolled in 1963.

About 2.2 million teachers in public and private elementary and secondary schools, an increase of 375,000.

A $9.7 billion increase in expenditures for elementary and secondary schools over the $23.3 billion spent in 1963–4.

A $7.2 billion rise in spending for colleges and universities above the $9.3 billion spent in 1963–4 . . .

With a predicted total of 62 million students in schools and colleges in 1973, there can be little doubt that any problem affecting education is of great national significance. Questions arise as we survey the impressive statistics before us. It is obvious that American schools are educating an imposing number of students each year; we are providing quantity education. These figures reveal nothing, however, of the quality of the education provided. What *kind* of education will these 62 million students receive? Are the teachers in our classrooms prepared to impart contemporary thinking, new concepts? Are they aware of research in education and of educational innovation?

And, furthermore, are we actually reaching all potential students? Are we educating all potential students to the the fullest extent of their abilities? Are we handling students who have special problems—the gifted, the creative, the culturally deprived, the dropout? Are we educating as efficiently and effectively as possible?

The problems of the educational establishment in twentieth-century America have been vastly multiplied by the large number of

EDUCATIONAL EXPENDITURES

Expenditures for education are estimated at $32.0 billion ($24.8 billion public and $7.2 billion private) for the school year ending in 1963. Between 1952 and 1962 educational expenditures increased by 160 per cent, and in the school year 1962 they comprised 5.5 per cent of gross national product.

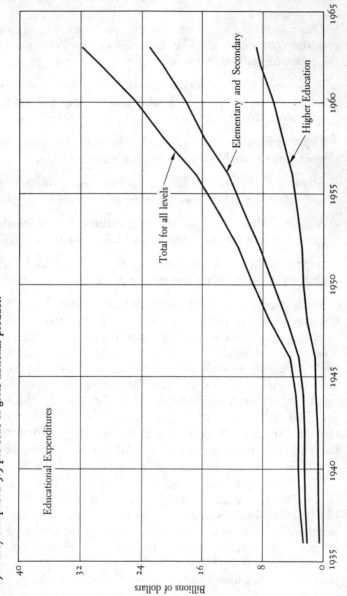

Educational Expenditures

Total for all levels

Elementary and Secondary

Higher Education

Billions of dollars

(Dollar amounts are in millions)

School year ending[1]	Total current expenditure, capital outlay, and interest									All educational expenditures as per cent of gross national product[6]
	All levels[2]			Elementary and Secondary[3]			Higher education[4]			
	Total	Public	Private	Total	Public	Private[5]	Total	Public	Private	
1920	—	1,156	—	—	1,040	—	267	116	151	—
1930	3,234	2,655	578	2,601	2,366	235	632	289	343	3.3
1932	3,057	2,474	583	2,423	2,192	231	635	282	352	4.5
1934	2,374	1,955	418	1,875	1,735	140	499	220	279	3.9
1936	2,746	2,271	475	2,157	1,986	171	589	285	304	3.5
1938	3,154	2,582	572	2,469	2,250	219	685	331	354	3.6
1940	3,352	2,756	597	2,594	2,364	230	758	392	367	3.5
1942	3,369	2,740	629	2,581	2,342	239	788	398	390	2.4
1944	3,742	2,974	768	2,741	2,474	267	1,002	500	501	1.8
1946	4,436	3,482	953	3,276	2,931	345	1,160	551	609	2.2
1948	7,066	5,476	1,590	4,876	4,341	535	2,190	1,135	1,055	2.9
1950	9,335	7,312	2,023	6,672	5,883	790	2,662	1,430	1,233	3.5
1952	11,312	8,967	2,345	8,438	7,402	1,036	2,874	1,565	1,309	3.3
1954	13,950	11,084	2,866	10,536	9,172	1,364	3,414	1,912	1,502	3.9
1956	16,812	13,352	3,459	12,632	11,005	1,627	4,180	2,348	1,832	4.1
1958	21,120	16,748	4,371	15,713	13,634	2,079	5,407	3,114	2,293	4.8
1960	24,722	19,447	5,275	18,106	15,694	2,412	6,616	3,753	2,864	5.0
1962(p)	29,430	22,870	6,560	21,200	18,220	2,980	8,230	4,650	3,580	5.5
1963(p)	31,980	24,760	7,220	22,960	19,660	3,300	9,020	5,100	3,920	

Source: U.S. Department of Health, Education, and Welfare; Office of Education; *Biennial Survey of Education in the United States*, Chapter 1, *Statistical Summary of Education*. National Education Association, Research Division; annual *Estimates of School Statistics*. 1/ Data include Alaska and Hawaii beginning with 1960. 2/ Includes capital outlay; excludes debt retirement. 3/ Includes Federal schools for Indians and on Federal installations; prior to 1956, also includes residential schools for exceptional children. 4/ Includes auxiliary enterprises and other noneducational expenditures as given in tables or footnotes of the Office of Education's *Biennial Survey of Education*. 5/ Estimated on basis of per-pupil expenditures in public elementary and secondary schools. 6/ Adjusted to a school-year basis by averaging data for two calendar years concerned [72 p. 60].

FIGURE 1

PUBLIC SCHOOL EXPENDITURES

Expenditures for public elementary and secondary day schools totaled an estimated $19.5 billion in the school year 1962–63. Current expenditures decreased from a high level of 93 per cent of total expenditures during World War II, when little construction of plan was being undertaken, to 75 per cent in 1954–55, but rose to 79 per cent by 1959–60 and remained at about that level through 1962–63. Some 35.7 million pupils are attending public schools daily at a current expenditure of $432 per pupil per year.

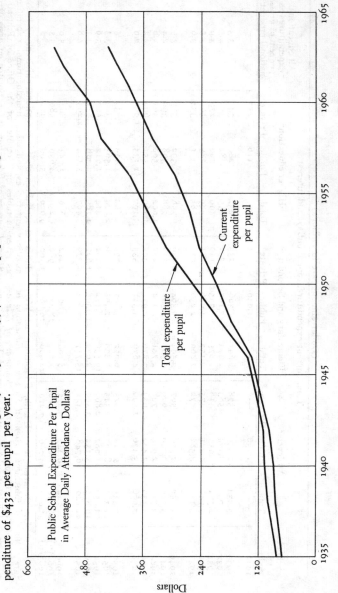

Public School Expenditure Per Pupil
in Average Daily Attendance Dollars

| School year ending[1] | Expenditures (millions of dollars) | | | | | Current expenditures for day schools as percent of total | Average daily attendance (millions) | Expenditure per pupil in average daily attendance[5] | |
| | Current[2] | | | Capital outlay[4] | Interest | | | Total (dollars) | Current (dollars) |
	Total	Day schools	Other[3]						
1920	1,036	861	3	154	18	83.1	16.2	64	54
1922	1,581	1,235	4	306	36	78.1	18.4	86	67
1924	1,821	1,369	5	388	59	75.2	19.1	95	72
1926	2,026	1,538	5	411	72	75.9	19.9	102	77
1928	2,184	1,706	4	383	92	78.1	20.6	106	83
1930	2,317	1,844	10	371	93	79.6	21.3	108	87
1932	2,175	1,810	13	211	140	83.2	22.2	97	81
1934	1,720	1,516	8	59	137	88.1	22.5	76	67
1936	1,969	1,657	8	171	133	84.2	22.3	88	74
1938	2,233	1,870	10	239	114	83.7	22.3	100	84
1940	2,344	1,942	13	258	131	82.8	22.0	106	88
1942	2,323	2,068	9	138	109	89.0	21.0	110	98
1944	2,453	2,293	9	54	97	93.5	19.6	125	117
1946	2,907	2,707	11	111	77	93.1	19.8	145	135
1948	4,311	3,795	28	412	76	88.0	20.9	203	179
1950	5,838	4,687	36	1,014	101	80.3	22.3	259	209
1952	7,344	5,722	30	1,477	114	77.9	23.3	313	244
1954	9,092	6,791	92	2,055	154	74.7	25.6	351	265
1956	10,955	8,251	101	2,387	216	75.3	27.7	388	294
1958	13,569	10,252	123	2,853	342	75.6	29.7	449	341
1960	15,613	12,329	133	2,662	490	79.0	32.5	472	375
1961(p)	17,029	13,147	272	3,106	503	77.2	33.4	501	393
1962(p)	18,223	14,338	351	2,958	576	78.7	34.5	528	415
1963(p)	19,544	15,454	379	3,083	627	79.1	35.7	547	432

Source: U.S. Department of Health, Education, and Welfare. Office of Education; Biennial Survey of Education in the United States, Chapter 2, Statistics of State School Systems: Organization, Staff, Pupils, and Finances. National Education Association, Research Division; annual Estimates of School Statistics. 1/ Data include Alaska and Hawaii beginning with 1960. 2/ Community services were shifted from "current expenditures" to "other expenditures" beginning with the school year 1953-54. 3/ Includes summer schools, adult education, and community colleges operated by local school districts. 4/ For land, construction, and equipment. 5/ For day schools only. Beginning with the school year 1945-46, excludes current expenditures not allocable to pupil costs [72, p. 65].

FIGURE 2

students and the complexity of contemporary education. It was inevitable that these problems would become a national concern. It is this concern which has repeatedly brought the federal government into the educational scene, but action by the federal government has consistently led to questioning and debate. Is education rightly the province of the federal government?

Dimensions of the Study

What should be the role of the federal government in education? Should the federal government control education? Should segregated schools receive federal assistance? Should federal aid be given to private schools? Should the federal government aid all schools equally? Is federal aid to schools necessary or advisable? Is the federal government's involvement in education unconstitutional?

These questions give some idea of the host of problems involved in determining the role of the federal government in education. The study of the federal government's role in education has become, moreover, even more complex, for the problem encompasses many other issues and institutions which are also of great consequence in American society; viz., Segregation, Finance, Federal Control, States' Rights, and Defense—issues that touch the very heart of our existing order. The number of articles in newspapers and magazines and the number of books published dealing with the various aspects of federal aid to education clearly indicate the strong feeling aroused by the arguments both pro and con.

The problem of federal involvement in education is so vast that the present study will analyze the role of the federal government only as it pertains to education in public elementary and secondary schools. The importance of this segment of education was noted by Felix Frankfurter, a justice of the United States Supreme Court, who asserted: "The public school is at once the symbol of our democracy and the most pervasive means for promoting our common destiny."

Although many decisions and arguments are the same for any

level of education and laws granting aid to institutions of higher education affect elementary and secondary education both directly and indirectly, the problem of federal aid for higher education is not specifically treated in this study. Nor is the extremely complex problem of separation between Church and State presented except as it is directly relevant to the discussion of federal assistance to elementary and secondary schools (Chapter V).

This book presents a sound academic analysis of a vital contemporary problem. The study focuses on education, not in an abstract theoretical sense, but education as it functions in classrooms across the nation, as it directly affects American children and American society.

The Organization of This Book

As we focus attention on the varied aspects of the role of the federal government in education, we shall employ the following organization:

   History of Federal Aid to Education
   Arguments Advocating Federal Aid to Education
   Arguments Opposing Federal Aid to Education
   Federal Aid for Private and Parochial Schools
   The Kennedy-Johnson Administration
   Contemporary Developments

HISTORY OF FEDERAL AID TO EDUCATION

The history of federal involvement in education spans approximately 180 years. In Chapter II we shall first examine a chronological description of various programs and enactments that have directly involved the federal government in education, beginning with the Northwest Ordinances of 1785 and 1787 and concluding with the National Defense Education Act of 1958. This background information also includes an analysis of other attempts to enact general federal aid to public elementary and secondary schools, beginning with the Hoar Bill in the nineteenth century and continuing to the proposals by the Kennedy administration.

The historical analysis concludes with a discussion of the themes recurring through these years—1785–1960.

ARGUMENTS ADVOCATING FEDERAL AID TO EDUCATION

Chapter III first offers a summary of the basic arguments of those favoring a greater degree of federal involvement in education. Following this summary is a presentation of the specific viewpoints of representative groups which advocate federal aid to education.

ARGUMENTS OPPOSING FEDERAL AID TO EDUCATION

Chapter IV presents the points made by those who object to federal aid to education. It includes papers indicating the positions of individuals and groups opposed to the government's greater involvement in this field.

FEDERAL AID FOR PRIVATE AND PAROCHIAL SCHOOLS

A separate chapter has been devoted to the controversial question of aid for private and parochial schools. Chapter V presents an analysis of the arguments of both its proponents and opponents, as well as pertinent Supreme Court decisions. Position papers are presented to illustrate the views of spokesmen on both sides of this complex issue.

THE KENNEDY-JOHNSON ADMINISTRATION

The Kennedy-Johnson administration's efforts to encourage the involvement of the federal government in education are analyzed in Chapter VI through a discussion of President Kennedy's first and second bills. An analysis of legislation that both directly and indirectly affects education is followed by representative statements by Presidents Kennedy and Johnson.

CONTEMPORARY DEVELOPMENTS

Chapter VII summarizes the activity of the federal government in education, and notes new approaches and attempts to solve the problem of federal involvement. President Johnson's statements and proposals are analyzed as indicators of future developments.

Never before has education loomed so important in the development of any nation. Record-breaking enrollments and expenditures cause the topic of education to be constantly newsworthy, for every family pays taxes to support schools, has someone attending school, or members who will be attending schools. The analysis of the role of the federal government in education is of concern to all. Let us begin our study of this problem by examining the historical precedents which have helped set the stage for present-day action.

II

THE HISTORY OF FEDERAL AID
TO EDUCATION

> Not to know what happened before
> one is born is always to be a child.
>
> CICERO

Education in this country, it is generally conceded, first developed in the Massachusetts Bay Colony as exemplified by the Massachusetts Bay Law of 1642 and the "Old Deluder Act" of 1647. These acts attempted through education, and more specifically through the reading of the Bible, to prevent the Old Deluder, Satan, from corrupting the minds and hearts of the good men of New England. These early laws required that communities establish common schools whenever it was warranted by the population:

It is therefore ordered that every township in this jurisdiction, after the Lord hath increased them to the number of fifty householders, shall then forthwith appoint one within their town to teach all such children as shall resort to them to write and read, whose wages shall be paid either by the parents or masters of such children, or by the inhabitants in general . . . [43, p. 208].

In this way the Massachusetts laws generated school development in the United States setting the precedent for education as a local responsibility. As one writer stated succinctly: "Education is a local responsibility, a state function, and a national concern." The extent of this concern and the direction it has taken are to be examined in this chapter, for with the growth of the nation and the development of the federal government, activities of the

14

national government inevitably have affected the nation's schools. The questions before us now are: "What has been the role of the federal government in education?" and "How has the federal government's role in education changed throughout the historical development of our schools?"

Organized chronologically, this brief review of the history of the federal government's involvement in education has been divided into three sections: (1) the Early Period (from the beginning of the country's history to the Civil War), (2) the Middle Period (from the Civil War to the Second World War), and (3) the Contemporary Period (from World War II to the Kennedy-Johnson administration in 1961).

The Early Period

The first suggestion regarding federal aid to education has been attributed to Colonel Timothy Pickering in 1783. Briefly stated, his proposal was that all surplus lands from the Ohio Territory should be the common property of the states and should be disposed of for the common good, that is, the laying out of roads, the construction of public buildings, and the establishment of public schools and academies. Although this suggestion was not enacted, it does indicate the thinking of this period, which resulted in the passage of the Northwest Ordinances.

THE ORDINANCES OF 1785 AND 1787

The first example of legislation specifically involving the national government in education is the Land Ordinance of 1785. The Continental Congress decided to sell the public lands in the Northwest and decreed that, preparatory to being sold, these lands were to be surveyed and divided into townships comprising 36 sections of 640 acres each. A section was the smallest unit that could be bought, and the price of one section of every township was to be used for maintaining public schools. This policy of governmental support for education was affirmed in 1787 with the passage of the Northwest Ordinance, which stated: "Religion, morality, and knowledge being necessary to good government and the happiness of mankind, schools and the means of education shall forever be encouraged."

The area provided in this ordinance was approximately the size of Texas and was of great assistance in helping to establish our public school system. There remains some question whether these grants were set up to dispose of public lands or whether their purpose was chiefly to aid schools. Daniel Webster, however, recognized the importance of the Northwest Ordinance when he stated:

I doubt whether any one single law, or any lawgiver, ancient or modern, has produced effects of more distinct, marked and lasting character than the Ordinance of 1787. It set forth and declared it to be a high and binding duty of government to support schools and the means of education.

THE UNITED STATES CONSTITUTION

The United States Constitution does not mention education either in its body or in any of the Amendments. There has been much scholarly discussion about this omission. Of the many reasons for the omission the most plausible appears to be that the writers of the Constitution could not foresee the complexity and immensity of the present system of education.

The Tenth Amendment, which reads, ". . . The powers not delegated to the United States by the Constitution, nor prohibited by it to the States, are reserved to the States respectively, or to the people," is usually cited as providing for a state or local system of education.

The General Welfare Clause of the Constitution, Article II, Section 8, reading as follows: "The Congress shall have Power to lay and collect Taxes, Duties, Imposts, and Excises, to pay the Debts and provide for the common Defense and general Welfare of the United States . . . ," is used by most authorities to justify the constitutionality of the federal aid programs.

The National Advisory Commission on Education, appointed by Herbert Hoover in 1931, reported finding fourteen warrants for federal activities in the field of education. Historically and legally there appears to be little validity in the argument that any involvement in education by the federal government is unconstitutional.

While education was not mentioned in the Constitution, interest in education was evinced by the founding fathers. Both Washington and Benjamin Rush advocated a national university to prepare young Americans for the duties of self-government. In his will Washington designated stock in the Potomac Navigation Company to be used in developing a university. (Unfortunately, the Potomac Navigation Company failed in 1828.)

Washington's Farewell Address, delivered on September 17, 1796, states clearly his concept of the connection between democracy and education:

Promote then as an object of primary importance institutions for the general diffusion of knowledge. In Proportion as the structure of a government gives force to public opinion it is essential that public opinion shall be enlightened.

ENABLING ACTS

Land grants were continued under the Statehood Acts, beginning with the Ohio Enabling Act of 1802 and continuing through the more recent statehood acts of Alaska and Hawaii. Thus Congress confirmed the validity of the Ordinances drawn up under the Continental Congress.

In later Statehood Acts the land grants became even more extensive, with some states receiving two sections and even four sections, as in the case of Utah and Arizona. A total acreage of 98½ million acres has been granted by the federal government to states for public schools. The largest grant of land was made in Alaska, with an estimated acreage of 21 million acres, approximately a fifth of the total acreage granted. The size of the land grant to Alaska may be accounted for by the size of the state and, too, its long status as a territory with the majority of the land being government owned.

The Middle Period

THE MORRILL ACT

The Middle Period is marked by the historic Morrill Act of 1862, which donated lands to the states and territories for the establishment of colleges. This act represents, according to Gordon Lee, the first attempt to establish through congressional action a national policy with regard to federal aid to education (39). Introduced first in 1857, and again in 1861, this act was finally passed by the 39th Congress in 1862. The differences between the first bill and the act as passed five years later consist of two points: (1) the original bill specified 20,000 acres per senator and representative in each state, while the final act allotted 30,000 acres per congressman, and (2) the original bill contained no provision for military training which was added later.

Passed by Congress when first introduced, the bill was vetoed by James Buchanan who explained his decision thus:

1. The bill was unconstitutional.
2. It interfered with states' rights.
3. It aided just one aspect of education.
4. The bill was extravagant.

The arguments for the bill as stated more than a hundred years ago were: (1) the need for scientific, agricultural, and industrial training; (2) the fact that most existing colleges were primarily classical; (3) the regional inequalities in the ability to support education; and (4) the belief that too much of the public land was falling into private hands.

The colleges and universities established under the Morrill Act now include sixty-eight institutions whose combined enrollment represents 20 per cent of all undergraduates, while they constitute only 4 per cent of the total number of colleges and universities in the country. Including such outstanding names as Massachusetts Institute of Technology, Ohio State University, and the University of California, these institutions grant close to 40 per cent of the doctoral degrees awarded in all fields of study (8). It is difficult to overemphasize the significance of the Morrill Act of 1862, which not only determined policy with respect to the federal government's role in education but also granted aid for specific educational purposes.

THE UNITED STATES OFFICE OF EDUCATION

The post-Civil War period saw President Andrew Johnson establishing a Department of Education in March of 1867, with Henry Barnard as its first commissioner. In 1869, Congress reduced the Department to a Bureau of the Department of the Interior. Later in 1930, it was shifted to the Federal Security Agency, and finally, in 1953, to the Department of Health, Education, and Welfare. It remains in the latter Department under the commissionership of Harold Howe.

The purposes in establishing a federal Office of Education included the collection and diffusion of information about education and the encouragement of education. These purposes were to be effected through the collection and publishing of educational data, through educational research, and through the administration of funds and various programs. The budget for the Office of Education for the fiscal year 1961–62, including salaries and expenses, was $11.5 million.

THE HOAR BILL

In 1870, George F. Hoar, Republican representative from Massachusetts, introduced the first postwar bill involving general aid to common schools. The purpose of this bill was to compel the establishment of a system of education throughout the country. Where this system was not provided by the state, the president was to be given the power to appoint a state superintendent of schools. The Secretary of the Interior was to be given the power to appoint all district superintendents. This bill also empowered the federal government to control school texts.

In defense of his bill Representative Hoar cited the then current census figures, which showed that of the people growing up in the South only one-fourth were being taught to read and write. The

Hoar Bill is one of the most far-reaching and restrictive bills in the history of educational legislation. In discussing this bill one must remain cognizant of the spirit of the times, for it was proposed during the Reconstruction Period when many northern congressmen were greatly concerned with the South, particularly with the education of Southerners.

The Hoar Bill represents the only attempt ever made by the federal government to legislate direct control over local systems of education. The bill never came to a vote, but it did serve to focus attention on the question of federal aid to common schools, and thus stands as a landmark in the study of the problem of federal aid to education.

THE PERCE BILL

In January, 1872, Legrand W. Perce, representative from Mississippi, introduced a bill "To establish an educational fund . . . The net proceeds of public lands are hereby forever consecrated and set apart for the education of the people."

The provisions of this bill were that the districts would receive money on the basis of population. This was later changed to read, "their school population from age four to twenty-one." To determine the question of need an amendment was added that would establish need by the illiteracy factor; that is, the greater the number of illiterates the greater the need. This bill was the last bill attempting to grant general aid to education to be considered by the House of Representatives for the next half-century.

THE BURNSIDE BILL

In March, 1879, Ambrose Burnside, Republican senator from Rhode Island, presented a bill which, like the Perce Bill, would have endowed schools with money received from land sales. Burnside's bill was similar to that introduced by Perce with the exception that only interest on the money from land sales was to be used for educational purposes, and not the principal. It proposed to use the money from land sales and the extra revenues from the Patent Office to buy United States bonds, thus providing a permanent educational fund. The Burnside Bill was not approved.

THE BLAIR BILL

First presented to the Senate by Henry W. Blair of New Hampshire, the purpose of the Blair Bill was, in the words of its author, "to aid in the establishment and temporary support of common schools." The bill passed the Senate three times in 1884, 1886, and 1888, but it was never approved by the House.

The main provisions of the Blair Bill included: (1) a system of direct financial aid to schools, increasing for a period of three years and then diminishing; (2) distribution of money based on rates of illiteracy of individuals over ten years of age; (3) appropriations governed by the matching of funds raised by local districts; (4) grants administered by state and local officials; and (5) aid for public common schools only.

The arguments, both pro and con, concerning the Blair Bill are of particular interest to us today because of their contemporary ring. Seven arguments or points were made in opposition to the passage of this bill:

1. The bill was unconstitutional.
2. It would be the first step toward complete national control of education.
3. Money from the federal government would serve to destroy a sense of self-reliance and would hinder the progress of popular education.
4. It is indefensible to legislate federal grants to states which don't need them.
5. Federal spending would result in vast wastes of public money, and politics would seep into the public schools.
6. There was no evidence of general support for the bill.
7. The bill would discourage local endeavor.

The proponents of the Blair Bill argued, on the other hand:

1. Universal, equalized education is essential to ensure free institutions.

2. The federal government is obligated to ensure to all children at least an elementary education.
3. It is constitutional because we have had other bills which have aided education.
4. Despite heroic efforts on the part of the South, it is impossible for the South to furnish means of education to its people.
5. The present economic conditions of the country demand that money be returned to circulation.
6. Aid would stimulate local effort, not reduce it.
7. Without national governmental participation too much control is left to other local agencies both public and private.

THE HATCH ACT AND THE SECOND MORRILL ACT

In 1887, the Hatch Act added agricultural experimental stations to the land-grant colleges which resulted in the encouragement of scientific investigation in the field of agriculture.

The second Morrill Act of 1890 introduced the principle of federal grants for instruction in certain branches of higher education. These permanent annual endowments set the stage for great expansion of agricultural and mechanical schools. The endowments of $15,000 per year were raised $1000 annually until the amount received reached $25,000 for each state. In 1908 the limit was further increased to $50,000.

THE SMITH-LEVER ACT

In 1914, Congress created the Agricultural Extension Service through the Smith-Lever Act, which was set up to "aid in diffusing among the people of the United States useful and practical information on subjects pertaining to agriculture and home economics."

The original act authorized $4,580,000 per year to be distributed on the basis of agricultural population; i.e., $10,000 to each state on a matching basis and $600,000 on the basis of rural population. Thus, for the first time an element of control was added. Standards and programs were outlined by the Department of Agriculture. Later enactments have increased this sum to an excess of $50 million per year.

THE SMITH-HUGHES ACT

The purpose of the Smith-Hughes Act was to foster vocational education and home economics training for high school students. This act stands as one of the first examples of federal aid provided to schools below the college level. It also involved the federal government in the payment of teacher salaries and included the principle of matching funds.

The original expenditure was $1.7 million in 1917, compared to the $7 million spent on vocational education through this act and others during the decade 1950–60. The Smith-Hughes Act also created the Federal Board of Vocational Education. Each state receiving monies was to submit its plan for vocational education to the Federal Board of Vocational Education for approval.

The money was allocated for the following uses:

1. To pay the salaries of teachers, supervisors, and directors of agricultural subjects.
2. To pay the salaries of teachers of trades, home economics, and industrial subjects.
3. To prepare teacher-trainees in these subject areas.
4. To study problems connected with the teaching of these areas.
5. To pay for the administration of the law.

SMITH-TOWNER BILL

The Smith-Towner Bill, first introduced in 1919, called for a department of education at the Cabinet level plus an appropriation of $100 million annually for teachers' salaries, for the teaching of illiterates, for the teaching of physical education, and for teacher training programs. These funds, too, were to be awarded on a matching basis. The Smith-Towner Bill was not enacted. It is interesting to speculate about what would have happened had the Department of Education been placed on the Cabinet level.

THE DEPRESSION DECADE

No general aid to education bills were enacted by Congress from 1930 to 1940. There were, however, several bills enacted which incidentally included educational undertakings. These depression bills, discontinued after World War II, represented noticeable departures from former federal policy toward education.

The Public Works Administration (PWA) was established in 1933 to aid in the construction of public works. This act of Congress also made grants and loans for school and college buildings.

The Civilian Conservation Corps (CCC) was set up in 1933 to provide employment and vocational training for older unemployed young men through development of natural resources.

The Works Progress Administration (WPA) distributed relief and supported a number of educational projects which gave employment to the unemployed.

The National Youth Administration (NYA) was the result of an executive order of Franklin D. Roosevelt in 1935. It gave relief and employment for young people from 16 to 25 years of age.

In February, 1934, Harry Hopkins, Federal Emergency Relief Administrator, quoted figures which revealed that 40,000 teachers were being paid from relief funds. He also estimated that from $2 million to $3 million was being spent each month for federal educational relief work. Congress allocated $48 million of relief money to employ unemployed teachers and authorized $75 million to pay overdue salaries of teachers. These loans did not include direct aid nor were school systems directly helped (46, p. 6).

The federal government's involvement in agricultural and industrial arts continued with the passage of the George-Dean Act in 1936. This act added other occupations to the list of trades and professions under the Smith-Hughes Act.

The Contemporary Period

THE LANHAM ACT

The Lanham Act, passed in 1941, was directed toward the alleviation of hardships in communities whose schools were expanding as a result of proximity to military establishments and war factories. The federal government thus accepted its responsibility for what, in many cases, amounted to disrupting community services almost overnight.

The Lanham Act also attempted to redress the imbalance in local communities resulting from the fact that the military installations did not appear on local tax rolls. Some communities were faced with suddenly increased school enrollment with no substantial increase in the local tax base. The Lanham Act helped to equalize this load with payments sometimes termed "in lieu of taxes." The act made funds available for school buildings, school services, and nursery schools for children of mothers who were involved in defense industries. The program initiated by the Lanham Act was further expanded in 1950 by the passage of the so-called Impact Laws (Public Law 815 and Public Law 874), which are discussed later.

THE SERVICE MAN'S READJUSTMENT ACT

The Service Man's Readjustment Act, commonly known as the GI Bill, was passed in 1944 to provide education and training for returning servicemen; that is, to assist these men and women in making a smoother transition to civilian life.

Approximately 7,800,000 veterans of World War II were sent to school under this act, which cost the government in the neighborhood of $14.5 billion. Public Law 550 extended the provisions of this bill, with some modifications to include 1.5 million veterans of the Korean War.

There were some inequities in the bill, and there were those, both veterans and institutions, who took advantage of the bill for personal gain, but it is generally agreed that the Service Man's Readjustment Act was a highly successful venture.

THE TAFT-THOMAS BILL

In 1943, Senator Robert A. Taft, an early opponent of federal aid to education, became convinced of the validity of the statistics presented by the proponents of federal aid. For this reason he joined forces with the National Education Association in proposing a bill which attempted to set up a national minimum foundation program, providing $300 million annually in aid to schools.

The Taft-Thomas Bill was approved by the Senate Education Committee in 1945. In 1948, under the 80th Congress, the bill was approved by the Senate, but it was never passed by the House.

THE IMPACT LAWS

In 1950, Congress enacted two laws—Public Law 815 for schoolhouse construction and Public Law 874, which provided funds to meet operating costs of school districts. They were essentially continuations of the Lanham Act of 1941, since the concept behind the three laws was roughly the same; namely, that the federal government had a responsibility to provide money for community services in lieu of taxes because federal property is not usually taxable on the local level. It was the Korean War which caused the increase in federal involvement with factories and military establishments, leading to undue pressure on communities in the vicinity of these installations and factories.

To illustrate the provisions of these laws let us examine the classification of students. All children attending schools are classified in three categories: (a) children who live on federal property and whose parents work on federal property; (b) children who either live on federal property or whose parents work on federal property; and (c) children whose parents have come into the district as a result of federal contracts with private firms. (These families do not live on federal property nor do the parents work on federal property.)

The Impact Laws, as they are commonly termed, are popular with school administrators because they serve to alleviate the financial difficulties of fast-growing districts and they are also free from any control or influence by the federal government. The laws are popular with Congress because of their geographic spread. Impact funds go to 316 of the 437 congressional districts. Twenty-five per cent of all students in public schools (elementary and secondary), or 7.5 million students, are covered by Public Laws 815 and 874 (77, p. 33).

Former Senator Barry Goldwater, who has opposed federal aid to education, stated: "The impacted areas bill purely and simply is an in lieu tax proposal." The Impact Laws, furthermore, are relatively inexpensive to operate and to administer. In the year 1953, for example, 0.9 per cent of the total grant was spent on administration. This compares favorably with the 2.4 per cent that was spent on the administration of highway grants (70, p. 171).

In the years since the passage of these laws there has been a continued increase of expenditures of funds under them. In 1950, for example, $52 million was appropriated. Eleven years later in 1961, expenditures had mounted to $312 million. Over a period of ten years $2,300,000,000 was spent on Public Laws 815 and 874 (68).

In spite of the general agreement about the validity of the Impact Laws, there are some admitted defects and inequities. Changes have been proposed, therefore, in recent years. The greatest inequities result, in part, from the fact that it is possible (in the case of category C) for school districts to receive government payments *in lieu of taxes* for property which is, in reality, on the local tax roll.

Public Law 874 exemplifies the first granting of federal funds to a school district for general operating costs. The funds issued under this law are not earmarked for any specific purpose or area of the curriculum. They may be spent for teacher salaries, or any of the operating costs incurred by a school district.

THE EISENHOWER ADMINISTRATION

The administration of Dwight D. Eisenhower began with his examination of two recommendations regarding education—the report from his Commission on Intergovernmental Relations and the recommendations of the White House Conference on Education. The majority of the bills recommended by President Eisenhower emphasized school construction. Reasons given for this emphasis include: (1) construction clearly limits the amount of money to be allocated, an important item to this administration in its attempt to balance the budget; and (2) there was less likelihood of federal control under provisions for construction.

Some pressure came for federal aid following the unexpected victory of the proponents of federal aid to education at the White House Conference. The conferees included in their recommendations general federal aid to elementary and secondary schools. President Eisenhower's proposals usually encompassed the buying of school bonds, both state and local, as well as some matching funds earmarked for federal aid.

An example of the kind of bill presented by this administration is the McConnell Bill (H.R. 3986), known as the School Construction Act of 1957. The specific purpose of the McConnell Bill was the financing of school buildings. The provisions included the spending of $325 million per year for four years, with the money distributed on the basis of a standard federal equalization formula.

THE KELLEY BILL

Augustine R. Kelley, representative from Pennsylvania, introduced his bill in 1955 as a compromise between the Eisenhower proposals and the proposals of the teachers' organizations. The bill was reported out of committee in 1955 and debated in 1956.

The bill ran into difficulty, however, on the floor of the House when the Powell Amendment, prohibiting all aid to segregated schools, was attached. Too, supporters of the Administration had already turned to another bill. On July 25, 1957, the Kelley Bill was defeated in the House of Representatives by five votes—208 to 203.

THE MURRAY-METCALF BILL

The Murray-Metcalf Bill was introduced in the first session of the 86th Congress (H.R. 22) with the backing of the National Education Association; the bill called for aid to teachers' salaries.

The McConnell Bill, presented by the Eisenhower administration, had proposed school construction. The Murray-Metcalf Bill functioned as a compromise bill and passed both the House and Senate. It "died," however, because the House Rules Committee failed to appoint a joint conference committee to work out differences between the House and Senate versions of the bill.

The Murray-Metcalf Bill, in its final form of 1959, was one of the most generous of all general federal aid proposals. It would have provided $25 per school-age child (five to seventeen), with the money to be used either for teachers' salaries or for buildings, depending on the need of the state. Money was to increase until it leveled off at $100 per child. It was estimated that this bill would have cost the federal government $1.1 billion during its first year of operation.

Explicit provisions were also made in the Murray-Metcalf Bill to prevent any control by the federal government. This bill was essentially simple, one of the least complicated bills proposing federal aid to education. The only complex feature was the requirement that states maintain their efforts, which were hard to measure. Any state whose *school effort index* fell below the national index would be deprived of some of the federal monies.

THE NATIONAL DEFENSE EDUCATION ACT

The National Defense Education Act came about in 1958, as a result of people's reactions to Soviet success in space (Sputnik) and scientific endeavor. This reaction caused some feeling of uneasiness about the adequacy of our educational system and resulted in the passage of an act which was meant to stimulate education in areas of science, foreign language, and mathematics.

The National Defense Education Act (NDEA) consists of ten parts, or titles, which indicate the provisions of this bill:

I. General provisions—purpose and definition.
II. Loans to students in institutions of higher education.
III. Financial assistance for strengthening science, mathematics, and modern foreign language instruction.
IV. National defense fellowships.
V. Guidance, counseling, and testing; identification and encouragement of able students; counseling and guidance training.
VI. Language development—centers for research and studies; language institutes.
VII. Research and experimentation in more effective utilization of television, radio, motion pictures, and related media for educational purposes.
VIII. Area vocational education programs.
IX. Science information service.
X. Improvement of statistical services of state educational agencies.

The October, 1963, issue of *School Life* summarized the achievements of the then five-year-old National Defense Education Act (75, p. 12). Some conception of the comprehensiveness of this act is given when it is pointed out that almost 500,000 students in 1500 colleges and universities borrowed approximately $330 million from the student loan fund.

Under Title V approximately $102 million in NDEA funds were spent during the same five-year period for guidance, counseling, and testing programs. These funds served to change the average counselor-student ratio from one counselor per 900 students to one counselor for each 540 students.

State educational agencies have approved more than 180,000 projects for local public schools, covering the purchase of equipment in science, mathematics, and foreign languages. The number of language laboratories, for example, has increased from 46 in 1938 to nearly 6,000 in 1963.

Under Title VIII approximately 30,500 technicians had completed training in vocational programs. It is interesting to note that states and communities overmatched federal funds by two to one in this area.

NDEA has touched nearly every level of public and private education. The major criticisms of this act rest on its emphasis on mathematics and science to the exclusion of the humanities and the fact that it aids both private and public institutions. Some persons comment, too, that this act has de-emphasized the need for general aid to elementary and secondary schools, thereby hurting the cause of federal aid to education. NDEA has been expanded to include other subject areas, as will be seen in later chapters.

Summary

This chapter has presented the historical background of the federal government's involvement in education. The material presented here has been selective, for there are many areas that have of necessity been omitted. The focus of this chapter has been on general aid to education.

This historical summary has presented the major bills enacted as well as the major bills proposed. Thus, we have the chronological treatment of both the successful bills and those that were never passed but did have great influence on subsequent legislation.

The federal aid story might be examined in terms of who gets what, when, and why? who, in this case, has included institutions of higher education, vocational and agricultural education, and, most recently, federally affected communities.

The what was originally the land grant, which later evolved into the matching of funds as land became more scarce. In general we note that specific grants have been favored by Congress. A recent example is the National Defense Education Act, which first focused on assistance to mathematics, science, and modern foreign languages.

when has usually occurred during a war or national emergency. The Morrill Act, for example, was enacted during the Civil War. The Smith-Hughes Act was passed during the First World War, the Lanham Act during World War II, and the Federal Impact Laws during the Korean War. Finally, the National Defense Education Act resulted from the Cold War.

WHY has federal aid been thought necessary? It has usually been the result of reaction to inadequacies in our educational system. These inadequacies have been pointed up, in many cases, by the draft rejection statistics. A theme that runs through many of the acts and bills, therefore, is that of wiping out illiteracy. Another theme is that of equality of opportunity in education. This problem has been examined in terms of broadening the curriculum through, for example, land-grant colleges, which provided vocational education, and in terms of equalizing educational opportunity on a geographic basis.

It should be noted further, that education has been used historically to solve many problems, but not until recently has education been considered a problem in itself. This point is brought out in the examination of the federal aid activities of the present and in an analysis of trends that will influence future legislation.

Selected Readings

Buehler, Ezra C. *Federal Aid for Education*. New York: Noble, 1934.

Cubberley, Ellwood P. *Public Education in the United States*. Boston: Houghton Mifflin, 1947.

Lee, Gordon C. *The Struggle for Federal Aid*. New York: Teachers College, Columbia University Bureau of Publications, 1949.

Mort, Paul R. *Federal Support for Public Education*. New York: Teachers College, Columbia University Bureau of Publications, 1936.

III

ARGUMENTS ADVOCATING FEDERAL AID
TO EDUCATION

> As I see the situation, national security
> and economic growth now change the
> need for a federal program in education
> from a desirable domestic goal to a
> deadly serious necessity.
>
> FRANCIS KEPPEL
> ASSISTANT SECRETARY FOR EDUCATION,
> DEPARTMENT OF HEALTH, EDUCATION,
> AND WELFARE

Chapter III presents the basic arguments made by those who favor greater federal involvement in education. In order to make these arguments as clear as possible, the first section of this chapter will analyze nine basic points argued by the proponents of federal aid to education. The second section includes representative statements of individuals and spokesmen for groups that advocate federal aid to education.

An Analysis of Arguments Favoring
Federal Aid to Education

Through examination of the positions taken by proponents of greater involvement of the federal government in education, we can observe several recurring points:

1. Equalization of educational opportunity.
2. Need for assistance.
3. National concern for education.
4. Broadening of the tax base.
5. Mobility of population.
6. National acceptance.

7. Historical background.
8. Local control.
9. Efficiency of federal taxes.

EQUALIZATION OF EDUCATIONAL OPPORTUNITY

Proponents of federal aid point out that grave conditions of inequality exist in our schools. Assistant Secretary for Education of the Department of Health, Education, and Welfare, Francis Keppel, for example, stated: "We must find ways to eliminate the inequality of educational opportunity. There are rural slums, backward areas, in which children don't have a fair chance to learn. There are growing, high-density areas where the schools don't keep up."

As an example of inequality of educational opportunity, writers point to school systems like that of New York, which in 1961–62 spent $778 per child each year on education, while the state of Mississippi spent only $288 per child per year (71, p. 69). Proponents of federal aid maintain that inequality in the amount spent per year is not due to any lack of willingness on the part of the respective states to spend the money; the inequality is due rather to a lack of fiscal ability. This lack of fiscal ability is clearly demonstrated by the application of the *Personal Income per Child Index*, on the basis of which the state of Mississippi was found, in 1959, to have approximately $4000 behind each child of school age, whereas the state of Connecticut had a personal income of approximately $13,000 per child. It is pointed out, furthermore, that in 1958 the number of school-age (5 to 17) children per 1000 adults was 612 in Mississippi, and 413 in Connecticut (53).

NEED FOR ASSISTANCE

At the present time, it is argued, there is a great need for increased educational facilities, equipment, and personnel to meet the needs of an overwhelming increase in school enrollment as more students attend school for a greater number of years. School population is increasing by approximately 3 million students each year; between

1946 and 1948, enrollment increased 50 per cent. At the turn of the century a mere 11 per cent of the potential high school population actually attended school, contrasted to 85 per cent in 1958.

The need for school buildings was made evident by a survey conducted in the spring of 1962 by the Office of Civil Defense, the U.S. Office of Education, the Bureau of the Census, and state departments of education. Covering 96 per cent of the elementary and secondary schools of the nation, this survey revealed a need for 375,477 new classrooms to replace those which were not fireproof, were only temporary, or were built before 1920.

It is pointed out, furthermore, that the supply of adequately prepared teachers is woefully insufficient, and one of the greatest problems in obtaining teachers lies in the inability to pay suitable salaries in many states. In 1961, Abraham Ribicoff, former Secretary of Health, Education, and Welfare, stated that the highest paid teacher in Mississippi was paid less than the lowest paid teacher in California. At that time 20 per cent of the teachers of the nation had no college degree.

NATIONAL CONCERN FOR EDUCATION

Another argument for increasing federal involvement in education is that our national welfare is directly related to our educational welfare. This point is illustrated in innumerable ways, the most publicized of which was Sputnik, which caused much consternation about the status of programs in mathematics and science. National concern led to the passage of the National Defense Education Act, passed in 1958 and extended in 1964; the title of the act indicates the nature of the concern. Many writers asserted that Khrushchev was the most influential man in American education at that time.

Advocates of federal aid also point to the concern for our national welfare on the domestic scene. Social problems—segregation in schools, automation, poverty, and so on—are named as reasons for greater federal involvement in education. Education is too complex, they contend, to remain a state or local responsibility.

BROADENING OF THE TAX BASE

Only the federal government, according to the proponents of federal aid to education, has the tax machinery for collecting the money needed to support education. The local revenues on which school expenditures depend can no longer bear the increased cost of education. Figures quoted from the U. S. Department of Commerce report in 1958 (4) substantiate this stand:

Who Collects the Tax Dollar?		Who Pays for Education?	
Federal government	65%	Federal government	4%
State government	15%	State government	40%
Local government	16%	Local government	56%

The federal government, it is pointed out, collects two-thirds of the taxes of the entire country; yet it pays only 4 per cent of the cost of education. Local governments, on the other hand, collect only 16 per cent of the tax dollar, but bear 56 per cent of the expenses of education.

Property taxes, on which most school districts rely, are particularly inflexible, it is maintained, and do not fluctuate with the increased needs of the school. Since property is no longer the index to wealth that it once was, the argument is that the federal income tax is a fairer tax, in that it is progressive and reflects a truer index to wealth. Over 81 per cent of our national income lies in corporate profits, which pay little to support local schools. Ninety-six per cent of taxes on personal and corporate income is paid to the federal government (55).

MOBILITY OF THE POPULATION

The educational neglect of one state may be inherited by another. We are presently involved in one of the largest mass migrations in the history of our country as each year 40 million people change their addresses and approximately one million youngsters cross state lines.

The poorly educated child in any state is a social and economic liability to every state and to the nation as a whole, and migration is toward civilization. People are no longer citizens of just one state; they live in many in their lifetimes. Enough people enter California each month to create a town of 30,000, and it has been said that California is importing its illiterates. In 1961, some 5.8 million Americans changed their state residence (52).

NATIONAL ACCEPTANCE

It is further maintained that the majority of people are in favor of federal aid to education. One source of support for this statement is Gallup's national public opinion poll, which found in 1960 that 65 per cent of the American voters favored federal aid to school construction. The Lou Harris Poll, as reported in the *Christian Science Monitor* of September 13, 1963, revealed that 70 per cent of voters favored federal aid to education.

Among teachers the percentage is even higher. In a survey conducted by the *Phi Delta Kappan*, an education journal, it was found that 84 per cent of the individuals surveyed (primarily male teachers and school administrators) were in favor of federal aid to education. A poll conducted in 1964 by the Los Angeles Teachers' Association showed that 80 per cent of teachers polled were proponents of federal aid to education.

HISTORICAL BACKGROUND

Historically, it is averred, there is nothing unprecedented about the involvement of the federal government in education, for the roots of federal aid to education probe deep into our historical past. Since 1785, Congress has passed almost 200 laws that give federal assistance to education. Proponents of federal aid point to these laws and the fact that they have resulted in little that could be termed "control."

According to a study conducted by Edith Green, congresswoman from Oregon (published in 1963 under the title, *The Federal Government and Education*), the issue of federal involvement in education was decided 100 years ago, and 42 federal agencies now provide aid to education in the amount of more than $2 billion each year.

Wrote statesman Adlai Stevenson in support of this position: "We hear those who would push aside federal action with the usual cries of 'socialism' and 'regimentation.' But there has been federal help for education ever since 1785 . . . and we are not closer to federal control of our schools than we were then" (49).

LOCAL CONTROL

The question of local control is one on which both opponents and proponents of federal aid to education agree, for most would leave control of the schools with local authorities. The question debated is, "Will federal aid entail control?" Proponents deny that local control will be affected, for in cases of federal aid there has been no federal control of the school district. Most bills, moreover, are drawn up with the express proviso that no type of federal control be included in the bill.

An examination of existing laws comprising federal aid to education reveals, for example, that colleges and universities have received more federal financial aid for a longer period of time than have most public school districts. By many standards, it is contended, the colleges and universities are freer than the public elementary and secondary schools. The question is asked, for instance, "Does Harvard lose its freedom of action when it receives a grant of federal funds for research?" Most observers would agree that this is far from the case.

EFFICIENCY OF FEDERAL TAXES

The cost of raising monies through federal taxation has been found to be less than that of any other method of taxation. We find, for example, that the cost of levying and collecting $100 through federal taxation is $.40, compared to $1.00 when levied and collected by state agencies, and $5.00 to $10.00 as levied and collected by local government agencies. It appears advantageous, therefore, to send tax monies to Washington rather than to local tax-collecting agencies.

Opponents of federal aid question the addition of costs, the so-called "freight bill," involved in sending taxes to Washington and then returning that money to the areas in which it is to be used. The Commission on Intergovernmental Relations, or the Hoover Commission, reports these statistics on administrative overhead for laws enacted (71).

School lunch program: 1.7 per cent
Vocational education: 2.0 per cent
Resident instruction in land-grant colleges: 0.5 per cent
Federal assistance laws: .9 per cent.

Others question whether, in light of the existing heavy tax load, the federal government can afford the expense of additional aid to education. Those favoring greater involvement of the federal government in education quickly assert that whereas the federal debt has increased 10 per cent in the 1950–60 period, local and state debts have increased 190 per cent during the same period.

Representative Statements

The last section of this chapter presents statements of individuals and spokesmen for major organizations that favor federal aid to education. The statements have been selected on the basis of their relevancy, recency, and repute. Varied arguments for federal aid to education are made by:

1. Dr. Benjamin C. Willis, Superintendent of Chicago Schools
2. Peter T. Schoemann, AFL-CIO Education Committee
3. Abraham Ribicoff, former Secretary of Health, Education, and Welfare
4. National Farmers' Union.
5. Carl J. Megel, President of the American Federation of Teachers
6. National Education Association
7. Senator Wayne E. Morse, Education Subcommittee Chairman

DR. BENJAMIN C. WILLIS

Dr. Benjamin C. Willis, as president of the American Association of School Administrators and superintendent of public schools in Chicago, testified before the Subcommittee on Education. His was one of the statements heard on behalf of the Public School Assistance Act of 1961, proposed by John F. Kennedy (84).

NEED FOR LEGISLATION NOW

That there is an ever-present and insistent need for education in a democracy requires no comment to men such as yourselves. I think it is self-evident that you, as legislators and citizens, and we, as educators and citizens, have a deep interest and concern, that extends beyond any local areas, to the obligations of society and of the Nation to provide a quality program of education for all of the children and all of the youth in all 50 States.

If we are to meet this challenge, there is much that needs to be done. National shortages of classrooms and of qualified teachers were reported in a survey in the fall of 1960 and are well known. Perhaps, less well known is the fact that of every 10 pupils who reach fifth grade, only 6 finish high school.

Predictions vary, but they all indicate tremendous and continuing increases in the population of the United States in the years just ahead. An economist of the Dodge Corp. estimates that within the next 40 years we will have two persons living in the United States for every one person living here now.

If this materializes, we would need an additional teacher and an additional classroom for every one we now have.

The school population, nationally, has been increasing at about 1 million annually. . . .

The national increase requires 40,000 more teachers and 40,000 more classrooms a year just to maintain education at the present program level.

.   .   .

. . . We need school buildings and we need teachers; but also we need a quality program of education planned for individuals and available to all individuals. Fundamental to any quality program of education is the quality of teachers available in adequate numbers. Of this I am certain; what was quality preparation for teaching in 1930 is completely inadequate in 1960.

At the very time when the world in which we live demands an increasingly well-informed and educated teacher, we are faced with a constricted group from which to recruit. Population figures reported by age brackets show that in the sixties about 47 percent or 1 in 2 will be young people under 24 years of age and that another 41 percent will be over 45 years of age.

In the 24–45 age group there will be only 12 percent; this is the group from which the majority of our teachers come. Not only will we have an exceptionally large enrollment of children, but we will have this very small group from which to draw our teachers.

In addition, as women move increasingly into other professional areas, competition for the services of the very able will be intensified. Teachers' salaries are going to have to be related to the skills required and, also, realistically, to the small supply available, and the great demand.

COSTS OF PROGRAM

As we look ahead, then, it is apparent that the cost of education must continue to rise not only to provide facilities and staff for growth in population, but also to provide education for all Americans, and to provide a quality program.

It has been estimated that the present total cost of education should double by 1970. Evidence has been given to support this position in the reports of many groups, among them the Report of the White House Conference of 1956 and the Rockefeller Report on the Pursuit of Excellence.

Problems involved in paying for education today are closely related to the fact that our population has grown faster than the tax base. In the early days of our history, real property accounted for 75 percent of our wealth; today, real property accounts for only 25 percent. Local governments still rely primarily on real property for their tax base especially for schools; this has meant a serious strain in relation to real estate.

Some of our problems stem from the fact that today property tax represents such a small part of our total wealth.

That the Federal Government by sharing tax revenue with the States and localities can provide the necessary funds to aid in seeking a quality program of education to reach all Americans is evident when we look at the report on our gross national product. It was $285 billion in 1950; it is reported as $500 billion today. Projection figures estimate over a trillion by 1975.

There are some who have equated Federal support with Federal control. The American Association of School Administrators believes in local control; I believe in local control; history has given evidence that local control can be compatible with Federal aid. We have had Federal support of education since the beginning of the land-grant colleges; since 1917, there has been Federal support to vocational education.

In this latter case, the program is so local that funds are granted to programs within schools. Recently, millions of dollars have been paid to teachers by the Federal Government while they attended institutes sponsored by universities. The universities select the teachers and determine the course of study; the Federal Government does not. I refer to institutions both through NDEA and also through the National Science Foundation.

Senate bill 1021 is a States rights bill because the State has a choice in the utilization of funds. It is a bill in which Federal aid and local control are compatible. Money allocated may be spent by States and localities to meet the major need in each State and the major need within each area of the State.

The skills of people make a people strong. At no point can we forget that vocational education is the acquiring of skills, and that the opportunity or the acquiring of skills, whether they be for entrance into teaching or machine shop, or for other skills when adjustment is needed, as a result of technology, must be available to all Americans.

Because of our belief in the work and dignity of the individual; our growing population, our interdependent national economy; our expanding scientific knowledge and today's technology; because of the insistent demands of our times for improvement, for quality in the program of education and for excellence in teaching—there must be more and better teachers, and more and better equipped classrooms.

PETER T. SCHOEMANN

As vice-president and chairman of the Education Committee of AFL-CIO, Peter T. Schoemann testified in favor of federal aid to education before the Subcommittee on Education (84). His testimony in support of the Public School Assistance Act of 1961 read as follows:

. . . from the time of the Survey Ordinance, back in 1785, it was recognized that the National Government had a proper role to play in assisting and encouraging educational effort.

The partnership of locality, State, and Nation in supporting education has continued. Even though local school problems have become national problems we nevertheless strongly favor local control, local operation, and local policy determinations for public schools. We are gratified that the American community is in nearly complete agreement on this basic premise. This general opinion removes any question of Federal control from serious contention.

The real problem facing America today, it seems to us, is whether the National Government is playing its fair part in support of education. We think it is not; we urge that it should. . . .

Trade unionists can, in 1961, restate their union's traditional dedication to the public school idea—the chance for a free education for all. The means of fulfilling the goal have, however, changed. They now require a substantial Federal participation in the effort. . . .

We are seriously concerned today with the status and the immediate future of public education in the United States. The challenge confronting the public schools is different and critical. Education must prepare us to solve the problems of a new age. Americans of the 1940's and 1950's helped to fight the greatest of wars, establish the United Nations, provide unprecedented aid to less fortunate peoples and fight the Communist world tyranny. These were monumental jobs. Compared to the jobs facing Americans of the 1960's and 1970's, however, these past accomplishments shrink in proportion.

Americans of the next score of years must help the many new independent nations into the family of free nations. We must work with our friends to eliminate starvation, illiteracy, mass disease, religious persecution, racial discrimination. We must control arms under law. We must resist the renewed threats to freedom from the dictatorial governments of the Soviet Union and Communist China. We must advance the space age. We must do these things at home and abroad, on earth, and in space, with the knowledge that we might not succeed, that we have no guarantee of success, but knowing that to fail is to commit mankind to extinction or to centuries of barbarism and slavery.

The issues, then, could not be more grave. The stakes could not be higher.

.   .   .

The central vehicle for advancing our way of life and rolling back the menaces of totalitarianism, ignorance, and hunger is our educational system. Where does it stand? What is its condition?

SCHOOL CONSTRUCTION

Pupils and teachers should have safe, well-ventilated classrooms in buildings designed to provide maximum opportunity for learning. The present situation is a national disgrace.

We in the AFL-CIO think that we can afford good schools. We believe that this marvelously productive economy, if operating near its capacity, can sustain the effort to provide all of our children with first-rate schools. If history's richest society must send its children to study the sciences and humanities in schools built before the turn of the century, then there sure is something out of kilter. If a substantial number of our children must be put on curtailed or half-day sessions to learn the humanities which reflect our fundamental value system, then we have a problem, and 685,000 pupils in 36 States and the District of Columbia do, in fact, go to school on just this basis.

We in the trade unions think that this "affluent society" should provide sufficient classroom space for our young people, yet we had 1,868,000 pupils in excess of classroom capacity when the present school year began. This was an increase of 122,000 over the year before.

The U.S. Office of Education reported that, as of last September, we had 76,000 classrooms which were unsatisfactory, and an additional 66,100 were needed to house the students in excess of the present capacity; in other words, a national shortage of 142,100 classrooms. Thus, an already critical shortage has worsened in the last year because the shortage in the fall of 1959 was 135,200. The problem is not that we fail to build. We built 69,400 new or converted classrooms last year. The fact is that we simply do not build enough.

For some years many have questioned these figures provided by the U.S. Office of Education. For our part, we have wondered if they were not too modest, too cautious to reflect the facts. However, I believe these new figures are better than those provided before. Heretofore, the national totals were based partly on State-level estimates of shortages. These latest figures, showing a shortage greater than before, are based on locally completed questionnaires. They are entitled to most careful consideration.

The problem, of course, is simply a failure to build sufficient new classrooms for the expanding school age population. Our public school enrollment went up 3.2 percent in the past year, an increase of 1.1 million of a total of 36.6 million pupils in the public elementary and secondary schools. The only answer is more classrooms; the only apparent way to get more classrooms is through substantial Federal financial aid.

TEACHERS' SALARIES

It is not certain how many teachers we lack in this country. There are various estimates. One of the more reliable seems to be an estimate by one of our affiliated unions. The American Federation of Teachers has estimated that as of September 1959 we lacked 250,000 public school teachers. But quality is even more important than quantity— in teachers. Whatever the total shortage, and it is plainly huge, one glaring fact stands out as a warning of impending peril: the legal measure of competence, the certification requirements for teaching, are not met by 24,300 high school teachers and 67,200 elementary school teachers. These 91,500 teachers—6.5 percent of our teaching forces— are on substandard certificates. These are issued on an "emergency" basis—to meet an "emergency" that stretches on, year after year.

It might be noted here that we are finding more and more opportunities for the fruitful use of American teachers overseas. It requires little imagination to see the boundless good that the free world would derive from the presence of thousands of dedicated, enlightened U.S. teachers in the newly independent communities of Asia and Africa and in the stirring nations of Latin America. But we cannot properly provide teachers for oversea missions when we lack so many here at home. Both needs must be met; they are twin aspects of the same need, the same shortage; they pinpoint with clarity another reason why this problem cannot be solved by the more than 40,000 local school districts, acting alone, without Federal assistance.

The failure of the law of supply and demand is classic in the case of teachers. Despite the patent need for teachers, local school districts have been unable even with State aid, to provide attractive salaries and conditions. Nevertheless, thousands of teachers who could earn far more in other fields, stay on in education, and thousands of new teachers join their ranks each year, but not enough.

The truth is that our teachers do not earn a full living wage. The U.S. Department of Labor's City Workers' Family Budget, updated to 1959, shows that a worker and spouse with two children require at least $6,130 per year for a modest but adequate standard of living. Thus the teacher's average annual salary of under $6,000 ($4,730 in 1958), leaves him with only a subsistence wage level. He is not meeting the minimum $118 per week required each week of the year. The way he most often makes ends meet is to spend the summer and holidays working in some routine job instead of using this period to improve his worth as an educator. Under these conditions, we cannot hope to attract an adequate number of top men and women into the teaching profession.

I would point out to the committee that the figures used here on classroom and teacher shortages are current figures, the latest we could find, and are taken mostly from Government sources. They do not involve baseless speculation, or even well-based projections. Any projection, either as to building needs at any level of the educational system, or as to teacher shortages, shows an even grimmer picture than that appearing now. The current figures, however, tell a story startling enough to demand immediate action. Further delay can be purchased only with the gravest of risks.

ABRAHAM RIBICOFF

As Secretary of Health, Education, and Welfare, Abraham Ribicoff testified in favor of federal aid to education under the Public School Assistance Act of 1961 (84). His statement read as follows:

The Federal Government is now—and has long been—deeply involved in the support of education. Four years before the adoption of the Federal Constitution, in the Survey Ordinance of 1785, the National Government provided that "there shall be reserved the Lot Number 16 of every Township for the maintenance of public schools in each Township." Two years later, the Northwest Ordinance of 1787 enunciated and further emphasized the principle that education of the people must be a requirement for the continued existence of a democratic society. Later enactments continued the principle of Federal endowment for public education in new Territories and States. In the Territories, the Federal Government itself organized school systems which were turned over to the States administration as they entered the Union.

In 1862, Congress created the great land-grant system of colleges and universities—a unique form of higher education which has contributed mightily to the growth and development of our country.

The Vocational Education Act of 1917, the so-called Smith-Hughes Act, establishing the program of Federal assistance for vocational education, was in direct response to widely expressed needs of the American people.

The GI bills, providing education for the veterans of World War II, have been a statesmanlike contribution to the education of American youth.

The National Defense Education Act of 1958 is helping our public schools to improve their programs in mathematics, science, and modern foreign languages, conceded by all to be areas of crucial national concern. The several programs of the National Science Foundation aimed to modernize and strengthen the teaching of science in the schools also represent a similar significant contribution.

ONE HUNDRED AND SEVENTY-FIVE YEARS OF FEDERAL AID TO EDUCATION

The Federal role has been a legitimate and accepted part of the American educational experience since the founding of the Republic. For 175 years, Federal aid to education has helped to serve the national interest.

These Federal activities have not come about by accident or to demonstrate a theory. The Congress has authorized Federal aid to meet certain specific needs, when other solutions were not deemed adequate or sufficiently timely.

These programs of Federal assistance to education have, in my judgment, been administered without evidencing one shred of Federal control. As a former Governor of a State, I have naturally been very sensitive to the question of Federal-State relationships and have been anxious to preserve the rightful responsibility of and independence of action by the States. In my 6 years as Governor of Connecticut, not once has the Federal Government exercised control directly or indirectly over education in my State. I doubt whether you will find any such interference in any of our 50 States.

THE ADMINISTRATION'S PROPOSALS

I have come before you today to explain and to urge you to support S. 1021 which embodies the administration's proposals to provide Federal assistance (1) for teachers' salaries, classroom construction, and

special projects in our public elementary and secondary schools and
(2) for maintenance and operation and classroom construction in
those school districts affected by Federal activities.

It is my firm judgment that S. 1021 embodies those two great principles which have been found in our long-continued tradition of Federal support of education. These principles are recognition (1) that
the Federal Government has an especial concern for programs which
are in the national interest and (2) that the basic responsibility for
the operation and administration of our school systems inheres in the
State and local communities.

The United States is the first nation in history to establish universal
public education as its goal. . . . Our future requires that appropriate
educational opportunities be freely available to all children and youth
no matter what their background, circumstance, or place of residence.

RISING ENROLLMENTS AND INCREASING COSTS

We have made substantial progress toward meeting this goal, but rising enrollments and increasing costs have placed great pressure upon
the States and local school districts. During the past decade, enrollments in public elementary and secondary schools have increased from
25.7 million to 37.6 million, or 46 percent. Annual expenditures have
increased during the same period from $6.5 billion to $16.5 billion, or
154 percent. The cost per pupil in our public education system has
jumped from $284 a year to $496 per year—an increase of 75 percent.

While Federal tax dollars have increased 85 percent in the postwar
years, State and local communities have had to increase their tax revenues by 221 percent. From 1946 to 1959, while the Federal debt increased by 6 percent, State and local debt soared by more than 300
percent. Property taxes, the traditional source of revenue for education,
are in many areas rapidly approaching the limits of reasonableness.

Another problem confronting many a school district is the great
mobility of our population. Each year more than 5 million people
move from one State to another. Today's resident of a high income
State with a better than average school system may well find tomorrow
that his children must attend a less than average school in a low income State.

Moreover, the States exhibit varying degrees of ability to support
education. For example, the State with the highest income enjoys
almost four times the income per public school pupil found in the
State with the lowest income. On the other hand, the lowest income

State has almost 50 percent more children in public schools for each 1,000 population as the highest income State.

PROJECTION FOR THE NEXT DECADE

The next decade holds no promise of lessened impact upon our resources available for support of education. Enrollments in public elementary and secondary schools will increase from 36 million in 1959–60 to 44 million in 1968–69. These increases in enrollment will require an additional 437,000 instructional personnel and 600,000 new classrooms by the end of the 10-year period. Of more striking importance, however, is the fact that greatest pressure will be placed upon us during the next 5 years. We cannot afford, in my judgment, to permit any of our children to go even 1 year longer than necessary without adequate instructional staff and classroom facilities.

We are therefore proposing in S. 1021 a measure which is aimed to focus especially upon the problem of providing adequately for the teaching profession and for the necessary facilities for public elementary and secondary school programs, with additional emphasis upon certain special and unique problems.

ALLOCATION OF FUNDS LEFT TO STATES

We are suggesting that the States themselves be authorized to decide in what proportion they desire to utilize the proposed Federal financial assistance for teachers' salaries or for classroom construction. We believe that the States are the best judges of the degree and incidence of educational need within their borders. For example, the State which has already made substantial progress in meeting its construction needs can turn to the problem of increasing the salaries of members of its public school instructional staff. Another State which has not yet surmounted the problem of constructing adequate classrooms may, while giving early emphasis to meeting these needs, also use a share of its allotment to increase the salaries of teachers.

TEACHERS' SALARIES

In order to have professionally qualified and competent teachers throughout our public schools, we are going to have to provide salaries that are competitive with those in other occupations requiring equivalent training and experience. Inadequate salaries for instructional personnel are a primary deterrent to the recruitment and retention of highly qualified persons to staff our public elementary and secondary schools.

In order to keep from losing ground on the basis of present qualification standards, the States and local school districts will be hard pressed in face of the need for increased numbers of teachers. To raise qualification standards in a tight market personnel with high professional training—and we should raise such standards—will require substantial improvement in the level of teachers' compensation.

While the States and localities must bear the main burden of such increase, the Federal Government can and should make a substantial contribution to assist the States and local communities in meeting their goals. Moreover, we must make it possible for our public elementary and secondary schools to bring the present instructional staff up to the requisite standards as promptly as possible. The 90,000 teachers now in our classrooms who fail to meet full professional certification requirements must be assisted to meet these requirements as promptly as possible.

CLASSROOM NEEDS

It is evident that we do not have enough classrooms to meet our needs. We should not allow a condition to continue in which several million pupils are studying under overcrowded conditions, in half-day or curtailed sessions or in substandard, obsolete, or dilapidated classrooms. The problem of meeting the need for instructional space is complicated and made more difficult by the fact that the bulge of school age population has now begun to be felt to the fullest extent in the secondary schools, thus increasing the cost of instructional facilities. The percentage of enrollment in secondary schools has increased from 27.9 in 1954 to 32.6 in 1960. The number of secondary school students reported in excess of normal classroom capacity in 1954 was 18.7 percent of the total, whereas the number so reported in 1960 was 36.8, or almost double.

NATIONAL FARMERS' UNION

A representative of the National Farmers' Union testified in support of the Public School Assistance Act of 1961 (84). The statement of this organization was as follows:

The current debate on Federal aid to education is much more than a discussion of declining educational excellence in the United States.

It is an economic question, one of the utmost importance, particularly to farmers.

Farmers are very much in the middle of it. The burden of education is falling on them more every year, although every year they have less to show for it.

Education is becoming more expensive. New classrooms, new facilities, new higher paid teachers are needed. The cost of education per pupil ran all the way from a low increase of 36.2 percent to a high of 142.9 percent since 1950. The average cost increase in just 10 years was over 60 percent.

This increase in cost does not take into consideration the increase in enrollment. Enrollment in U.S. public schools has increased 18.5 percent since 1950. The Committee for Economic Development, in a conservative projection of growth in the United States, puts the enrollment increase at 29 percent for the next 10 years.

The committee estimates that school costs will rise by 47 percent during the sixties.

Who is paying the education bill today?

The question is of particular interest to farmers, particularly farmers in the agricultural and Southern States.

The property tax since the advent of the income tax has lost importance as a source of government income. Yet, due to the other costs of government, the property tax has borne a bigger share of the education burden.

Last year, 54 percent of the financial burden of supporting schools was placed on the property tax. Although many States put the property tax into a general fund and pay their education bills from that, it has been estimated that at least 70 percent of the property tax collection goes toward education. Many farm States earmark funds directly to education. Kansas and Utah, for example, turn 100 percent of the money collected through property taxes to education. In Texas, 95 percent of the property tax goes to education; 94 percent in Indiana; and over 80 percent in Montana and Wyoming.

Who pays the property tax? Farmers in farm States are paying more and more of it. Over one-third of the total property tax collected in South Dakota, North Dakota, Iowa, and Nebraska is paid on farm property and farm real estate. Farmers in Idaho, Kansas, Montana and Minnesota pay one-fifth or more of the property tax in their State. This is despite the fact that the number of farms to be taxed have been reduced in every one of these States.

The Agriculture Research Service of the U.S. Department of Agriculture reports that in 1958, State and local governments levied $1.1 billion in tax on farm real estate, almost double the amount levied 15 years before. An additional quarter of a billion dollars was levied on farm personalty, such as automobiles, farm machinery, and livestock.

The size of farm property tax has almost doubled in 15 years although the number of farms in the United States has been almost cut in half during the same period, from 6,089,000 to 3,703,000.[1]

In recent years, taxes on farm property have been rising at an average rate of more than 5 percent annually. The USDA sees no letup in sight unless new sources of income are found.

Despite the fact that agriculture is asked to shoulder a growing amount of the educational burden and the rural and Southern States are putting forth a greater effort toward education than are the industrial States, these States are unable to keep the pace and the quality of their education is falling behind.

A State's educational effort is computed by taking the percentage of the educational bill in the overall expenditures of the State, divided by the number of students. The effort of the agricultural and Southern States is higher in every instance than the effort of the large industrial States.

Yet, despite the added effort, the quality of education in these States is falling further behind the standards set up by the industrial States.

The average salaries of classroom teachers in the farm States rank below the national average, and some are near the bottom. For example, North and South Dakota rank in the lowest five States with South Carolina, Arkansas, and Mississippi.

With the lower salaries comes high migration by teachers and a lower percentage of qualified teachers remaining. Only 17.4 percent of the elementary schoolteachers in South Dakota have 4 years of college education, less than one-fifth of the teachers have a basic requirement in many of the other States. Wisconsin, Montana, Iowa, Nebraska, and Minnesota rank among the lowest of the States studied as far as teachers' qualifications, ranking below all the Southern States studied.

The quality of a State's education is based largely on the qualifications of its teachers.

The above figures were taken on a statewide basis. The situation in

[1] U.S. Department of Commerce and Agriculture figures.

the rural areas of the States is subject to even more serious support problems.

Rural schoolteachers average about $1,000 less per year in salary than do city teachers. The percentage of qualified teachers in rural areas is lower, in every instance, than the number in the city. Rural schools are older, facilities are more limited, scope of courses is more limited, scholastic accreditation is more difficult, thus scholarships for advanced education are more difficult to come by in rural areas than in urban sections.

This is the educational situation today. There is no possible way for it to improve except through Federal aid. Education is a growing strain on the State budget, and the strain on local tax capability is even greater. Educational deficiencies, particularly in rural areas, are growing despite the fact State budgets are at the breaking points. The only possible way to spend more than is being spent on education now—outside of Federal aid—is by raising State and local taxes, particularly property taxes.

Were this the only consideration, it would be reason enough for the farmer to realize how important Federal aid is to him and his operation. Farm profit has nothing to do with property taxes, except to the farmer. Growing property taxes are becoming more important in the overall cost-price squeeze on the farm. It is possible that a farmer could be taxed right off the farm.

The Federal aid to education plan proposed by President Kennedy is aimed at areas where the need is greatest—in the Southern States and farm States where the current effort is greater but not enough. The Kennedy plan would add to the overall effort and bring it into better balance with the results being achieved in other States. For example, under the plan, the amount of money per student is almost double in the Southern States and agricultural States (such as North and South Dakota) as it is in the leading industrial States (such as New York, Illinois, and Pennsylvania).

The Kennedy plan would not bring schools under Federal jurisdiction. This is a weak argument by critics of the plan. The Federal grants would go to the States to do with what they want—build schools and facilities, raise teachers' salaries, etc. The Federal Government has helped support land-grant colleges and a number of other institutions and programs for a great many years, and there has been no interference from the Federal Government in the operations of these institutions and programs whatsoever.

CARL J. MEGEL

Speaking for the American Federation of Teachers before the Subcommittee on Education was Carl J. Megel, president of the organization (84). His statement was as follows:

. . . Education can no longer be retarded by those who view with alarm; who demand that the bill include unconstitutional provisions, or who contend that State and local ox-cart school financing methods can be adapted to this space age.

There have been many authoritative estimates of the number of new classrooms needed—150,000 to 500,000. I submit to you that whichever of these estimates may be correct is beside the point. So long as groups of American boys and girls are crowded into classrooms —40 to 50 in a class—American education is not serving America or American youth.

Estimates of the shortage of qualified teachers also vary—from 100,-000 to 350,000. Which of these estimates is correct is also immaterial, so long as American children anywhere lack competent instruction.

And I cannot emphasize enough the necessity of having a portion of Federal aid appropriations mandated for teachers' salaries. It is foolhardy to consider aid for education only in the area of school construction, for the teacher and the pupil are the keys to education in the final analysis. Bricks without brains constitute national folly.

Certainly our States and localities must recognize the need for higher teachers' salaries and so apply a portion of the Federal allotment. Today, under State and local financing, only 21 percent of all classroom teachers are paid more than $5,000 a year; 17 percent are paid $3,500 or less, and 62 percent are paid from $3,500 to $4,999. Of necessity, this must be corrected if we are to staff our public schools with competent, qualified career teachers.

Total financing of the public schools by the States and communities is no longer possible. The property tax method is inadequate and obsolete. It no longer spreads school costs over the majority of the people, and only the Federal taxing system can do so.

The Federal Government receives 74 cents of the total of every tax dollar. A teacher who earns $5,000 pays approximately $874 in income tax. Yet at the present time only $11 of that amount is spent by the Federal Government for education.

It is true that certain States such as Illinois will pay more than they will receive in return if the aid bill is enacted into law. In 1940 the assessed valuation of property in the United States was $144 billion whereas the national income was $81 billion. In 1956 the assessed valuation of property rose 1⅞ times to $272 billion, but the national income increased 4⅙ times to $343 billion.

Property taxes should therefore be supplemented so as to be relieved of the increased demands made upon it because of the enlarged and expanded school system we now must support.

. . . .

Additionally, such funds from the Federal Government should not be construed to relieve State or local communities of their responsibility, but rather, increase education and not reduce taxes. Our school population is growing so rapidly that only by increasing the funds for education can we hope to maintain a satisfactory and stable educational system.

Our 40 million students now in school are in critical need of the help the bill before you would provide. School districts able to completely finance themselves in these days, in every way, simply do not exist. Our largest and wealthiest cities have the largest classroom and teacher shortages.

Federal aid for education should not be evaluated in terms of its cost, alone, but in terms of an investment that will increase the national wealth and the individual's earning ability many times over the amount of the expenditure.

Education is the basis of our national progress and prosperity. From now on, in days of world rivalry among nations, in days when man will compete to reach the stars, while communism threatens us—it is also our hope for national security.

NATIONAL EDUCATION ASSOCIATION

The testimony of the National Education Association before the Subcommittee on Education in support of Public School Assistance Act of 1961 was entitled: "Can Our States Support Good Schools?" This presentation favored federal aid as the solution to some of the problems of education.

Following is the resolution adopted at the 1964 National Education Association's Convention at Seattle, Washington, on July 3, 1964 (56): *

The National Education Association seeks legislation to provide federal support of public education in line with the following principles:

(a) That there be substantial federal support of the whole of public education at all levels and of all types.

(b) That federal programs of specific aids be continued or improved in addition to comprehensive federal support.

(c) That the general federal-support funds be allocated without federal control to state school authorities to be commingled with state public education funds.

(d) That distribution of the federal funds within states permit the same administrative discretion as for state public education funds.

(e) That expenditure of the federal funds be only for the purposes for which the states and localities, under their constitutions and statutes, may expend their own public education funds.

(f) That the legislation be consistent with the constitutional provision respecting an establishment of religion and with the tradition of separation of church and state.

(g) That the legislation contain provision for judicial review as to its constitutionality.

The National Education Association urges its officers, directors, affiliates, and Legislative Commission to develop, seek, and continuously review legislative programs to realize these principles.

Testimony given by the National Education Association in 1965 (54) supported President Johnson's Elementary and Secondary Education Act as follows: *

. . . The National Education Association, with its more than 903,-000 members, represents the broad spectrum of American education. Its membership ranges from kindergarten teachers to college professors. It includes administrators, supervisors, school principals, county and state superintendents of public instruction and their staffs, and other individuals. Ninety per cent of the NEA members are classroom teachers.

* Reprinted by permission of the National Education Association.

The National Education Association is concerned over the increasingly critical needs of education at all levels, and throughout its more than 100 years of existence has sought to meet those needs through a comprehensive legislative program.

The NEA applauds the educational accomplishments of the Eighty-eighth Congress and is heartened at the prospect that the Eighty-ninth Congress will make even greater contributions to education.

Despite the achievements of the last session, there remains unmet the most urgent educational problem of all—the provision of substantial Federal support to the states for elementary and secondary schools.

This need, most dramatically manifest in a critical shortage of well-trained teachers and an alarming lack of adequate classrooms, would be realistically attacked by the President's program and the provisions of this bill.

The National Education Association, while remaining committed to the belief that broad-scale general Federal support of the schools is the ultimate and ideal solution to these problems, is dedicated also to the expansion and improvement of existing programs of specific aids.

Basic to the NEA's policy is an unalterable insistence that the Federal funds be allocated to the states and school districts without Federal control. General Federal-support funds, the NEA policy suggests, should be commingled with state public education funds and their distribution within states should permit the same administrative discretion as for state public education funds.

Central to the Association's policy on Federal support is the position that expenditure of the Federal funds be only for the purposes for which the states and localities, under their constitutions and statutes, may expend their own public education funds.

NEA policy likewise insists that legislation providing general or specific aids be consistent with the constitutional provision respecting an establishment of religion and with the tradition of separation of church and state.

The President's proposals do not, in my opinion, violate these principles. In its approach and emphasis the program has the whole-hearted support of the National Education Association.

We believe that Mr. Johnson's message constituted one of the strongest commitments to meeting the urgent needs of education ever to come from the White House. We believe the President has forthrightly faced up to the practical problems of getting a school support bill enacted and has offered a proposal which should have the backing of all individuals and groups interested in the educational welfare of the nation.

The approach embodied in Title I of the bill is compatible with policies of the National Education Association. In fact, the NEA last December 16 proposed a program to increase Federal support by $1.5 billion a year, the exact amount of the Administration's proposal. Central to that recommendation was a plan to expand the so-called "impact" program under which the Federal Government for many years has aided school districts bearing an abnormal educational load caused by the presence of Federal defense and military installations.

The NEA proposed, as does the President, to channel Federal funds to school districts impacted by the presence of large numbers of children from low income families. Last year the NEA testified in favor of proposed legislation to accomplish this. We are gratified that the major part of H.R. 2362, $1 billion of it, and its companion measure in the Senate, S. 370, are based on this concept.

The national need for help is undeniable. The financial ability of the states to furnish good education varies widely, and the disparity of geographic regions and individual communities is fantastic. The resulting school facilities and opportunities for children to learn range from excellent to grossly inadequate. And even in areas of presumed plenty, pockets of shocking educational poverty exist where not even minimum desirable standards prevail.

The correlation of expenditures and educational excellence is well established. The ill-financed school is almost certain to produce a low-quality educational product, despite the dedication and effort of the teachers. Conversely, the best opportunities for intellectual and cultural attainment almost universally are found in schools which can afford top quality facilities, superior instructional materials and well-paid, competent teachers.

As described so dramatically by the President in his message, the areas of educational deficiency are not to be found exclusively in regions commonly recognized as economically depressed. They exist everywhere, perhaps surprisingly in States and sections of supposed wealth as well as in regions of low income and generally inadequate resources. The slums of ignorance exist everywhere. They can be eliminated only by utilizing the total resources of the nation through the broad, efficient—and I might add—amazingly economical tax collecting facilities of the Federal Government.

The legislation being considered by this Committee proposes to do that. It provides for placing the money where it is most needed—at the elementary and secondary levels—with special emphasis in areas of low economic ability and deprived cultural opportunity.

This legislation has much to commend it.

With its appropriation of $1.255 billion it gives enough money to substantially improve the quality of education nationwide.

It distributes the money on the basis of need.

It leaves control at the state and local levels.

It's realistic. It gives a practicable basis for resolving some of the thorny controversies which have surrounded earlier efforts to provide Federal support of education.

In short, it makes a lot of sense.

The National Education Association enthusiastically supports all of the purposes of the legislation.

(1) The bolstering of programs in low-wealth areas.

(2) The provision of school library resources and instructional material to all children.

(3) The creation of supplemental educational centers and services.

(4) The expansion of research activity.

(5) The strengthening of State Departments of Education.

Inherent in the NEA's position is the assumption that only materials approved for use in the public schools will be made available to children in communities benefiting from these Federal funds and that guarantees that none of the funds be used to support any sort of religious observance, indoctrination or sectarian education will be retained. The provisions of Titles II and III which place their operations under public control provide sufficient safeguards and restraints, in my opinion, to protect this fundamental principle.

It is a real pleasure to record the support of the National Education Association for this legislation which well may prove to be the most significant ever enacted in the field of education.

SENATOR WAYNE E. MORSE

Senator Wayne E. Morse of Oregon is chairman of the Subcommittee on Education under the Committee on Labor and Public Welfare. He has introduced bill after bill before the Senate in an attempt to further the cause of federal aid to education.

On April 5, 1964, he delivered this speech, "Federal Support for Education: Now and in the Future," to the National Conference on School Finance: *

. . . Prediction is a most hazardous business in politics. It is made so in part by the very institutions of government of which we are most proud. A very witty state senator, the late George Woodward of Pennsylvania, once put it this way:

> We all know that it was Thomas Jefferson, or some one of the Fathers who could read French, who read M. Montesquieu's essay on three compartments of government. The Fathers thought it over in English and put it in all our constitutions. It is, therefore, customary for the legislative, executive and judicial compartments to abstain from one another's society and to try to misunderstand one another as far as possible. This promotes business in the art of government and adds zest to elections.

So when I discuss with you the various measures we have passed, are currently considering or hope to enact, in this and successor sessions of the Congress, I want you to know that I have some biases. In others they would be convictions, but in me they are biases about education which you should allow for. I want you also to discount my inclination to speak highly of the Senate of the United States in the field of educational legislation, because frankly, I think that we have in this last year taken tremendous strides toward meeting some of the problems. The acts themselves may be initially modest, but I surmise they are but the seed bed of greater accomplishment in the future.

WHAT HAS BEEN DONE TO DATE

As you know, the late President sent to the Congress an omnibus education bill containing some 24 major provisions with his 1963 Education Message. I was pleased to introduce the bill, which was co-sponsored by many of my colleagues on the Education Subcommittee, and I conducted some 17 days of hearings upon it last spring. The hearings were opened by my comment that the important thing for the Congress to do was to enact the substance of the President's program without too much regard for the legislative wrapping paper used. S.580, the number assigned in the Senate, as introduced was

* Reprinted by permission of Senator Wayne E. Morse.

identical with the companion measure H. R. 3000, upon which the House committee took testimony. Since only one Senate subcommittee is involved in education legislation, we had less difficulty with the omnibus approach. The House Committee on Education and Labor found that the contents of the omnibus bill overlapped a number of their subcommittee jurisdictions; hence the bill was broken up by them into separate measures at an early date. Separate hearings were held on these components of the original bill by the appropriate House subcommittees and from this process there emerged a vocational education bill and a higher education construction bill.

In our subcommittee sessions we took the House-passed measures, re-wrote them substantially, passed them through the Senate and went to conference. We also passed a major revision of the Library Services Act under the Senate number 2265, which we sent over to the House, where it was re-worked and passed. Rather than go to conference on that bill, the Senate accepted the amendments and sent the bill to the President. It is now Public Law 88-269.

The higher education bill and the vocational education bill, to which we had added major changes in the National Defense Education Act and an extension of the impacted areas legislation, Public Laws 815 and 874 were the subject of some pretty hard nose-to-nose bargaining in conference. More than once we came very close to losing both bills. From the outset, I had warned the conference that the fate of both bills was inter-related in the Senate and that without the vocational bill, great difficulties would lie in wait for the higher education bill.

What did we get in these major educational advances? For one thing, in the higher eduction bill, for the first time, the government has recognized the construction needs of all institutions of higher education from the community college through the graduate school.

The $179.4 million in categorical matching grants to four-year institutions means that more than $500 million in facilities can be built. The $50.6 million earmarked for public community colleges should generate an additional $126.5 million worth of unrestricted classroom construction and the $60 million a year federal graduate construction grant will add a further $180 million.

The $806.5 million worth of collegiate construction joined to the facility which can be erected by the $120 million a year low-cost loan money in the bill means that almost $1 billion a year can be used to do a part of the job ahead that needs to be done. The magnitude of that task can be judged by the statistic we quoted time and time again in our debate. It is that by 1980, in a little more than 15 years, we need to double the size of every existing college and university and, in addition, to construct 1,000 new institutions of higher education to accommodate in them a student body on the average of 2,500 each.

Indeed, perhaps the least appreciated, but in the long run, perhaps the most important, aspect of the measure was the recognition of the growing importance of the public community college. Twenty-two percent of the grant funds were earmarked for the public community college and technical institutes which last year accommodated almost 28 percent of the first year students. I hazard a guess that these institutions, which are meeting a pressing need for low-cost, community-based introduction to higher education, and which, in addition, offer training beyond the high school for the many newly developing technical specialties needed by our increasingly automated society, will continue to burgeon. In the future I feel they will be the academic portals through which will go an increasingly larger percentage of our young people.

The concept which many of you in the National Education Association have endorsed, and which is attracting great support from many other segments of our society, that the free public school system should be expanded in this century to encompass at least the first two years of collegiate training will, in my judgment, command the necessary support of the majority of the taxpayers of this country within the next decade. California is blazing the trail which was pioneered by the City of New York. The people of Oregon have adopted a very generous program of combined local and state effort through their legislature.

Federal funds in P. L. 88-204, the Morse-Green Higher Education Facilities Act of 1963, which, since they are on a matching basis, are designed to supplement but not supplant the grass roots financial support, should offer to more and more areas the encouragement and incentive needed to get such programs started.

As you are all aware, one of our most difficult problems in passing educational legislation is the resolution of the church-state controversy which seems always to develop. In the Morse-Green Act, we feel that we have worked out a formula—so far as higher education is concerned —with which we can live. It is based upon the Article I power granted in the Constitution of the United States to the Congress: ". . . To

lay and collect Taxes . . . to pay Debts and provide for the Common
Defence and general Welfare of the United States; . . ."

Although a good case could probably be made for basing the legislation solely upon the "general welfare" part of the clause—and I,
for one, would very much like to see the Supreme Court breathe into
that clause the scope of meaning I feel it legitimately contains—as
a lawyer and teacher for some few years of constitutional law, I felt
that we were buttressed in our categorical grant position by the
"common Defense" power, since the categories of construction we
covered for the private and church-related schools were the mathe-
matical, scientific, engineering, modern foreign language and library
areas, most of which are parallel with the categories of the National
Defense Education Act of 1958, Title III provisions, or as in the
case of the one-third matching grant for libraries, closely related to
these fields. The graduate school grants are justified on the basis
that they produce the teachers of our scientists, mathematicians,
engineers and language specialists. As you know, the act also contains
specific prohibitions against the construction with federal funds of
facilities to be used in connection with the program of a school or
department of divinity.

Be that as it may, this whole area is a muddled and grey area of
our constitutional law. It should be clarified, but only the Supreme
Court can speak with finality on these points. I am hopeful that the
Maryland case which was instituted by the Horace Mann League can
bring us into the legal light of day through a clear and precise decision
on the point. My own bill for judicial review which would accomplish
the same purpose is pending before the Judiciary Committee. Since
Senator Ervin, who serves on that Committee, has also deep convictions on this matter which I honor though I cannot share, I feel
confident that the bill will be brought to hearing, as will, I trust, the
companion measure which was introduced by Representative Green
in the House and is now before Representative Cellar's committee.

Vitally important as was the higher education bill, to my mind the
four-fold and more expansion of the vocational education programs
under federal financing will have greater impact. In particular, the
re-definition of the term "vocational education" to include "training
or retraining which is given in schools or classes . . . under public
supervision and control . . . and is conducted as part of a program
designed to fit individuals for gainful employment as semi-skilled
or skilled workers or technicians in recognized occupations (including

any program designed to fit individuals for gainful employment in business and office occupations, . . .)" will in my judgment lead to a wholesale re-evaluation by the secondary school authorities of their present programs. This is a permanent and continuing program. The $225 million annually which will go into it by fiscal year 1968 is to be matched 50-50. At present slightly more than $50 million is expended annually by the federal government for the limited vocational programs authorized under prior legislation. Thus you can see that for this new program at least $550 to $600 million for programs and construction of area vocational schools will be flowing into our great public school plants throughout the country. Here, too, the junior and community college, which can qualify as an area vocational school, will find a source of revenue to supplement but not supplant the local and state effort.

Why do I think that the Morse-Perkins Vocational Act is of such great importance? Because I believe it will start young men and women seriously thinking about their future in an automated society while they are still in high school.

We know that scientists and engineers feel that there should be about four technicians providing each professional man with the necessary back-up services. Currently, according to testimony we received, the ratio now is more like one to one. The National Science Foundation publication, "Scientists, Engineers, and Technicians in the 1960's—Requirements and Supply", last Wednesday states: ". . . in recent years the available supply of well trained technicians appears to have fallen short of meeting the demand for these workers. With the large increases in demand anticipated in the decade of the 1960's, it seems fairly certain that the number of technicians being formally trained will continue to be much smaller than the number required."

We will need about 700,000 new technicians, the report estimates, in the ten-year period which will end in 1970. We won't get them unless and until training programs both on the job and in our schools are expanded. The Vocational Education Act of 1963, carrying as it does, substantial sums—10 percent of the appropriation—for research and demonstration projects should revitalize the existing curriculum and give to this extremely important field of educational activity the same type of a thrust forward given to the mathematics, science, and modern foreign language field by the National Defense Education Act of 1958.

The National Education Association has had an automation

project which has done excellent work. You are familiar, therefore, with the problems which flow from this technological revolution we are going through which we term automation.

If, as Secretary Wirtz has said, we are losing each year 2 million jobs through automation, it is plain that we need as quickly as possible to restructure our preparation of young people so that they can enter into American life ready to work in jobs that will be there when they come out.

I have mentioned my biases. One of the biggest of them is against allowing our young people to become unemployable. Not unemployed—that presupposes the possession of skills which can be used, and will be used, when a job is located. No, when I talk about the pool of unemployability, I refer to the dropout who did not acquire the necessary skills, or the person whose skills will never again be needed.

The human and societal waste involved in unemployability is morally shocking and politically indefensible. We have a mutual obligation, you and I, to see to it that our efforts, yours to educate and ours to finance your work, will result in training with meaning and relevance to the remaining decades of this century. If objections are raised to this on the basis of the cost, I say to you that our cash investment in the boys and girls of America is the soundest possible investment and one which will bring a return a thousand fold. Not only is our course right and farsighted; it is also, in cold cash terms, a very sound investment with high return.

Dr. John F. Morse, formerly vice-president of Rensselaer Poly-technic Institute and currently Director of the Commission on Federal Relations of the American Council on Education, in an article published last winter in the *Association of College Admission Counsellors Journal* entitled: "They Do Not Serve Who Only Stand and Wait", had this to say about the return to our country of the one time in our history, "and that for a fairly short period of time, we came close to achieving the Jeffersonian dream of providing education for all as far as their talents would take them." Dr. Morse was speaking of the two GI bills which did so much to help almost 8 million young Americans realize their talents through education. He says in his article:

> Almost eight million young people went on with their educa-
> tion at levels appropriate to their ability and pursued programs
> which cannot fail to have lifted their sights and developed

their talents to a far higher level than could otherwise have been achieved. The youngsters of yesterday who were educated under this program are now in their early- and mid-forties. In this age of youth, they are the leaders in virtually every field of human endeavor.

Have you ever wondered where this nation would be if it had not been for this tremendous, almost revolutionary program of a generation ago? Last year I assembled from the relatively small number of documents and reports in my office on the Hill over forty pages of short quotations from speeches and other public statements deploring the shortage of trained people in almost every conceivable field. I wonder what those shortages would have been like without the GI bills. Or to put it another way, I wonder whether we would have known we had shortages. Is it not possible that the technological revolution and the industrial development through which we have passed and are passing has been the very creation of those whom we trained a generation ago?

WORK IN PROGRESS

I am sold on the desirability of heavy national investment in education. That is why I am still going to do all that I can to see to it that a general federal aid to education bill becomes a law. That is why I am also advancing wherever I can, modification of existing authorities to make them more effective and to increase their scope of application.

We are now providing more than $320 million a year in operation and maintenance money, which includes teachers' salaries, to school districts which qualify as impacted areas under P.L. 874. These school districts educate about one-third of all of our youngsters. Yet you know and I know that there are a great many school districts which badly need additional money if they are to do their job properly. They are "impacted" with children; they are impacted in poverty areas, rural and urban; they are impacted with special teaching problems, since many of their children hear and speak the English language only in school. These are the districts which most need our immediate help. To try to bring to these districts the money so badly needed, so that the quality of education offered in them can be raised and so that their students can have an equal break, vocationally and educationally speaking, I have introduced legislation on which I hope to have hearings as soon as the floor situation in the Senate will permit, to bring to these poverty districts federal payments predicated on the number of children in the school district whose families are federally connected through the Aid to Dependent Children program and the Unemployment Compensation program.

This bill of mine is no substitute for general federal aid which we ought to have; it is, rather, just an advance payment on the general bill I hope we can get through. I am encouraged by the fact that Congressman Dent on the House side, whose subcommittee would have jurisdiction over the bill, has joined with me in this endeavour. He, too, has introduced an identical bill and has expressed to me his intention to proceed with it as rapidly as the committee schedule will permit.

I know you share with me the heartfelt sympathy that all Americans extended immediately to our brothers in Alaska and on the sea-ravaged portions of the West Coast as a result of the earthquake and the tidal wave which followed. I shall, of course, support every effort to provide financial assistance to the State of Alaska and the affected communities. This terrible news caused me to think, however, that perhaps we should explore the utility of an automatic standby authority which would release federal funds for the replacement of schools damaged by such acts of God. Three to four schools a week in this country, I am advised, burn or are destroyed. The replacement of these schools in a great many cases, where tragedy has also wiped from the tax rolls the land values in the community, poses a terrible problem to the local communities. I am therefore exploring with the Office of Education the possibility of broadening of P.L. 815 so that the construction authority contained in it might apply under such circumstances. I have asked that a bill be drafted to take care of such contingencies, and I am sure that many senators will be interested in it.

Currently, my subcommittee is conducting hearings upon S. 2490, introduced by Senator Hartke of Indiana, which, if enacted, would strengthen our program of financial assistance to students attending colleges and universities. In addition to expanding the present title II student-loan provisions of the National Defense Education Act, the Hartke bill would establish a program of insured or guaranteed loans for students whose economic circumstances preclude the direct loan, and he has added to this a scholarship program and a work-study program. The combination of these student financial aids when they become law should make it easier for the hard pressed student to complete his education. Shortly after our hearings close on April 15th, I plan to act in subcommittee on this bill.

The recommendations of the President regarding the war on poverty are also under consideration by the select subcommittee which the Labor and Public Welfare Committee has established. As you are aware, a great many of the programs advanced in the draft legislation have educational implications. I feel sure that this measure, S. 2642, of which I am proud to be a sponsor, will be given full and careful consideration by the Congress prior to our adjournment.

OUR FUTURE GOALS

In 1787, in a letter to James Madison, Jefferson said: "Above all things, I hope the education of the common people will be attended to; convinced that on their good senses we may rely with the most security for the preservation of a due degree of liberty."

These are wise words with present application. Thirty-five years will see us approach the end of the century. What must we do if we are to assure to the best of our ability that the patrimony we pass on to our children and to our grandchildren has under our stewardship increased in value, materially and, more importantly, spiritually?

The concept of equality which is enshrined in the great documents of our republic is being polished and burnished in the controversies in the courts, in the Congress, and, to be frank, in the streets of our great cities. Surely the application of this concept to education can only mean that we must, and shall, find the way to provide to each and every young American the education which will bring his unique collection of God-given talents and abilities into full realization. We cannot afford and should not tolerate the waste of potential ability.

This means that the walls of economic Jericho which bar the young from effective education must be blown down. Before the turn of the third millennium, the sole criterion for educational opportunity should be the ability to profit from it.

We have accepted the concept of the graduate fellowship, we are striving to obtain the federal scholarships. May I suggest that an expansion of the work-study programs in high school and college may lead us to the belief that educational virtue should not be the sole reward of academic excellence, but that strong positive financial incentives to the young, which will permit them to live comfortably as undergraduates, might be feasible. Surely by 35 years from now, we will have found the formula whereby the costs of tuition and books are shifted from the student and his family and instead will be borne by the commonwealth. This is the path of the Morrill Act, the California program, and that of the City College of New York.

For our future elementary and secondary schools, I hope that the teaching requirements, not the budget, will determine what the architect can create. And in our schools, I trust that the keystone of the educational arch, the classroom teacher, will have been freed, through automation, from the non-essential routines so that he or she can concentrate and give to the pupil all the professional help he needs. Here, too, the budget requirements should be subordinated to the child requirements. We do not ask a doctor to qualify and restrict his professional services when he deals with the body of the child. Why then should we not adopt a similar attitude when it comes to the precious mind psyche and soul of the child?

It will cost a great deal, but I verily believe that it will cost us far more if we don't do it. No one really can count the cost of a thwarted and frustrated talent which becomes twisted to anti-social ends. What price tag can we place on an Einstein or an Edison, a Steinmetz or a George Washington Carver? Had one of these not reached fulfillment of potential, we all would have been far poorer. We cannot afford for our future to echo the tragedy of Gray's poignant lines:

> But Knowledge to their eyes her ample pages,
> Rich with the spoils of time, did ne'er unroll;
> Chill penury repressed their noble rage,
> And froze the genial current of the soul.

> .   .   .

> Full many a gem of purest ray serene
> The dark unfathomed caves of ocean bear:
> Full many a flower is born to blush unseen,
> And waste its sweetness on the desert air.

Let us then together commit ourselves again to the noblest pursuit of man, the conquest of darkness born of ignorance.

Selected Readings

Committee for Economic Development. *Paying for Better Public Schools*. New York: Commission for Economic Development, 1960.

Harris, Seymour E. *How Shall We Pay for Education?* New York: Harper, 1948.

Harris, Seymour E. *More Resources for Education*. New York: Harper, 1960.

Rivlin, Alice M. *The Role of the Federal Government in Financing Higher Education*. Washing, D.C.: Brookings Institution, 1961.

Serdner, F. J. *Federal Support for Education; The Situation Today*. Washington, D.C.: Public Affairs Institute, 1959.

IV

ARGUMENTS OPPOSING FEDERAL AID
TO EDUCATION

> The fiscal case for federal school aid is contrived, unsubstantiated, and fallacious.
>
> ROGER A. FREEMAN
> *Taxes for the Schools*

> Public education is and should continue to be a state and local responsibility.
>
> DR. K. BRANTLEY WATSON
> U.S. CHAMBER OF COMMERCE

> The underlying thesis of NAM's approach . . . is that the federal responsibilities should be limited to the truly national tasks.
>
> HARLEY LUTZ
> NATIONAL ASSOCIATION OF MANUFACTURERS

Chapter IV sets forth the cause of those who oppose federal aid to education. In order to analyze this position, a summary of the basic arguments is first presented. Statements of prominent spokesmen illustrating these arguments are included in the last part of the chapter.

An Analysis of Arguments Opposing
Federal Aid to Education

The following analysis summarizes the major points presented by those who oppose federal involvement in education. We shall examine these arguments in depth to determine the parameters of each point:

1. Impossibility of equalizing educational opportunity.
2. Lack of need for federal assistance.
3. Threat of federal control.
4. Unconstitutionality.
5. Cost of the program.
6. Discouragement of individual initiative.
7. Opposition by the people.
8. Lack of historical precedent.
9. Infringement on individual freedom.

IMPOSSIBILITY OF EQUALIZING EDUCATIONAL OPPORTUNITY

Opponents of federal aid to education maintain that any attempt to equalize educational opportunity on a national level would fail, for the task is far too complicated for the government to devise any feasible system for equalization. Tax monies should not be allocated to attempt to equalize education in this manner, since this effort would have the effect not of bettering national education, but rather that of dragging the educational standard in the best school systems down to the average or mediocre level. To attempt to equalize as a method of betterment, they assert, would actually prove detrimental to the nation's entire system of education.

Schools have always reflected society, it is maintained, and it is only natural that these schools should differ somewhat from each other. This diversity has been one of the strengths of the American educational system. To equalize education it would be necessary first to change our entire society in all its aspects—economic, political, social—an obviously impossible and undesirable end. Efforts along these lines would lead certainly to a measure of conformity which has never before existed in the United States educational system.

LACK OF NEED FOR FEDERAL ASSISTANCE

The basic issue is not of quantity but one of quality, argue opponents to federal financial assistance for schools. What we need, they assert, is a whole new theory of education, a new philosophy, a re-examination of the curriculum. We need to eliminate the frills, to tighten up the present curriculum, and to use existing facilities to better advantage. Our aim should be the attaining of more education for the same amount of money.

Nor is there a lack of financial ability on the part of the states, as many claim. Each state can do the job at hand; it is simply a matter of desire. Data show, in fact, that the gap in potential abilities between states has actually been closing in recent years without aid from the federal government. A statement of March 8, 1963, by the U.S. Chamber of Commerce supports this position:

The least wealthy region of the Nation, for example, in 1930, had per-capita income only a little more than 50 per cent as large as the Nation's average, and the most wealthy region almost 150 per cent of the Nation's average. In contrast, the per-capita income in the least wealthy region in 1960 was 75 per cent of the Nation's average and that of the most wealthy region was only 118 per cent of the Nation's average [13, p. 3].

State governments are in a better fiscal position to finance education than is the federal government, for is it not true that at the present time states are actually handling the job of educating? When a national survey revealed, for instance, that 600,000 classrooms were needed throughout the nation in the past 10 years, almost 700,000 classrooms were built to fill that need. School enrollment has increased 42 per cent, compared to the increase of 581 per cent in school expenditures. In addition, teachers' salaries have increased tremendously, without federal assistance, and the ratio of pupils per room has declined from 27.8 per cent in 1950 to 26.4 in 1960. States the American Farm Bureau: "There is massive evidence to demonstrate that we are making real progress at the State and local levels in meeting the educational needs of our Nation" (84).

THREAT OF FEDERAL CONTROL

Control inevitably goes with the purse strings. With the advent of general aid to education must certainly come federal control.

When the last strong bastion of states' rights, the school, falls to federal control, individual rights will soon diminish. Aid to education is simply the opening wedge for an all encompassing move on the part of the federal government to enslave the American people and to seize control in all areas of endeavor.

Even when the aid might be construed as beneficial, as in the National Defense Education Act, there is still a measure of curriculum control, because the act provides aid for specific areas. Opponents of federal aid also point to the inevitable "red tape" which would be involved in a national school system controlled by the federal government. Time-consuming and expensive filing of forms would necessitate the adding of staff members to handle administrative detail.

It is also pointed out that the cost of the federal government's involvement in education has in the past followed the escalator principle. Programs, modest in their beginnings, have expanded with the passing years, and very few of them have been terminated. The histories of the federal Impact Laws and the National Defense Education Act support this statement.

UNCONSTITUTIONALITY

The major spokesman for the position maintaining the unconstitutionality of proposed federal aid to education has been former Senator Barry Goldwater of Arizona, who stated: "There can be no question but that federal intervention in our school system through aid programs is unconstitutional" (28).

Proponents of this position point out that education is not mentioned in the Constitution in any way. The Tenth Amendment to the Constitution, they contend, has the effect of reserving education to the states and thereby prohibits the federal government's interference. Article X states: "The powers not delegated to the United States by the Constitution, nor prohibited by it to the States, are reserved to the States respectively, or to the people."

Senator Goldwater pointed out, in a speech before Congress in 1961, that: "No constitutional amendment to extend Federal powers or responsibilities into education has ever been considered. If proposed, it would be overwhelmingly rejected" (28).

COST OF THE PROGRAM

Opponents of federal aid to education maintain that the government is facing serious financial difficulties. They note the huge national debt, and see education as our most expensive domestic service. The government, they say, is in no position to finance something as expensive as a nation-wide program of aid to education.

The federal income tax, moreover, is already as high as it can safely be pushed. Presently confiscatory at the higher levels, this tax threatens to damage individual initiative. The property tax, on the other hand, whose potential yield is much underrated, represents only 3 per cent of the total national tax bill. If better administered and used, this tax, which is not available to the national government, could provide sufficient tax revenue to cover the needs of education.

It should be obvious, too, that all sources of tax money are the same, that is, the individual citizen. The aggregate wealth of the citizens of the United States is the same as the aggregate wealth of the individual states. In other words, there is no tax money available to the federal government, that is not available to the states.

DISCOURAGEMENT OF INDIVIDUAL INITIATIVE

The purpose of any aid to education should be to help people to help themselves, it is argued. No bill should take away this opportunity. Putting students on "the dole" is not the way to ensure a high level of individualism or scholarship. The federal government's assistance to individual students is competing directly, moreover, with small companies which offer effective programs for commercial loans, and private endeavors cannot compete with federally subsidized loans requiring little or no interest.

With federal interference, too, any sense of local pride or sense of responsibility for community schools will disappear. Individuals will lose a feeling of personal involvement in schools financed and "run" by a remote federal government. Federal control of the schools will bring bigness, impersonality, and standardized conformity. Schools will lose any warmth; they will no longer belong to the people.

The tremendous increase in centralization would eliminate the citizen's right to take part in curriculum decision-making. Individual and community responsibility are essential to ensure academic freedom and to guarantee the best education for all children, for do not the parents and citizens of the local community know these children best? Writes John R. Miles, Manager of the Chamber of Commerce's Education Department:

If the Congress decides to provide funds to finance general education, it will not "aid" local authority, but will weaken the people's prerogative to make decisions about their schools. It will be a major step in the transition sought by those educators who believe that the people should be forced to "do right" by their children, the definition of right, henceforward, to be determined by the profession— not parents and the general public [84].

OPPOSITION BY THE PEOPLE

It is pointed out, furthermore, that federal aid to education is not actually wanted by the general public. For well over fifty years demands for federal aid have come from teachers' groups and educationalists, but in all these years no general program of federal aid to education has been enacted. Here lies proof that the demand for federal aid to education originates with a small group of educators who do not represent the feeling of the general public.

An example of a group which is very close to the educational firing line is the School Board Association. Reported in the *New York Times* of April 12, 1962, was the polling of the members of this group at their national convention. Over half, 55 per cent, indicated opposition to any federal aid to education.

Other groups opposed to federal intervention are the U.S. Chamber of Commerce, the National Association of Manufacturers, the Farm Bureau Federation, the National Grange, the

American Legion, the Daughters of the American Revolution, and the Association of Physicians and Surgeons. In 1946, for example, the DAR adopted a resolution opposing federal aid to education on the grounds that it would tend toward further regimentation and centralization of government. The American Legion has consistently opposed proposals for federal aid on the grounds that they are "unreasonable, unsound, unnecessary, and dangerous to the preservation of local initiative and vitality." Excerpts stating the positions of these groups are included in this chapter.

LACK OF HISTORICAL PRECEDENT

Opponents of federal aid agree that all so-called *education bills* have been passed primarily to solve problems other than education. Stated Harley L. Lutz, government finance consultant of the National Association of Manufacturers:

The advocates of Federal support of public education have sought to rely on various Federal actions, back to the Ordinance of 1785. to confirm a Federal obligation in this field. However a review of the record shows that neither any separate action nor the entire collection of them together was motivated by a primary concern with public education as such. There were always other objectives for the realization of which education was used as a medium [84].

From the earliest relevant bills, i.e., the Ordinances of 1785 and 1787, education has played a very minor role, benefiting only indirectly. Recent historical research has highlighted the point, for example, that these ordinances were really enacted to provide free land and to encourage settlement of large sections of our developing country, rather than to aid education *per se*.

Through these and other enactments many segments of our society were helped to a far greater extent than was education. More land was allocated, for instance, to our railroads than was ever given to the schools. More recently, concern for our military preparedness and our competitive position in the space-race led to the passage of the National Defense Education Act. The Impact Laws, passed during the Korean War, were meant to help school districts which had had an unexpected growth because of federal activities in their immediate vicinity. These payments were made in lieu of taxes, from which the federal government is exempt. In the same manner the Morrill Act was intended to assist the development of agriculture, and the School Lunch Act provided a way of disposing of federal surplus foods.

INFRINGEMENT ON INDIVIDUAL FREEDOM

Those who oppose federal aid to education point to the expanding role of the national government as yet another step toward, loss of intellectual and political freedom. Historically, the family has been the basic unit of our society, and this has been true in education. Nevertheless, the family has had to relinquish to government some of its freedom in exchange for certain services, among them education. The individual has chosen to give the right to educate to the government which is in the best position to provide education for each child, and the government selected was the local government.

Professional freedom, too, is threatened as emphasis is placed on the college professor's ability to collect government research contracts rather than on his skill in teaching. The professor cannot devote his time to teaching, for his professional standing is determined by the research he has undertaken. High school and college students are influenced in their selection of a profession, and in the light of federal grants available, is it any wonder that students will tend toward careers in fields which carry government assistance?

Representative Statements

In this section we shall examine statements of individuals and spokesmen for major organizations which oppose federal aid to education. The statements have again been selected on the basis of pertinency, currency, and cogency.

To illustrate the varied arguments opposing federal aid to education statements are included for the following:

1. United States Chamber of Commerce

2. National Association of Manufacturers
3. Investment Bankers Association of America
4. American Farm Bureau

UNITED STATES CHAMBER OF COMMERCE

Dr. K. Brantley Watson, speaking for the Chamber of Commerce, testified against federal aid to education under the proposed Public School Assistance Act of 1961 (84). His statement before the Subcommittee on Education (Committee on Labor and Public Welfare) read thus:

. . . public education is and should continue to be a State and local responsibility. It is our belief that the intrusion of Federal support and consequent control into the discharge of this responsibility is unwarranted. Furthermore, it would be contradictory to the principles of our democratic processes and could well lead to a nationalized school system which is the antithesis of our American approach to education which has produced the highest educational level of any nation in history.

. . . . .

. . . Forcing decisions on local education from a central bureaucracy is contradictory to the practice of freedom and inconsistent with the American approach to education. Our system has advanced because it reflected diverse cultures and yet a common acceptance of responsibility by many citizens for education.

This pluralistic concept of decisionmaking identifies the unique basis of American education. It is unlike and not subject to the hazards of centralized standardization of education as practiced in Europe. History shows that such centralized systems of education become easy instruments for indoctrination which can be exploited by political demagogs.

In the chamber's view, Federal subsidies mean Federal decisions about school problems which should be left to the States or their communities to make. Proposals as comprehensive as those before this committee, especially those providing grants such as in S. 8 and in title I of S. 1021, are thus a retrogression toward centralized planning at a time when our State systems, uniquely cast in the image of maximum diversity and free enterprise, are enjoying a more rapid acceleration than at any time in our history. Never before have our people been more alert to technological and economic progress. Never have they shown more interest in education and its essential importance.

In quantitative terms, the expansion and improvement in our educational system during the last decade through State and local responsibility are unprecedented. Over 47 million persons, more than one-fourth of the Nation, now participate in full-time formal education. Ninety-nine percent of the children aged 6 to 15 and almost 85 percent of those aged 16 and 17 are enrolled in school. One-third of our young people enter college; two-thirds of those who enter graduate. One and a half million high school diplomas and a half million college degrees are awarded each year. No nation on earth ever did, does now, or has a reasonable prospect to approach these achievements.

School expansion required by the baby boom of World War II has been met effectively by State and community action. In the last decade, the number of teachers employed and the number of classrooms in use have increased faster than enrollment. While school enrollment increased by 48 percent since 1950, the total number of classrooms available increased by 60 percent. They are taught in smaller groups by better trained teachers, whose number increased by 51 percent. The certification requirements for teachers have shown a significant rise. Every State in the Union now requires a bachelor's degree or better as a qualification for teaching in high school. All but eight States require a college degree for teaching in the elementary school. In 1950, only 17 States required 4 years of college for beginning teachers.

Average annual salaries of the instructional staff rose in proportion to quality: From $3,126 in 1950–51, they are estimated to reach $5,389 this year, an increase of over 72 percent.

These records are only part of the phenomenal advancement this Nation has enjoyed in education—without Federal direction. The people at the local level on whom the power of decision has rested have had the wisdom to give the priority to education which it deserved. Neither should we write off these accomplishments as matters of the past because they augur for an even better future. The new record in school-bond approvals in the year 1960 is an indication that school-bond sales will continue at a high rate justifying the assumption that there will be a greater rate of classroom construction and larger outlays per pupil in the years ahead. . . . Instructional staff rose to 1,455,000 in 1959–60 from 962,000 in 1949–50. In terms of increase in numbers and monthly earnings, education led all other categories of State and local government employees. Teacher-pupil ratio actually improved while student enrollment increased by 15 million. In 1949–50, each teacher taught an average of 26 pupils, but only 25 pupils in 1959–60. In secondary schools the record was even better. The teacher-pupil ratio dropped from a high of 27.2 to 1 in 1937–38 to only 22.7 to 1 in 1958–59. Expenditures per pupil are estimated at $390 this year while in 1950–51 expenditures per pupil in average daily attendance amounted to $224 annually.

In just 1 year (1959–60)) students meeting requirements for certification to teach rose as follows:

Elementary	up 1.6 percent to	52,567 in 1960
High school	up 12.4 percent to	80,465 in 1960
Mathematics	up 31.9 percent to	5,650 in 1960
Science	up 26.4 percent to	7,797 in 1960
Foreign language	up 21.1 percent to	2,200 in 1960

In 1959–60, Americans 25 years of age and older averaged 11 years of education compared with 9.3 years in 1950 and 8.4 years in 1940. Illiteracy dropped to only 2.2 percent of the population in the last year.

These facts are conclusive proof that people can and will provide for greater quality and quantity education as the needs demand. They also show that satisfying our educational needs will be much more easily accomplished in the next decade than was the case in the fifties.

Enrollments since the bulge brought on by the baby boom of World War II were at a rate of growth approximating 5 percent while the rate of economic growth was 3 to 4 percent. The situation will reverse in the decade of the sixties wherein enrollments will drop to a rate of growth slightly above 2 percent while the rate of economic growth will at least continue at the same rate of 3 to 4 percent.

In the first instance, maintenance of school expenditure levels which existed before the enrollment growth meant that a higher percentage of national income had to be earmarked for school revenues. As indicated by the statistics just cited, levels were not only maintained, but surpassed during this period of demand through State and local taxation. In the 1960's, when economic growth will exceed enrollment growth, even continuation of the present high levels of school revenue through State and local treasuries cannot only maintain but improve standards of education.

Moreover, on the horizon are exciting dividends from the experimentation in education which the public interest has encouraged since World War II. Current innovations in the improvement of instruction, if accepted, can spread the value of a good teacher over many more students. Increased teacher efficiency through team-teaching methods, the use of educational television, refinements in guidance counseling and improved laboratory techniques in science and language instruction will afford teachers the opportunity to concentrate on their professional specialties while clerical and administrative duties are assigned to personnel qualified to assume the nonteaching responsibilities.

Trends of this nature plus the progress within the States to consolidate and reorganize small school districts into more efficient units promise to make it easier to provide education of higher qualities financed within the existing framework of resources at the community and State level.

These improvements in organization and instruction methods are the key to quality in education through more efficient use of facilities, personnel, and funds. Herein lies the futility and the dilemma of Federal action. The fundamental improvements in the efficiency and effectiveness of our schools can be achieved either through voluntary acceptance and local support, or by the compulsion of Federal directives. Advocates of Federal intervention in education believe it is too late for local freedom of action; that expert authority must be given the power to speed up the evolutionary process. While they may rationalize this resort to Federal direction on other grounds, they are in reality convinced that State and local autonomy in education is a risk we can no longer afford to take; that we must move toward a nationalized school system, standardized as to method, content and organization.

If the Congress authorizes general Federal support for all State school systems, it must understand that it is confirming this judgment of some professional educators. Such congressional action will not merely be a matter of authorizing funds for one or more of the general needs of education; it will be the beginning of the end of local responsibility based on community understanding and belief in "our local schools."

While the present Congress may deny most sincerely any intention of Federal "takeover" in education, subsequent Congresses will find that both more Federal money and more Federal direction are necessary—and the precedent and the mechanism—a Federal bureaucracy

—will already exist to move on toward greater centralizing of responsibility in Washington. While this, too, will fail to resolve the many complex problems of education, the local apathy or tax-impoverishment brought on by Federal usurpation of responsibility will leave no recourse but to go on ever further in Federal direction of the cause of education.

. . .

State and local financing has been and will be available to provide what the people of each State believe to be the right or best approach to their different school problems. The fact that professional experts disagree, or may believe the State-local process too slow, should not becloud the issue faced by the Congress. That issue is the control, the decision making about the priority in and between construction, methods, personnel, organization in and between education and other socioeconomic demands. The basic meaning of a "free" society is that the people set such priorities based on their own definitions and decisions; and that no central agency has the power to make such decisions and use the power of the Federal purse to enforce them. The bills before this committee establish the latter course of action as the future way of determining how education is to be financed in this country and what aspects of education shall have priority.

. . .

In light of the massive evidence that exists to the contrary, it is hard to believe that any emergency has been demonstrated to exist which would justify Federal intervention into the support of our schools. The U.S. Office of Education with the support of research from the National Education Association has issued figures that show the teacher-pupil ratio is lower than it was 10 years ago. It is a fact that over one-half of the children in school today are attending in classrooms which were built since World War II—almost as many new ones as were in existence in 1946. The following is a graphic presentation of the number of classrooms built in each year since World War I. It shows that classrooms built since 1946 will be an estimated total of 755,100.

This is proof that indictment of voluntary local effort in the building of schools is grossly unjust and a pure fiction when matched against the record.

We believe that the pretense of an emergency in school housing is based upon faulty conclusions from accounts of half-day or double

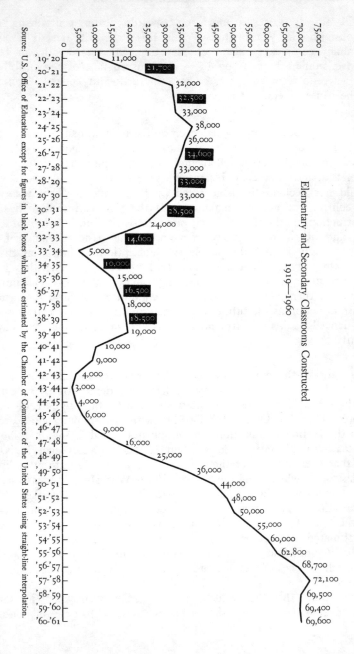

Elementary and Secondary Classrooms Constructed
1919—1960

Source: U.S. Office of Education except for figures in black boxes which were estimated by the Chamber of Commerce of the United States using straight-line interpolation.

'19-'20 — 11,000
'20-'21 — 21,700
'21-'22 — 32,000
'22-'23 — 32,500
'23-'24 — 33,000
'24-'25 — 38,000
'25-'26 — 36,000
'26-'27 — 34,600
'27-'28 — 33,000
'28-'29 — 33,000
'29-'30 — 33,000
'30-'31 — 28,500
'31-'32 — 24,000
'32-'33 — 14,600
'33-'34 — 5,000
'34-'35 — 10,000
'35-'36 — 15,000
'36-'37 — 16,500
'37-'38 — 18,000
'38-'39 — 18,500
'39-'40 — 19,000
'40-'41 — 10,000
'41-'42 — 9,000
'42-'43 — 4,000
'43-'44 — 3,000
'44-'45 — 4,000
'45-'46 — 6,000
'46-'47 — 9,000
'47-'48 — 16,000
'48-'49 — 25,000
'49-'50 — 36,000
'50-'51 — 44,000
'51-'52 — 48,000
'52-'53 — 50,000
'53-'54 — 55,000
'54-'55 — 60,000
'55-'56 — 62,800
'56-'57 — 68,700
'57-'58 — 72,100
'58-'59 — 69,500
'59-'60 — 69,400
'60-'61 — 69,600

sessions involving a small number of students. Figures on these are very misleading when presented without analysis. For example, the U.S. Office of Education reported 156,840 secondary school pupils were on double sessions in 1958–59. Analysis of the distribution of these pupils revealed that nearly a third of them were located in New York State and another 11,000 were in Connecticut—two of the so-called wealthy States. This example underscores our contention that in most instances the crowding which exists occurs in growing suburban areas where classroom shortages are not a matter of poverty but an inability to predict the rate at which a community will populate as the local economy expands.

The number of children has been increasing rapidly in high-income States and little if any in low-income States. Almost three-fifths of the national increase in school enrollment between 1955 and 1970 is projected to take place in the 12 wealthiest States, only 5 percent in the 12 States at the bottom of the income scale. Thus most of the school load occurs where the taxable wealth and income are. A recent report of the Bureau of the Census (P–25 No. 194) showed substantial gains in the number of children under 5 between 1950 and 1957 in the high-income States and losses in such States as Arkansas, Mississippi, Alabama, West Virginia, Kentucky, etc. Certain areas in California, although they have money committed to schools already under construction, report classroom shortages because the bricks and mortar cannot be put in place as fast as enrollment changes. Significantly all 3 of the States mentioned, plus 14 others, are among the wealthy States which will be carrying the load in the proportion of Federal income taxes they will contribute toward the cost of the programs such as those proposed under title I of S. 1021.

NATIONAL ASSOCIATION OF MANUFACTURERS

Included here is a concise statement of the views of the National Association of Manufacturers. Published in 1962 in leaflet form, "Why We Believe Education Should Remain a State and Local Responsibility" sums up the position that education is "a matter of national interest but it is not a federal function." *

* Reprinted by permission of the National Association of Manufacturers.

WHY WE BELIEVE EDUCATION SHOULD REMAIN A STATE AND LOCAL RESPONSIBILITY

The National Association of Manufacturers, throughout its organizational history, has supported the expansion of both public and private education. Why, then, are we opposed to federal aid?

Because, *as a matter of governmental principle*, education is not a federal function but a responsibility of state and local governments and voluntary bodies.

Because, *as a matter of fiscal principle*, state and local governments are in a better position to finance tax-supported education than is the federal government. Non-public education, which is a matter of choice, should be voluntarily supported.

Because, *as a matter of political principle*, intellectual and political freedom are best nurtured by the education system which is least subject to conformity in content and teaching practices and most responsive to the needs and preferences of the community supporting it.

Because, *as a matter of educational principle*, federal aid is more likely to aggravate than to solve our educational problems.

Because, *as a matter of fact*, it is not needed.

THE PROPOSALS: PAST AND PRESENT

Suggesions for generalized federal aid to education are not new. They have been debated seriously in Congress for at least a century. The specific proposals, the attempted justifications for them and the degree of political support they could muster have varied. However, several things have remained unchanged:

. . . The demand for federal aid comes primarily from the educators, not from the public.

. . . No bill for general federal aid has become law.

. . . The proposals that have been enacted have been specific and, at least in their origins, associated with some national emergency, real or alleged.

In the post-World War II period we have seen an intensive campaign to achieve generalized federal aid, waged on the basis of a series of presumed crises (extrapolated from obvious needs).

. . . During the late 40's and early 50's, the supposed crisis was one of shortages—of classrooms, of teachers, of money for adequate salaries to attract and retain teachers. Population was increasing rapidly and, with shifts in population and the accumulated needs of the war years, many communities did need schools. The proposals approximated general aid but, except for those dealing with the so-called "federally impacted areas" and college housing, they have been consistently rejected. Undoubtedly they will continue to be offered in various forms. However, the achievements of the last decade make it increasingly hard to justify them on the basis of need.

. . . In 1957, the first Soviet Sputnik fortuitously presented the federal aid proponents with a new crisis. They argued that our national prestige had suffered this blow because we had not been educating enough scientists and technicians. Education, in a technological age, was a matter of national defense. This time they were successful. The National Defense Education Act was passed in 1958 as a 4-year "emergency" measure. It has already been extended. The expectation is that its proponents will seek to expand its provisions (particularly to introduce scholarships in addition to loans). Having achieved the precedent —and with the youngsters who crowded the elementary schools in the early 1950's coming of college age and causing another kind of crisis— it would be unrealistic to anticipate anything except such pressure. That has been the history of grant programs. Once enacted, they are extended and expanded. Ultimately they are "depended upon"—and become permanent.

And new themes are developing to replace or supplement the appeal of ephemeral crises. The U.S. Office of Education has reported that 72,000 classrooms were built in the year 1960–61; 69,000 in the previous school year. With this type of activity—*without* federal aid— they must admit that the shortage has "eased."

The growing trend toward centralization of government for its own sake is filling the void. The argument of national "emergency" is slowly but surely being replaced by that of national "purpose." Education is good for the country. Ergo, education is a federal responsibility. What may become the basic document in this approach is a report, issued in April 1961, entitled A *Federal Education Agency for the Future.* This is a 56-page plan by members of the career staff of the United States Office of Education for expansion of their functions and responsibilities. It reenforces the impression many people have had that the real goal of the educator-proponents of federal aid *to* education is federal control *of* education. To some extent the report is summarized by the proposal to change the name of the Office of Education to the United

States Education Agency in recognition of "the more active role of this unit of government."

In anticipation of the return of Congress, Secretary Ribicoff announced his "new" package for federal aid. The headline item was an attack on "illiteracy" among adults and the inclusion of adult education a—term that has been used to cover everything from bridge lessons to the return to school of serious students—in the federal program. Included also were projects for medical education and aid to education television, in addition to the more familiar suggestions. This seems to us to indicate two things:

. . . The progress of local and voluntary education has been such that the proponents of federal aid are looking for new projects.

. . . A small group, dedicated to the idea of federal aid—rather than to the meaning of education for our nation and our time, will continue to wage a persistent and determined battle to achieve that end.

Undoubtedly the new and old proposals will find Congressional sponsors and will be presented and debated. The important questions for every citizen to consider are:

. . . Under our political system would federal aid to education be an acceptable solution?

. . . If it were, could it solve the educational problems that do exist?

The first question is basic because we must solve specific problems within the framework of the political system to which we are committed. As a nation, we have always stressed local control of public education. The federal aid advocates are aware of this and most of them insist that federal money can be provided without federal control. This is unrealistic. When government has the power to decide *whether* and *how much* support to give, control is implicit. It would be neglectful for the federal authorities not to provide for inspection and supervision of the use of federal funds.

The control that must follow is more than cost accounting, important as that is. Federal funds will, sooner or later, mean federal standards —for curriculum, teaching methods, teachers' salaries, college admission standards and a host of other items. Those who consider this to be an exaggeration might pause to realize that the aim is to nationalize education, although the proposals are made in terms designed to be more tolerable to the electorate. For example, in the U.S. Office of Education report, referred to above, a connection was made between the federal government's responsibility for conducting foreign affairs and the teaching of foreign languages: ". . . national observers are especially well qualified to assess the international deficiencies of our domestic educational system. . . . And for precisely the reason that the Federal Government feels these deficiencies most acutely, it has a unique responsibility to sponsor and subvene their remedies." This type of reasoning leads to curriculum control and curriculum control limits intellectual freedom.

The issue of the distribution of responsibilities between federal and state governments has been discussed pro and con since the beginning of the Republic. Viewing the area of governmental functions and responsibilities as a whole, the basic line of cleavage is between those tasks which can be performed *only* by the national government and all of the other matters which can be dealt with elsewhere. Certainly education falls into the latter group. It is one of the functions obviously reserved for the states by the Tenth Amendment.

Even if such issues were not involved, we would still be left with the second question: could federal aid solve our educational problems?

What are the educational problems of the United States in the second half of the twentieth century?

. . . Providing *quality* education at all levels for an increasing number of young people.

. . . *Providing financial support for institutions* at all levels.

. . . In some instances, rendering *financial assistance to qualified students* who could not otherwise attend college or professional school.

It is our belief that increasing the federal government's role in public and private education will not contribute to the solution of these problems and may, even, aggravate them. What follows is an explanation of that belief. Because the focus of the argument seems to be shifting to higher education, we start with the third problem.

FINANCIAL ASSISTANCE TO STUDENTS

One of the loudest post-Sputnik alarms has centered around the idea that we are wasting talent because "too few" of our "top" students go to college. The quotation marks are used because there is some need for definition or clarification of terms. Who should go to college— and do they?

The discussions center around the proportion of the top quarter, or top third, in ability who are not in college. In other words, it is assumed that the approximately 30 per cent of young people of college age who are in college are not identical with the top one-third in ability. This assumption may be correct. However, it ignores the possibility that some young people are slow starters intellectually, just as it ignores the possibility that the high school evaluation of ability may be incorrect. Nevertheless, we can agree that some number of the most capable young people do not go to college.

We cannot, however, agree with the next assumption that is usually made—that all those who "should be" in college, but are not, are absent for financial reasons. Many are not in college because they do not want to be. A recent survey showed, for example, that more bright girls than dull ones drop out of school to marry. Some bright young people are anxious to begin to earn money; others want to be independent of parental and educational discipline. They may later regret this decision—sometimes enough to return to school. However, it is certainly the young person's choice. If he does not want to develop his capacity—and if his parents and teachers cannot persuade him to do so—it is hardly appropriate for the federal government to use its taxing power to bribe him to do so.

The argument that we need full utilization of the talent of the nation has become the rationale for federal aid in a Cold War context. We want to meet the challenge offered by the communists. We must meet it.—But not by becoming authoritarian and telling our young people what they *must* do.

Another aspect of the argument that "they don't go to college for financial reasons" involves a definition of the financial reasons. Although loan funds have been available for many years, NDEA loans were more readily accepted than those from other sources had been. Some of the attractiveness of this program is undoubtedly to be found in the fact that the law permits cancellation of part of the debt if the recipient becomes a teacher in the public elementary or secondary school. Between the demands to extend the bases for forgiveness of the debt and the demands to replace loans with scholarships, it may be that there are some who anticipate that all of this money will eventually become a gift. It is significant that the demand from many educators and politicians has not been for financial *aid* (which a loan is) but for an outright *gift*. There is no evidence that there is comparable pressure from the students and their parents.

In the course of making these demands the federal-aiders contradict their own propaganda. One of the arguments put forth to convince us that everyone in the top third among high school graduates should go to college is that they will then contribute more, because of higher skills, to the development of the economy—and they will earn more. It has become almost axiomatic that the more education, the higher the life income. However, when loans are offered to enable the student to go to college, many of the federal-aiders are horrified: "These young people cannot be asked to borrow the money because they may not be able to pay it back."

The federal government is already in the business of financial aid to college and graduate students—via the NDEA, the National Science Foundation and Atomic Energy Commission programs and the whole complex of research grants. These are largely programs enacted originally on an "emergency" basis. The problem is one of holding the line and, hopefully, minimizing the activity.

To the fiscal reason for doing this we must add the educational one that the availability of funds in some disciplines results in an overemphasis of those disciplines. Making funds available to all subject matters would only be the first step toward that federal control of curriculum that most people still decry. There is an analogy here to the economic situation in which "planning" replaces freedom of choice. When students choose to study in departments that are well-provided with scholarship and other special funds, rather than in those of their major interests, there is a depressing effect on quality and effort. If we are to accept the analogy that education is "investment in human resources," we must ask whether the individual with no risk in or responsibility for that investment will be as zealous as he would otherwise be.

One last point must be made about the special problems of college students. A great deal has been made, in the advocacy of federal aid, of rising tuition and living costs. For the truly interested student, from a family that cannot afford the current costs, there are such solutions as commuting to college or attending a tax-supported institution. However, some families want the private college and life-away-from-home experience for their children. If the cost of this has not risen significantly in relation to family income (and it has not because of the growth of income), why does it seem a greater burden than it did a generation ago? One obvious answer is found in the tax burden that the average family now bears. Doing something about this by reforming tax rates, thus permitting the family to give its children the type of education it prefers, seems to be a more practical and direct solution than adding another major government project that must be paid for out of additional tax revenues.

FINANCIAL SUPPORT OF INSTITUTIONS

This is really a series of problems, involving elementary and high schools as well as colleges and universities, and the financial needs of public and private institutions. Although we have public and private educational institutions at all levels, there is a tendency to think of the elementary and high schools in terms of tax support and of the colleges in terms of private support. Partly to simplify the discussion— and partly because the available data on tax support are largely on the lower schools—we shall follow this pattern.

The argument that federal aid is necessary for elementary and high schools was built on the assumption that the states and localities do not have the financial capacity to provide more for educational purposes. The most cogent answer to that is found in the accomplishments of the past decade, which have made it necessary for federal aid proponents to look for new programs and reasons for intervention.

A decade ago the "crisis" was three-fold: a shortage of classrooms, a shortage of teachers and inadequate salaries for teachers. The states and communities have not just made progress in one or another of these areas—they have made dramatic progress in all three:

. . . Average annual salaries of classroom teachers rose 70 per cent between 1950–51 and 1960–61 (while gross weekly earnings in manufacturing rose by 53.2 per cent).

. . . Pupil enrollment increased 44.4 per cent in the decade; the number of teachers increased 51.9 per cent, making possible reductions in the average pupil-teacher ratio.

. . . The generally accepted projection of classroom needs through the 1960's is for 60,000 new classrooms a year. During 1960–61, 72,200 were built. The U.S. Office of Education reports the yearly average was 69,100 a year in the last six years.

. . . And, at the same time, expansion of tax-supported colleges, including community colleges, was taking place.

Obviously the claim of state-local fiscal incapacity has been overworked. It thrives on the illusion that federal money is free—provided by someone else. Yet it is a simple fact that the aggregate income of all of us is what must support all government. The states have broad taxing power and less debt than the federal government. Although the projected demand for education is impressive, so are the tallies of recent accomplishment and the ability of states and localities to supply even more education.

Nor is the situation of the private institutions as gloomy as the federal-aiders would have us believe. And this despite the facts that inflation has cut down the buying power of income from endowment and operating costs have increased sharply. Some colleges operate in the black. According to a 1959–60 survey by the authoritative Council for Financial Aid to Education, this report is made on *voluntary* giving to a group of 72 institutions in the six-year period, 1955–1960:

. . . voluntary support more than doubled;

. . . alumni giving up 102.5 per cent;

. . . business corporate support up 96.8 per cent;

. . . support to professional and specialized schools up 147.9 per cent;

. . . voluntary support for 64 institutions included in all surveys over this period increased by 117 per cent; GNP over this period was up 26.6 per cent.

This is hardly the picture of a society that must be taxed still more heavily to provide for its colleges and universities.

QUALITY OF EDUCATION

This may be the most crucial of our educational problems. It is one thing to have all of our youngsters of school age in school; it is quite another to see to it that they are taught so that they become intelligent citizens, skilled employees and reasoning adults.

Quality in a custom-designed, hand-wrought, high-priced product is neither surprising nor very difficult to achieve. Quality in a mass-produced and inexpensive product is another type of achievement—and one that has become characteristic of our economy.

We have faced an analogous situation in education. Education of high quality for a small elite group has been available since civilization began. Quality education, available to everyone in free schools, presents another type of challenge. We have done less well here than on the production line.

The fact that all children are not equally able to benefit from education need not have a negative influence on the quality of education. During the past half century, however, many professionals in education have tried to minimize, or ignore, intellectual differences. We have seen automatic promotions from grade to grade; eventual, and equally automatic, graduation from elementary and high school; and, in some areas, automatic admission to tax-supported colleges. The face-saving device has been the minimizing of the basic—often the "tough"—

courses and the substitution of standards of "adjustment" for standards of achievement. We deplore the situation of the youngster who drops out of high school without receiving a diploma much more thoroughly than we inquire into the significance of that diploma.

Universal education is a proud national objective. It should be a challenge to the ingenuity of our teachers. Instead it has too often been used as the rationale for allowing quality to take second place to quantity. Those who, in the name of democracy, abandon the slow or disinterested student to automatic promotion and graduation are, in effect, saying that he cannot be taught—that he can only be helped to "adjust" to his mediocrity.

And it is the proponents of the educational philosophy which put us in this dilemma who would have the most to say about the administration of federal programs in education. They are the leaders who have insisted that "professionalism," rather than subject-matter knowledge, dominate teacher-training curricula and teacher-certification standards. They are the spokesmen for the educators' organizations which, more than any other group, have repeatedly demanded federal aid for education. It is their panacea; they have the plans for administering it. They are an excellent example of the general tendency of *expertise*, once entrenched, to perpetuate itself.

BY WAY OF CONCLUSION

. . . Education of our youth is a matter of national interest but it is not a federal function.

. . . The states and localities are able to meet the financial needs of education. Thus, there is no validity to the argument that their financial problems make federal aid to education necessary.

. . . Education requires money. But the end-products of our educational system will not be improved by money alone. Many of the important things that money cannot accomplish can best be achieved by local and voluntary effort.

. . . Federal aid is advocated by the National Education Association, by the U.S. Office of Education and by non-professionals who welcome any accretion of federal power. It is opposed by school boards, many educators, farm and business groups and those who believe in preserving the identity and integrity of state and local units of government.

. . . Although many educators claim that we can have federal aid without federal control, this is just not so. And the federal control will eventually involve the content and method, as well as the financing, of education.

The citizens of this country want education of high quality for all students. We are willing to pay for it. We respect the role of the teacher. However, we are not willing to transfer to the professionals in education our responsibilities for education or to relinquish our judgments on matters of political principle. We know that there are educational problems but we do not believe that they are incapable of solution by traditional local and voluntary means.

INVESTMENT BANKERS ASSOCIATION OF AMERICA

The statement of the Investment Bankers Association of America was read before the Subcommittee on Education during its hearings on the Public School Assistance Act of 1961 (84). This organization stated the following reasons for opposing federal aid to education:

In our view, the first and basic issue to be decided by the Congress is whether there is really any need for the proposed Federal aid. Since the primary emphasis has been placed on the need for additional classrooms, the answer to this question rests upon an informed consideration of (1) the present need for additional classrooms, (2) the growth rate in enrollment in public elementary and secondary schools which will determine the future need for additional classrooms, and (3) the efforts and ability of State and local educational agencies to finance construction of additional classrooms. As we have up-to-date pertinent factual data on these questions which we believe will be helpful to the committee, this statement is directed particularly to this issue.

(1) CONSTRUCTION OF CLASSROOMS FOR PUBLIC ELEMENTARY AND SECONDARY SCHOOLS CONTINUES AT A HIGH LEVEL WITHOUT FEDERAL ASSISTANCE

The U.S. Department of Health, Education, and Welfare prepares annual tabulations of the number of additional classrooms reported to be needed in each State. These estimates of needed classrooms are generally accepted as the most accurate available, but it should be recognized that they represent maximum estimates of need. These estimates of classrooms needed to accommodate pupils in excess of normal capacity are inflated because they indicate needed classrooms in many cases where the classrooms are almost completed. For example, the figures for the fall of 1960 for a junior high school in Montgomery County, Md., show 2,180 students on double session in that school; but the facts reveal that a new high school scheduled for opening in September 1960 was not completed on schedule because of construction delays so that the 740 pupils scheduled to attend the new high school were put on double sessions with the 1,440 pupils in the junior high school until the new school was completed in December 1960. This situation undoubtedly occurred in many communities throughout the country with the result that the reports thus showed large numbers of students in classrooms in excess of normal capacity simply because schools which had been financed and scheduled for opening in September 1960, were not completed by the scheduled date.

The estimates of classrooms needed to replace "unsatisfactory" facilities are also suspect as maximum figures. In some States there are arbitrary standards which provide that after a school building has been in use for a specified number of years it automatically is classified as obsolete. In this connection, it might be observed that age alone does not make a classroom unsatisfactory. Many of our finest institutions of higher learning, both in this country and abroad, take great pride in classrooms that have been in use for over 100 years.

In 1955 it was estimated by the Department of Health, Education, and Welfare that about 300,000 additional classrooms were needed (and certain advocates of Federal aid then placed the estimate much higher).

In a release on January 19, 1961, the Department of Health, Education, and Welfare announced that its latest tabulation for the fall of 1960 showed a shortage of 66,100 additional classrooms needed to accommodate pupils in excess of normal capacity and 76,000 classrooms to replace unsatisfactory facilities.

This same January 1961 release by the Department of Health, Education, and Welfare reported classrooms completed during the past 4 years for public elementary and secondary schools as follows:

Year	CLASSROOMS COMPLETED
1956–57	68,700
1957–58	72,100
1958–59	69,500
1959–60	69,400
1960–61 (scheduled for completion)	69,600

Thus, over 279,700 classrooms have been completed during the last 4 years and an additional 69,600 classrooms are scheduled for completion during the 1960–61 school year, a total of over 349,000 classrooms during the 5-year 1957–61 period.

These facts serve dramatically to disprove the prophesies of the advocates of Federal aid at hearings before a subcommittee of the House Committee on Education and Labor in February 1957. One stated that "we will be very lucky if this year we build as many schools as we did last year and next year we won't build as many as we did this year unless there is assistance, stimulation, and financial incentives from the Federal Government" (pp. 128–129 of hearings on Federal Aid to States for School Construction before a Subcommittee of the House Committee on Education and Labor, 1957). Another advocate of Federal aid in 1957 stated, "And most serious, without substantial Federal aid, it is doubtful that even the present inadequate level of school construction can be maintained" (p. 226 of the same hearings). Today, 4 years later, we have an additional 279,700 classrooms without Federal aid.

In any community with a growing population it is a normal situation to need a few additional classrooms every year, and this normal level of additional classroom need—which may total thousands of classrooms when aggregated for the United States—does not indicate any "crisis" or inability to finance additional facilities. Classrooms usually are built only when they are needed, simply because taxpayers do not authorize the construction of classrooms and the required tax levy for payment of debt service until the need exists. In most communities the need for classrooms may be reaching what is considered a normal level of additional classroom need.

In short, the alleged "crisis" in need for additional classrooms for public elementary and secondary schools has been met by the construction programs which are continuing at a steady rate without Federal aid.

(2) RATE OF GROWTH IS DECREASING IN PUBLIC ELEMENTARY AND SECONDARY SCHOOL ENROLLMENT

A preliminary projection of enrollment in the public schools, included in a report on "Staffing and Constructing Public Elementary and Secondary Schools," issued by the Department of Health, Education, and Welfare, dated December 14, 1960, shows that the total enrollment in public elementary and secondary schools increased from

31,162,843 in 1955–56 to 37,196,000 in 1960–61, a total increase of 6,033,157, or an average annual increase of 1,206,631.

The projection estimates that the enrollment in 1960–61 will increase to 41,880,000 in 1965–66, an increase in the 5-year period of 4,692,000, an average annual increase of only 938,400.

The important fact from these figures is that the rate of growth in enrollment in public elementary and secondary schools during the 5-year period from 1961 to 1966 is estimated to be down 35.1 percent from the growth rate during the 5-year period immediately past. In absolute terms, the increase in enrollment in the next 5 years is estimated to be down over 22 percent from the average annual increase in enrollment during the past 5 years.

AMERICAN FARM BUREAU

John C. Lynn, legislative director of the American Farm Bureau, presented testimony for this organization before the Subcommittee on Education (84). His statement opposing the Public School Assistance Act of 1961 warns of federal control and questions the real need for federal assistance:

The financing of public elementary and secondary education is quite properly a State and local responsibility. We oppose expanded Federal aid to education because it would be a "foot in the door" toward a federally controlled system of education. It is unrealistic to contend that the mere insertion in a legislative proposal of a pious clause disavowing any intention of authorizing Federal controls would prevent Federal encroachment. The Supreme Court has ruled that the Federal Government can regulate that which it subsidizes. The greatest control available to the Federal Government is its power to allocate funds.

Federal aid to education would stymie local initiative, a very necessary ingredient to an adequate school system, and would increase overall school costs. To transfer general educational costs to the Federal Government would result in increasing Federal taxes or a boost in the current national debt, thus feeding the fires of inflation. Either of these consequences would undermine our educational system and all other aspects of our economy.

·   ·   ·

Our testimony deals primarily with the proposed aid to public primary and secondary schools since our policy deals mainly with this aspect of the proposed legislation.

This program is presented as an emergency to deal with public education. We do not believe an emergency exists except in a few special areas. There is no demonstrated emergency. There is massive evidence to demonstrate that we are making real progress at the State and local level in meeting the educational needs of our Nation.

It is fallacious to conclude that more schoolrooms will be constructed by the use of the Federal dollar than we will with State and local dollars. In fact, we believe that in the long run we will get fewer schoolrooms and less increase in teachers' salaries if we go the Federal aid route for public education.

Anyone who has traveled through this Nation must be impressed by the number of schools being constructed in many, many communities. Counties and communities throughout the Nation are spending unprecedented sums for schoolroom construction and efforts are being made to increase teachers' salaries and to improve overall conditions. Local people understand this challenge and will meet it through local taxation, without Federal assistance and without Federal control. Federal aid could slow down this process by taking away local initiative.

Never before have our people been more alert to technological and economic progress. Never have they shown more interest in education and its essential importance.

The expansion and improvement in our educational system during the last decade through State and local responsibility are unprecedented. Over 47 million persons—more than one-fourth of the Nation—now participate in some form of full-time formal education. Ninety-eight percent of children aged 6 to 15, and almost 85 percent of those aged 16 and 17 are enrolled in school. One-third of our young people enter college; two-thirds of those who enter graduate. One and a half million high school diplomas and a half million college degrees are awarded each year. No nation can reasonably hope to approach these achievements.

Another fact which points to existing State and local initiative is the sale of new school bond issues. Sales of new issues of school bonds for public elementary and secondary schools in 1960 aggregated over $2,183,870,000—an increase of more than 13 percent over sales of

$1,927,600,000 of such bonds in 1959. Sales of school bond issues during each of the last 4 years have been as follows:

1957	$2,357,700,000	1959	$1,927,600,000
1958	2,315,000,000	1960	2,183,870,000

Sales of such bonds in January 1961 aggregated over $305 millon— the largest amount of school bonds ever sold in a single month. The proceeds from the sales of these bonds are used for construction and expansion of school facilities.

At school bond elections in 1960 voters approved more than $1,756,975,000 of additional bonds for elementary and secondary schools. This represents approval of over 81 percent, by value, of the school bonds submitted for approval at bond elections. This was the largest amount of school bonds approved at bond elections in any year and indicates the possibility of a continuing high level of sales of school bonds to provide facilities in public elementary and secondary schools. The amount approved at bond elections in 1960 would be supplemented by unused authorizations from prior years and by bonds for which voter approval was not required.

FACTS ABOUT THE TEACHER SHORTAGE

Low birth rates in the 1930's and the baby boom of the postwar years have caused a scarcity of persons in the age group which normally enters teaching and an overflow of children to be educated. The number of persons between 20 and 29 years for every 100 children 5 to 17 years shrank from 78 in 1950 to 25 in 1960.

Schools have been remarkably successful in attracting a larger percentage of the smaller supply of potential candidates. The percentage of college students choosing a teaching career has grown from 21 percent to 32 percent of all graduates in the past 10 years.

The civilian labor force increased only 12 percent between 1949 and 1959, but the public schools were able to expand their instructional staff by 51 percent. One of the major factors that attracted applicants to teaching jobs was an increase in public school teachers' pay of 45 percent, compared with a raise for all employed persons of only 29 percent (in constant dollars) over the 10-year period.

For some time there has been clear evidence that the teacher shortage is rapidly diminishing. Four years ago the National Education Association, in its 1956 teacher supply and demand report predicted an end to the teacher shortage—by the early 1960's.

Shortages of teachers are concentrated in a few fields like mathematics and science. Teachers trained in those fields often receive offers of better paying jobs in industry.

In the past 5 years (1954 to 1959), while the number of all college graduates prepared to teach increased 47 percent, the number of those prepared to teach science or mathematics jumped by 100 percent.

The number of pupils per teacher has been consistently reduced, from 35.6 in 1900 to 29.2 in 1930 to 26.1 in 1950 and 25 in 1959–60. The decline was 6.4 pupils per teacher between 1900 and 1930, and 4.2 pupils between 1930 and 1960.

. . .

Teachers' salaries are not uniform throughout the United States. Neither are other incomes, living standards, or other economic and social conditions. But the range in teachers' salaries has shrunk dramatically. The ratio between the highest and lowest State average was 1:5.1 in 1941–42; in 1959–60 it was 1:1.9. This is a narrower range than in per capita income.

But in 1941–42 teachers in the lowest State received about one-third of the national average pay; in 1959–60 they received about two-thirds of the national average. This is a remarkable reduction in the differential. Relative to other citizens, the teachers are generally better off in the low-income States than in high-income States.

FACTS ABOUT CLASSROOM CONSTRUCTION

The major responsibility for the existence of a classroom shortage is generally attributed to two factors:

(a) The slowdown (sometimes called "standstill") in school construction during the 1930's and 1940's. School building activity was low during the depression and war years; so was everything else According to statistics of the Office of Education about 288,000 classrooms were built in the years 1929-30—1948-49 while the number of children attending public schools fell half a million. It is likely that replacement of old schools proceeded at a somewhat slower pace than if there had been no war or depression.

(b) The unprecedented influx of children between 1949–50 and 1959–60 swelled public school enrollment by 10.8 million. The presence of those children required a net addition of 370,000 classrooms. Actually, 567,000 classrooms were completed in the years 1949-50—1958-59. That left about 200,000 classrooms for the replacement of old buildings, and for the reduction of whatever shortage existed in 1950.

The classroom picture which the various conflicting and internally contradictory reports of the Office of Education present is no less confusing than the teacher shortage situation. The Commissioner of Education testified before the House Education Committee on October 8, 1954, that, at the prevailing construction rate, the classroom shortage would total 470,000 by 1959–60. The chairman of the Senate Committee on Labor and Public Welfare predicted on January 27, 1955, that the shortage, within 3 years, would climb to 600,000. But 2 months later the Secretary of Health, Education, and Welfare stated before the House Education Committee: "We find that the estimated classroom deficit by the year 1959–60 would be 176,000 classrooms rather than 407,000."

On December 23, 1959, the Secretary of HEW released at a news conference a report stating there existed a shortage of 132,400 classrooms in the school year 1959–60. Is this total more reliable than the erratic reports in earlier years? Analysis reveals that it is no better—and probably no worse—than the other shortage claims. It was arrived at by fundamentally the same process: by asking State departments of education about the size of the shortage in their respective States. Some State departments made their own estimates; others communicated with local school systems. No uniform national standards were prescribed and reliance was placed upon a local judgment of need. The replies were just as dependable as they would be to a survey of the need for automobiles which asked every man, woman, and adolescent whether he or she needed one or several new cars (with the prospect of getting them for free or at half price if the survey reported a big enough "need"). Close study of the annual classroom shortage reports of the Office of Education reveals sharp changes—amounting to thousands of classrooms—up or down in several States, from year to year.

The outlook for meeting future school building needs is excellent in view of the fact that annual enrollment increases will decline to half their present size in the course of the 1960's.

The classroom need in the coming decade was computed as follows by Louis H. Conger, Jr., Educational Statistics Branch, U.S. Office of Education.

ILLUSTRATIVE PROJECTION OF THE NUMBER OF PUBLIC SCHOOL
CLASSROOMS NEEDED TO BE BUILT IN THE 10 YEARS 1959–60
THROUGH 1968–69—48 STATES AND DISTRICT OF COLUMBIA

Classrooms needed for increased enrollment (8.7 million
pupils) 312,000
Classrooms needed to eliminate existing shortage (to eliminate excess enrollment and to replace unsatisfactory
facilities) 131,600
Classrooms needed for future replacement and abandon-
ment 166,400
Total classrooms needed to be built (1959–60—
1968–69) 610,000

This projection places 10-year needs at 610,000 classrooms, for an
annual average of 61,000.

Actual construction was reported by the Secretary of HEW on
December 23, 1959, as follows:

	Classrooms
1955–56	63,300
1956–57	68,700
1957–58	72,100
1958–59	70,000
1959–60	62,700

The average annual construction during these 5 years was 67,360—
which is 10 percent more than will be needed in the next 10 years.
That means that the recent and current rate of classroom construction
is ample to take care of the requirements of the public schools.

This is strong evidence of the ability and the desire of Americans
to finance schools at local levels of government.

We do not believe large sums of Federal funds are the answer
to our educational needs. There is no special magic in a federally
appropriated dollar. Enactment of Federal aid to education in the
form of assistance for school construction and teachers' salaries will
actually prove to be a great disservice to our public school system.
The result of intervention by the Federal Government could be to
stymie initiative on the part of the local people who might get the

impression that if they wait long enough the all-powerful Federal Government will assist them.

We will build more schoolrooms, pay our teachers better, and improve the education of our children if we promote local initiative and continue to finance our schools through local effort.

The public school system of this country is the envy of the world. The unprecedented progress in our public education system has been accomplished by State and local effort. Local control of our school system has made it possible for programs to be developed to fit local needs. A temporary or permanent program of Federal aid for school construction and teachers' salaries, by necessity, would involve Federal control over our public education system.

. . .

The American Farm Bureau Federation views with considerable concern Federal intervention in an increasing number of fields which formerly were the responsibilities of State and local government. With the Federal debt at an alltime high, with the need to balance the Federal budget to avoid more inflation, we think that citizens throughout the Nation are becoming more and more conscious that they don't get something for nothing from Washington.

Selected Readings

Freeman, Roger A. *Federal Aid to Education, Boon or Bane?* Washington, D. C.: American Enterprise Assn., 1955.

Freeman, Roger A. *School Needs in the Decade Ahead.* Washington, D. C.: Institute for Social Science Research, 1958.

Freeman, Roger A. *Taxes for the Schools.* Volume II. *Financing the Public Schools.* Washington, D. C.: Institute for Social Science Research, 1960.

Friedmann, Milton. "The Role of Government in Education," in: Solo, Robert A., ed. *Economics and the Public Interest.* New Brunswick, New Jersey: Rutgers University Press, 1955.

V

FEDERAL AID FOR PRIVATE AND PAROCHIAL SCHOOLS?

> Congress shall make no law respecting an establishment of religion or the free exercise thereof.
>
> THE CONSTITUTION
> FIRST AMENDMENT

The relationship of Church and State has always been a matter for national concern. Seymour M. Lipset, in his book *Political Man,* cites three major controversies of the American political scene. Church and State leads the list, which also includes Enfranchisement and the Distribution of National Income (40).

Why is the question of Church and State presented in a book which focuses on aid to education from the federal government? The basic reason is that the question of Church and State has been a major point of dispute with respect to most recent proposals on federal aid to education, and the consensus is that this question must be answered to the satisfaction of all before federal aid, that is, in the form of general aid, will be possible. The problem to be discussed in this chapter, then, is whether the federal government *can* (constitutionality) or *should* (public policy) assist private as well as public schools. If it can and should, then *how* (means) can this aid be effected?

Both historical and constitutional perspectives of this problem are first analyzed in this chapter in order to develop a better background than is commonly provided in a discussion of this complex issue. A delineation of the current situation leads directly into a presentation of representative arguments both pro and con, followed by position papers by individuals and spokesmen for major organizations. In order further to assist in the outlining of an objective, reasonable, and reasoned approach to this issue, the chapter also introduces Supreme Court cases which are relevant to the problem.

Opposing Views on Aid to Non-public Schools

Presented in this section are the basic arguments for the two conflicting positions. They reflect, at least in part, the sometimes acrimonious feelings aroused by this question of federal involvement with private and parochial schools. The most commonly heard arguments will be analyzed prior to the presentation of the representative statements in order to provide the reader with a "roadmap" with which to organize his own thinking on this highly complex issue.

PROPONENTS OF AID TO PRIVATE AND PAROCHIAL SCHOOLS

Following is a summary of the arguments used to substantiate the view that aid should be extended to include private and parochial schools. These arguments focus on: (1) Justice, (2) Freedom, (3) Size and Growth, (4) Precedent, and (5) Pluralism.

Justice. Officials of private and parochial schools want recognition for educating a substantial number of students. It is contended that the parochial schools perform a public function and that they are as highly regarded academically as are the public schools, that they teach citizenship and patriotism, and in some ways offer a broader cultural perspective than do the public schools.

The point is also made that if parochial schools in some of our larger cities were to cease to exist, these cities would be put in an impossible position, for it is estimated that enrollment would increase by 30 to 40 per cent in many cities. In several of our larger cities; e.g., Pittsburgh, 47 per cent of the enrollment is in private schools, while in Chicago the percentage is thirty-four. It is estimated that American taxpayers are actually saved $2 billion each year because of the enrollment of over 5 million students in private and parochial schools.

Joseph Cardinal Ritter asserts: "If public funds are received for the educational benefit of the children of America, then all children should share in the benefits." It is felt that private and parochial schools, as contributors to the American school system, justly deserve a share of the federal bounty.

Freedom. Catholic leaders maintain that it is fair and proper to have the separation of Church and State, but they do not believe in a rigid adherence to this wall of separation. Implicit in the freedom of religion, they point out, is the understanding that this freedom should not cost money. Writes Father Neil G. McCluskey: "Within the somber shadow of that wall there is no place for further discussion. So the mystical wall remains high, the public conscience is smoothed, and each succeeding year the Catholic community feels itself more aggrieved" [42, p. 53]. He concludes that separation of Church and State was not meant to be an end in itself, but a means of obtaining complete religious freedom.

Many Catholic authorities think that if Catholic schools are not included in federal benefits and grants, they are, in effect, victims of discriminatory practices. It is unfair, they feel, to provide a constitutional guarantee that has, in reality, a price tag—a price tag incidentally, that is disproportionately high for many Catholic families.

Size and Growth. The tremendous growth in private and parochial schools is cited as yet another reason for reconsideration of their position in requesting federal aid. Since 1950, for instance, parochial schools have increased 500 per cent, while, at the same time, public schools have increased only 132 per cent. In 1900, only 5 per cent of the total school enrollment was in the parochial school; in 1961, 14 per cent of the total school enrollment was in private and parochial schools.* Almost six million children attend the Catholic parochial school system alone. If funds were available to assist the construction of schools and the hiring of teachers, it is estimated that approximately 25 per cent of the total school enrollment would be presently attending these schools.

Not only has this growth in enrollment entailed an increase in general costs as would be expected, but it has also caused a dis-

* In 1960–61 there were 18.8 per cent enrolled in non-public elementary schools; 8.5 per cent were enrolled in non-public secondary schools (41, p. 16).

proportionate increase in the amount spent for teaching staffs because increased enrollment has necessitated the hiring of a large corps of lay teachers, which had not hitherto been required. It is estimated, for example, that 35 per cent of all teachers in parochial schools are now lay persons. From this tremendous growth in student population there has resulted, too, because of a shortage of space and facilities, the actual denial to many students of their right to attend the school of their choice.

Precedent. The argument is that private and parochial school leaders are not asking for anything new, since aid already exists in many areas. At present, there is federal aid to schools for school lunches, school transportation, and school texts. There is already aid for other institutions similar to the schools; e.g., aid is given hospitals operated and administered by Catholic orders. There is also aid in the form of tax exemptions for church properties and exemptions for amounts contributed to a church by individuals. There is aid in the form of the provision of chaplains to the armed forces, and more recently, parochial schools have been eligible for loans under the National Defense Education Act for the construction of classroom facilities in science and mathematics. States David Fellman in reviewing the variety of aids to religion already in existence:

There are many "aids" to religion in this country at all levels of government. To mention but a few at the federal level, one might begin by observing that the very First Congress which wrote the First Amendment provided for chaplains in both Houses and in the armed services. There is compulsory chapel at the service academies, and religious services are held in federal hospitals and prisons. The President issues religious proclamations. The Bible is used for the administration of oaths. N.Y.A. and W.P.A. funds were available to parochial schools during the depression. Veterans receiving money under the "G.I." Bill of 1944 could attend denominational schools, to which payments were made directly by the government. During World War II, federal money was contributed to denominational schools for the training of nurses. The benefits of the National School Lunch Act are available to students in private as well as public schools. The Hospital Survey and Construction Act of 1946 specifically made money available to non-public hospitals. The slogan "In God We Trust" is used by the Treasury Department, and Congress recently added God to the pledge of allegiance. There is Bible-reading in the schools of the District of Columbia, and religious instruction is given in the District's National Training School for Boys. Religious organizations are exempt from the federal income tax and are granted postal privileges. Up to defined limits—15 per cent of the adjusted gross income of individuals and 5 per cent of the net income of corporations—contributions to religious organizations are deductible for federal income tax purposes. . . . This list of federal "aids" could easily be expanded, and of course there is a long list in each state [88, p. 125].

There is in effect, therefore, nothing new in the recent request for aid to parochial schools. Furthermore, if higher education is considered, there is an even more impressive list of aids to private and parochial schools. The classic example is that of the land grant aiding Brown University, which was a Baptist institution.

Pluralism. Pluralism in religion has long been recognized in the United States, for it is protected in the Bill of Rights. The argument expressed regarding pluralism is that to maintain the diversity inherent in our society, it is fair and just that people not be penalized for sending their children to private and parochial schools. In keeping with this sentiment is the following quotation from an editorial in *Life* magazine: "Education needs all the concerns it can get. The greater the variety, the better, and the more religious schools, the better, too."

American society, it is stated, can retain its variety only through extending an equal opportunity to people of different preferences. Because equal educational opportunities are essential to this concept of equality, private and parochial schools should receive federal aid comparable to that given public schools.

ARGUMENTS OPPOSING AID TO PRIVATE AND PAROCHIAL SCHOOLS

Presented here is a summary of the arguments expressed by the opponents of federal aid to private and parochial schools. Five recurring points are made to substantiate this viewpoint: (1) American Tradition, (2) Fiscal Accounting, (3) Double Taxation, (4) Fragmentation, and (5) Unconstitutionality.

American Tradition. The American tradition of separating Church and State is embodied in the letter written by Thomas Jefferson, then President of the United States, to the Danbury Baptist Association:

Believing with you that religion lies solely between man and his God, that he owes account to none other for his faith or his worship, that the legislative powers of government reach actions only, and not opinions, I contemplate with sovereign reverence that act of the whole American people which declared that their legislature should "make no law respecting an establishment of religion or prohibiting the free exercise thereof," thus building a wall of separation between church and state [58, pp. 518–19].

Historically, the schools in our country have remained free, universal, and non-sectarian. Throughout American history there has developed a great freedom within this traditional separation, and, it is pointed out, separation represents the only means to co-existence in our pluralistic society. The state, it is felt, must remain neutral; otherwise, cleavage and strife will automatically develop. It is generally believed that the very existence of our country has been based on the idea that complete separation is best for the state and best for religion, and that the state's neutral friendliness toward all faiths is the only practical policy. In the words of James Madison, the government should never "intermeddle with religion."

Fiscal Accounting. This argument concerns the question of public policy. Good fiscal management requires, it is frequently noted, that any expenditure of funds involve a certain amount of control either through locally elected representatives or through state or federal officials. In effect the expenditure of money for private and parochial schools would place these schools under some measure of control by public officials, although the extent and nature of this control cannot always be determined in advance.

It is pointed out, that not all groups operating schools are desirous of aid for this very reason. The Lutheran Church, for example, which operates a nation-wide system of parochial schools, specifically denies wanting assistance. Other groups concede that aid might lead to control of school policies regarding admissions, curriculum, qualifications for teachers, and so on.

This argument is exemplified by Cardinal Cushing's statement in 1955: "We are not looking for any federal or government aid to build schools. I would absolutely refuse the offer because I cannot see how any government of state would build schools without expecting to control them."

Opposition to financial assistance from the federal government also comes from those who fear pressures to enforce desegregation in areas where existing schools are non-public; i.e., they do not accept all students.

Double Taxation. In many ways one of the strongest arguments for federal involvement in private and parochial schools is the question of double taxation. Those opposing this point of view, however, stress the fact that all of us suffer some form of double taxation; e.g., unmarried persons are required to pay taxes to support schools. Individuals who join private clubs and private swimming pools are also suffering a type of double taxation.

The point is argued, furthermore, that this added burden is self-imposed. This is the major point of the Dickman Case which was decided in Oregon in 1961 (37, p. 24):

We are not unmindful of the fact that parents who send their children to Catholic schools must bear the double burden of supporting not only their own parochial schools but the public schools as well. But the added burden is self-imposed; instruction in the public schools is available to all. Catholic schools operate only because Catholic parents feel that the precepts of their faith should be integrated into the teaching of secular subjects. Those who do not share in this faith need not support the cost of nurturing it.

Non-discriminatory, non-sectarian public schools are available to all who wish to use them and, as such, are supported by public tax monies paid by all individuals as citizens and taxpayers of the nation. All taxpayers may vote on matters pertinent to the school —bond issues, elections, etc. The person paying taxes to support public schools does not necessarily have children attending the schools; taxes paid, therefore, cannot be construed as tuition. Payments made to private and parochial schools, by contrast, must clearly be termed tuition payments, for the church has no power to levy or collect taxes. There is, therefore, no question of double taxation.

Fragmentation. Those who oppose federal assistance to private and parochial schools feel that the public schools in this country provide an excellent means for unifying our diverse society and that, while they represent a fragile compromise in terms of political, social, religious, and philosophical values, they do offer a common ground where all can meet. A system of financing any or all private and parochial schools would mean that any group could and would establish its own school system which would result in the relegation of the public school system to a minority position.

To support this argument, it is pointed out that the Black Muslims maintain full-time parochial schools in both Chicago and Detroit. A socialist group, the Workman's Circle, maintains elementary schools in several cities; and other political and economic groups, e.g., the John Birch Society and the Minutemen, could establish their own schools as well. Even very small religious groups have established schools. The Christian Reform Church, with 242,000 members, has a nation-wide school system, and the Pillar of Fire Church in Chicago, with only 5000 members, operates an elementary school. How can the quality of the education offered by these small groups equal that offered by the public school system?

Those who fear fragmentation frequently cite the situation in the Netherlands, which, since 1921, has subsidized religious schools. As a result, attendance in the Dutch public schools has decreased from 56 per cent to 32 per cent of the student population. The effect of this decrease has been to divide the country so that not only the schools but also other institutions represent religious segregation, and whole communities or towns are homogeneous with respect to religion.

When we consider that the United States has more than 300 religious denominations, the fragmentation argument appears to have substantial validity. In the last ten years, while Catholic school enrollments increased 66 per cent, the entire group of private and parochial school enrollments increased 340 per cent, which indicates a sharp rise in the number of schools supported by smaller religious groups.

Unconstitutionality. "There can be no question of federal funds being used for support of private and parochial schools. It is unconstitutional under the First Amendment as interpreted by the Supreme Court." These are the words which the late President, John F. Kennedy, a Catholic, spoke many times. In several news conferences, in his speeches before being elected to the presidency, and under close questioning, he consistently maintained this position.

Supporting the argument of unconstitutionality is the decision of the Supreme Court in the Everson Case (1947) which stated in part:

No tax in any amount, large or small, can be levied to support any religious activities or institutions, whatever they may be called, or whatever form they may adopt to teach or practice religion. Neither a state nor the federal government can, openly or secretly, participate in the affairs of any religious organizations or groups and *vice versa* [67, pp. 210–11].

In the words of Jefferson, the First Amendment was intended to erect "a wall of separation between Church and and State." The Everson Case clearly enunciates this doctrine with respect to the federal government's relationship to religious activities.

Supreme Court Decisions

This section describes relevant Supreme Court cases involving decisions on the question of the relationship between Church and State. The Supreme Court, in its business of deciding cases, has developed a large body of literature which is not always readily available to the student.

Many writers have noted the Supreme Court's significant educational role. Walt W. Rostow, for example, wrote: "The justices are inevitably teachers in a vital national seminar." Lawrence Cremin, noted educational historian, describes the Court opinions thus: "[They] have embodied some of the most cogent and compelling discussions of educational policy set before the American public." It is apparent even to the casual observer that all of our contemporary social problems sooner or later come to rest at the foot of the courts. This is certainly true in terms of the question presently before us.

Representative cases that are relevant to the question of Church and State, as this problem relates to federal aid to education may, for purposes of analysis, be divided into four categories: those which deal specifically with (1) religious freedom, (2) governmental assistance, (3) co-operation, and (4) religion in schools. Particularly relevant to the problem of religious freedom is the case of *Pierce v. The Society of Sisters* (often called the Oregon Case). Regarding governmental assistance, we can study the Cochran Case (the Louisiana Textbook Case) and the Everson Case (the New Jersey Bus Case). Under the grouping "co-operation," we shall examine the McCollum and the Zorach Cases, both of which involved released time. Discussing the place of religion in the schools are *Engel v. Vitale* (the Regents' Prayer Case) and one of the more recent decisions, the *School District of Abington Township, Pennsylvania v. Schempp; Murray v. Curlett* (sometimes termed the Lord's Prayer and Bible Reading Cases) on which the Supreme Court ruled in 1963.

None of these cases directly treat the complex question of federal aid to private and parochial schools. The Supreme Court is somewhat restrictive in its appellate jurisdiction; hence it is not always possible to have a direct ruling on a specific question or point of law. Supreme Court cases must stem from real cases rather than from abstract issues or theories.

In 1923, in *Massachusetts v. Mellon* (262 U.S. 447), the courts ruled that citizens, as such, do not have sufficient standing to challenge federal spending. As a taxpayer, an individual does not have sufficient financial interests to challenge federal appropriations. In some ways this decision has increased the difficulty in obtaining judicial review on specific questions. Concerning this position is the memorandum from the legal department of the Department of Health, Education, and Welfare: ". . . there appears to be no realistic likelihood that Federal legislation raising the constitutional issues discussed in this memorandum will be resolved by judicial decision" (79, pp. 27–8).

One other significant point should also be noted; i.e., only since 1925 has the Court ruled that the First Amendment is applicable to the states. It made the First Amendment applicable to the states through the use of the Fourteenth Amendment.

PIERCE V. SOCIETY OF SISTERS
268 U.S. 510 (1925)

In the earliest (1925) major case relevant to federal aid to private and parochial schools, Justice McReynolds, writing for a unanimous Court, ruled that the state of Oregon had no right to require all of its students to attend the public schools. In making this ruling the Court stated: "The child is not the mere creature of the State; those who nurture him and direct his destiny have the right, coupled with the high duty, to recognize and prepare him for additional obligations."

In 1922 Oregon passed, by initiative, a law which required all students to attend public school from the ages of eight to sixteen. There were some exceptions noted, but these were very few. The appellee, the Society of Sisters, an Oregon corporation, involved in the care and education of orphans, including the maintenance of a school system for primary grades, brought suit, as did the Hill Military Academy. The appellees stated that enforcement of this law would greatly diminish the value of their properties, and would interfere with the liberty of parents to direct the upbringing and education of children under their control.

The Court's ruling in this case was basic to many later cases, since if the decision had been reversed, those cases which follow in this discussion would, in all probability, not have come to the Supreme Court for decision, for public schools would have had a monopoly on all of education, with private and parochial schools virtually non-existent. The Court in its ruling, therefore, established the precedent for the existence of private and parochial schools and also indirectly led to the following cases. In the history of American Church-State relations, it is clear that the case of *Pierce* v. *The Society of Sisters* is crucial.

COCHRAN V. THE LOUISIANA STATE BOARD OF EDUCATION
281 U.S. 370 (1930)

The United States Supreme Court in 1930 unanimously upheld a Louisiana court's decision defending the right of the state of Louisiana to lend public school texts to children whether they attended public or private schools.

The Supreme Court was asked in this case (similar to *Borden* v. *Louisiana State Board of Education*) to judge whether a Louisiana law passed in 1928, one of Huey Long's welfare measures that provided public funds for textbooks regardless of the school that the child attended, was constitutional. The First Amendment was not then considered applicable to the states, and the case was decided on the basis of the Fourteenth Amendment, which forbids any state to "deprive any person of . . . property without due process of law." In this case the appellant brought suit to restrain the state from providing free textbooks, bought with public tax monies, to all children, since this act was considered the use of private property for private purposes, the purposes being to aid private religions in sectarian schools.

The crucial point in this decision is that the schools were not judged the beneficiaries of these appropriations. The school children and the state were considered the sole beneficiaries. Here, for the first time, we note the Court stating that the taxing powers of the state have been exerted for a public purpose in issuing these textbooks. Chief Justice Hughes wrote: "The schools, however, are not the beneficiaries of these appropriations . . . The school children and the state alone are the beneficiaries."

EVERSON V. BOARD OF EDUCATION
330 U.S. 1 (1947)

The majority opinion found that a state (New Jersey) may provide transportation as a general welfare item and that such transportation is not to be construed as an aid to education or to any particular group. The New Jersey statute was thus held to be constitutional.

In 1941, New Jersey enacted legislation which made it possible for school boards to provide transportation for all school children, including those attending non-profit private and parochial schools. Specifically, the Board of Education authorized payments to parents of money spent on transportation to whatever school they deemed desirable.

Justice Black expressed the majority opinion which compared transportation to the fire and police protection available to all citizens and to all groups and institutions, private as well as public. Extensive historical research was conducted in the Everson Case to determine the framers' intention at the time of the writing of the First Amendment. Probably due to this research, indicated by Justice Black's opinion, the Everson Case is the most important Supreme Court case dealing with the question of aid to private and parochial schools. This decision is cited by more writers than any other, and has been used in at least three subsequent cases. It was also cited by the late President Kennedy in support of his school bills. Of particular note are these words by Justice Black:

The "establishment of religion" clause of the First Amendment means at least this: Neither a state nor the federal government can set up a church. Neither can pass laws which aid one religion, aid all religions, or prefer one religion over another. Neither can force nor influence a person to go to or remain away from church against his will or force him to profess a belief or disbelief in any religion. No person can be punished for entertaining or professing religious beliefs or disbeliefs, church attendance or non-attendance. No tax in any amount, large or small, can be levied to support religious activities or institutions, whatever they may be called, or whatever form they may adopt to teach or practice religion. Neither a state nor the federal government can, openly or secretly, participate in the affairs of any religious organizations or groups or vice versa. . . .

In the Everson Case, which was a 5-4 decision, there were several strong dissenting opinions written. Justice Rutledge wrote:

Two great drives are constantly in motion to abridge, in the name of education, the complete division of religion and civil authority which our forefathers made. One is to introduce religious education and observances into the public schools, the other is to obtain public funds for the aid and support of various private religious schools. In my opinion both avenues were closed by the Constitution.

The Court in the Everson Case attempted to differentiate between types of aid and to set up a kind of aid which might be considered in addition to the child benefit theory upheld in the Cochran Case, i.e., aid as a public welfare item. While granting aid for transportation, the decision of this case appears to clarify a position opposed to any direct form of aid to religion *per se*. Black's opinion concludes: "The First Amendment has erected a wall between church and state. That wall must be kept high and impregnable. We could not approve the slightest breach. New Jersey has not breached it here."

MC COLLUM V. THE BOARD OF EDUCATION
333 U.S. 203 (1948)

In 1948 the Supreme Court found the released time arrangement used in Illinois to be unconstitutional because of (1) the excessively compulsive nature of the requirement and (2) the use of school buildings and school teachers in this particular arrangement.

In 1940 the public schools of Champaign, Illinois, had initiated a program of released time for attending religious education classes. In this program the board of education allowed the Council of Religious Education, a group of representatives of the Protestant, Roman Catholic, and Jewish faiths, to allocate teachers to 10 elementary schools and 1 junior high school in order to conduct religious classes for 30 minutes each week. The children whose parents provided written permission were released from their regular school curriculum to attend these classes of religious instruction.

In 1945 Mrs. Vashti McCollum complained to the local board of education that her son was embarrassed by being the only pupil in his class not taking religious courses. Her major complaint was that these classes took time from the regular school day and from the regular school subjects. Mrs. McCollum complained that the religious classes constituted a union of Church and State which was unconstitutional. The board of education ignored her complaint, and the McCollum Case made its way to the Supreme Court.

The decision of the Supreme Court indicated extreme concern with the separation of Church and State. The majority opinion states in part: "Designed to serve as perhaps the most powerful agency for promoting cohesiveness among a heterogeneous, democratic people, the public school must keep scrupulously free from entanglement in the strife of sects." Thus the Court anticipated in 1948 some of the questions it would face in the 'fifties and 'sixties.

Also illustrative of the difficulties involved in eliminating religious influences from the public school are the words of Justice Jackson, who wrote in a concurring opinion:

Music without sacred music, architecture minus the cathedral, or painting without the scriptural themes would be eccentric and incomplete, even from a secular point of view. Yet the inspirational appeal of religion in these guises is often stronger than a forthright sermon. Even such a "science" as biology, raises the issue between evolution and creation as an explanation of our presence on this planet. Certainly a course in English literature that omitted the Bible and other powerful uses of our Mother tongue for religious ends would be pretty barren, and I suppose it is a proper, if not an indispensable, part of preparation for world life to know the roles that religion and religions have played in the tragic story of mankind.

In this 8-1 decision, Justice Black stated for the Court: "The facts in the case show the use of tax-supported property for religious instruction and a close cooperation between the school authorities and the religious Council in promoting religious education."

Thus the central point made by the McCollum Case was that the use of public buildings for religious purposes is a violation of the First Amendment. This ruling raised many issues and aroused greater feeling among the American people than had previous decisions.

ZORACH V. CLAUSON
343 U.S. 306 (1952)

In the Zorach Case the Supreme Court declared constitutional (in a 6-3 decision) the released time program utilized in New York State in which students were released to attend religious classes held elsewhere than in school buildings or on school grounds. The conditions laid down by this case, one of the so-called "released time cases," include three; namely, the released time classes may not involve (1) coercion, (2) meeting on school property, and (3) support by public tax money.

The crucial words in this decision were delivered by Justice Douglas in the majority opinion sustaining the released time program in New York:

We are a religious people whose institutions presuppose a Supreme Being . . . When the state encourages religious instruction or co-operation with religious authorities, by adjusting the schedule of public events to sectarian needs, it follows the best of our traditions. For it then respects the religious nature of our people and accommodates the public services to their spiritual needs.

In the dissenting opinions, we find some ringing statements by Justices Jackson and Frankfurter. Justice Jackson's strong dissent illustrates the fervor that Church and State decisions arouse. To the writer's knowledge, this is the only time that a justice of the Supreme Court has utilized his own children to substantiate an opinion:

As one whose children, as a matter of free choice, have been sent to privately supported church schools, I may challenge the court's suggestion that opposition to this plan can only be anti-religious, atheistic, or agnostic. My Evangelical brethren confuse an objection to compulsion with an objection to religion. It is possible to hold a faith with enough confidence to believe that what must be rendered to God does not need to be decided and collected by Caesar . . .

The unwillingness of the promoters of this movement to dispense with such use of the public schools betrays a surprising want of confidence in the inherent power of the various faiths to draw children to outside sectarian classes—an attitude that hardly reflects the faith of the greatest religious spirits.

Through this decision the Supreme Court found a way of accommodating the religious groups and their religious programs (commonly called "released time"), as well as of maintaining the separation of Church and State through conditions which would assure that public monies were not spent in support of private and parochial institutions.

ENGLE V. VITALE
370 U.S. 421 (1962)

In *Engel* v. *Vitale* the Supreme Court declared unconstitutional the use of a prayer (stated to be non-denominational) in the New York public schools. The brief prayer, sometimes called the "Regents' Prayer," is here quoted in its entirety:

Almighty God, we acknowledge our dependence upon Thee, and we beg Thy blessings upon us, our parents, our teachers, and our country. Amen.

On July 25, 1962, in a 6-1 decision, the Supreme Court declared the required use of the prayer in the public schools to be unconstitutional, and a new storm suddenly broke over the Supreme Court, the Constitution, and the issue of religious activities in the public schools and other public institutions.

In his far-reaching statement, Justice Douglas, concurring with the majority opinion, asserted:

It is customary in deciding a constitutional question to treat it in its narrowest form. Yet at times the setting of the question gives it a form and content which no abstract treatment could do. The point for decision is whether the government can constitutionally finance a religious exercise. Our system at the federal and state levels is presently honeycombed with such financing. Nevertheless, I think it is an unconstitutional undertaking whatever form it takes.

SCHOOL DISTRICT OF ABINGTON TOWNSHIP, PENNSYLVANIA V.
SCHEMPP; MURRAY V. CURLETT

371 U.S. 807, 907, 944 (1963)

In June, 1963, the United States Supreme Court (examining two similar cases at one time) declared both Bible reading and the recitation of the Lord's Prayer in public schools to be unconstitutional. The major opinion, written by Justice Hugo Black, stated in part: "It is neither sacrilegious nor anti-religious to say that each separate government in this country should stay out of the business of writing or sanctioning official prayers and leave that purely religious function to the people themselves and to those the people choose to look to for religious guidance."

In *Engel* v. *Vitale* (1962) only the issue of prayer in the school had been involved, while the Schempp Case involved both prayer and Bible reading. The Engel Case concerned, moreover, a state-composed prayer, "The Regents' Prayer," while in the Schempp Case the prayer was taken from the Scriptures. The issue in the Schempp Case was derived from a Pennsylvania statute that provided: "At least ten verses from the Holy Bible shall be read or caused to be read, without comment, at the opening of each public school on each school day . . ."

It should be noted that in this case there were no provisions, either by law or in the administration of this law, for the excusing of a student who did not wish to participate in the opening exercises. The law was enforced, furthermore, by the requirement that a teacher who did not comply with its provisions was subject to dismissal.

In its decision the Court reaffirmed the neutrality of government by saying, "while protecting all, it prefers none, and it disparages none." It is interesting to observe that the majority opinion was written by Justice Clark, a Presbyterian, and concurring opinions were by Justice Goldberg, the Court's only Jewish member, and Justice Brennan, the Court's only Roman Catholic. In an opinion by Justice Brennan there is an extensive review of the history of the Church-State issue and an attempt to show the relationship between this case and the long line of previous Court decisions.

STATE SUPREME COURT DECISIONS

Other cases, decided by state supreme courts, have also ruled on the question of Church and State. In two areas—the provision of textbooks and the provision of transportation—there are a number of cases to be cited briefly.

In many ways the individual state constitutions are more specific than is the United States Constitution. As an example, the following is a statement in the constitution of California: "No public money shall ever be appropriated for the support of any sectarian or denominational school or any school not under the exclusive control of the officers of the public schools." As their constitutions are in many ways more specific, so are the decisions made by the state courts. They are generally considered to be of a more separative nature.

Transportation. The states of Iowa, Washington, New Mexico, Missouri, Alaska, and Wisconsin have ruled that provision of transportation to private and parochial schools is unconstitutional under their existing constitutions. In only one case, *Schneider v. Newton* (1961), has the provision of transportation been upheld.

Textbooks. Since the Cochran Case in 1930, many state courts have been involved with the textbook issue and its constitutionality. South Dakota, New York, New Mexico, and Oregon have declared the provision of school textbooks to be unconstitutional. One state, Mississippi, has declared the providing of school textbooks to be constitutional.

Of particular interest is *Dickman v. School District, Oregon City, Oregon* (1961), which reversed a thirty-year-old law which had permitted the state to provide elementary textbooks to both public and private schools. The textbooks, secular in nature, were loaned to the schools. This was judged a violation of the Oregon Constitution which prohibits the use of school funds "for the benefit of any religious or theological institution." In its ruling the court considered the issue: "Can the religious aspects of parochial school education be separated from the secular aspects?" The Oregon Supreme Court ruled that the use of the textbooks was inextricably connected with the teaching of religion through the use of syllabi, courses of study, etc. issued by the religious authorities of the state, so the point was made by this case that even when the textbooks did not contain any religious material, they were used in a religious context with religious motives and a religious educational setting. The United States Supreme Court has refused to review this case.

The Vermont Supreme Court, in *Swart v. South Burlington School District* (1961), also ruled on a question which had not come into cases before, i.e., state payment of tuition for students attending private and parochial schools where communities do not maintain public high schools. Vermont's constitution does not deal specifically with education, so the decision was based on the federal constitution and the First Amendment. The Vermont court held that it was unconstitutional for the state to make these tuition payments. The U.S. Supreme Court has refused to review this decision, although this refusal cannot be construed as marking either approval or disapproval of the state court ruling.

Representative Statements

Presented in this section are two statements relevant to the question of federal aid to education as it pertains to private and parochial schools. Included first is Father Neil G. McCluskey's succinct argument advocating federal aid to parochial schools. Following is the equally effective statement by R. Freeman Butts, opposing the extension of federal aid to private and parochial schools.

FATHER NEIL G. MC CLUSKEY

Education editor of the Jesuit magazine, *America*, Neil G. McCluskey, S.J., presented his views on federal aid for parochial schools in a paper read at the annual convention of the American Association of School Administrators, at Atlantic City, New Jersey, on February 15, 1960. This paper was adapted for presentation in *Teachers College Record* as it appears here.*

* Reprinted from *Teachers College Record*. 62:49–56, by permission of the author and the *Teachers College Record*.

PUBLIC FUNDS FOR PAROCHIAL SCHOOLS? YES!

The question of public support for church-related schools has been debated and discussed and argued over for generations. Over the years, most of the arguments that I have listened to about parochial schools have no direct bearing on the problem of support. These arguments rather hit another point—the very existence of such schools.

For example, all that class of argument which calls parochial school education "divisive" or "un-American" or "undemocratic" should conclude by demanding the suppression of these schools. It has nothing to do really with the question of support. If the common good of the American nation and the future of democracy depend uniquely on public schooling (as we know it now), then no competing system of schools should be tolerated. It is not the further growth of nonpublic schools that should be questioned but the propriety of their remaining in existence. This is the point to which critics of the growth of nonpublic schools should honestly address themselves. Either nonpublic schools have the right to exist and to multiply according to the wishes of their patrons, or they do not. If they do not have the right, the state should, at the very most, allow only a few schools of this type to operate in widely separate areas as a symbol of America's traditional tolerance—showcases, on the model of the churches left open in some Communist countries. Those who agree with a former president of Harvard University that, "The greater the proportion of our youth who attend independent schools, the greater the threat to our democratic unity," should logically insist on a quota or cut-off point, a percentage beyond which nonpublic schools become an intolerable menace.

THE BASIC ISSUE

At the beginning of the year, the New York *Times* (January 12, 1960) carried a news story to the effect that New York City's expanding parochial school systems are cutting into enrollment in the public schools. The article reported that:

> The Roman Catholic schools, with 37 per cent of the current enrollment of the public schools, expect to enroll about four times as many new pupils next fall as the public schools.
> Top officials of the Board of Education do not attribute this to any general dissatisfaction with the public schools. Rather,

they say, it reflects the desire of some parents to give a parochial school education to their children. And they note that in recent years the construction of new parochial schools, particularly on the secondary level, has given more children the opportunity to attend.

This story could have been carried in many other newspapers. In dozens of towns and suburban communities, the parochial school now enrolls, 40, 50, and even in some cases, 60 per cent of the school population. One-half the children of Green Bay, Wisconsin, and 52 per cent of the Manchester, New Hampshire, children are in Catholic schools. The Catholic school systems in many of the largest cities of the United States enroll one quarter or more of the total school population. Here are a few of the percentages: Chicago, 34; Philadelphia, 39; Detroit, 23. The figure for Hartford is 24 per cent; for Cincinnati, 28; for Boston, 30; for Milwaukee and New Orleans, 33; for Buffalo, 40; for Pittsburgh, 42.*

At the beginning of the century, there were 854,523 students enrolled in Catholic primary and secondary schools in the United States. This represented 5.2 per cent of the entire elementary and secondary school population of the nation. Today, the number has grown to over five million or about 14 per cent of the total enrollment. The trend shows no sign of abating. It seems to be limited only by available resources. Very many, perhaps most, of the other five million Catholic school children that are now in public schools would not be there if there were enough desks and schools to accommodate these children within the Catholic system. These figures invite reflection.

The public school, at least as presently constituted, has been judged by the American Catholic parent as incapable of providing the kind of education he desires for his child. The history of the American public school has made it painfully apparent that the American people have been caught in an unresolved ambiguity. They insist that the common school assume a certain responsibility for character education, but the 250 different religious bodies and the millions of unchurched Americans do not agree on what should comprise character education or form its basis. The people have given the common school a moral mandate, therefore, whose subject remains in dispute among the different groups served by the school. This is not to blame

* Figures furnished by the superintendents of Catholic schools in the respective dioceses.

the school or to suggest that the school staff is derelict. Public school administrators and teachers did not create this problem; they inherited it and are helpless to cope satisfactorily with it. The central problem is the contradiction inherent in the very idea of one common school's attempting to serve a religiously pluralistic society. Correlative to this problem, of course, is the place of the independent, church-related school in the total scheme of things and, specifically, the claim this school has on appropriate public support.

I respectfully submit that it is in the best interests of the American nation that the church-related schools, which have assumed a generous share of America's educational burden, receive appropriate recognition and support. My two basic reasons are that (1) only in this way can the constitutional guarantee of freedom of religion be effectively safeguarded, and that (2) only in this way can the nation's youthful talent be fully realized.

RIGHT OF FAMILY CHOICE

That freedom of choice in education is an integral part of freedom of religion requires no involved proof. The family right in education is prior to the rights of civil and ecclesiastical society because it is based on the natural relation of parents to their offspring. Common sense, a venerable tradition in Western free society, and several important U. S. Supreme Court decisions have put the priority of family right beyond dispute.

Need we do more than recall that the Supreme Court has, on several occasions, unqualifiedly reaffirmed the principle that "the child is not the mere creature of the state" (*Pierce v. Society of Sisters,* 1925); and that "the custody, care and nurture of the child reside first in the parents" (*Prince v. Massachusetts,* 1944)? Or to remind ourselves that unambiguous support for the primacy of the family right is likewise to be found in the *Universal Declaration of Human Rights,* proclaimed by the General Assembly of the United Nations (December 10, 1948): "Parents have a prior right to choose the kind of education that shall be given to their children" (Article 26, 3).

To state this truth is not to deny or diminish in any way the state's rights in education. A modern democratic state rests on the intellectual alertness and moral maturity of its citizenry. The state, accordingly, is obligated, directly or indirectly, to maintain a level of universal education sufficient to ensure its own economic, political and cultural well-being. However, this obligation can be discharged in many ways. It does not follow that the state itself must invariably set up its own quasi-monopolistic system of schools. An imposing number of countries, whose traditions and sympathies are as liberal and democratic as America's own, have long accepted—and subsidized —the assistance of other agencies in achieving the goal of accessible universal education.

The American state has passed compulsory school attendance laws, and to assist parents to comply with such legislation, has established a system of free public schools, but without any provision in them for religious training. In pursuit of the common good, the state taxes all citizens alike to form a common pool for the support of education, so that it may provide for its school children the substantial benefit of free education and certain auxiliary benefits related to education. But this can only take place within the type of school the state itself chooses. Catholic parents judge that in all conscience they must, if at all feasible, send their children to a Catholic school. For Catholics believe that secular education during the child's formative years must be integrated with religious training. The Catholic parent looks to the public school not reproachfully but regretfully. As a policy statement issued only a few years ago by a commission of the NEA-AASA has solemnly told him, "As public institutions, the public schools of this nation must be nondenominational. They can have no part in securing acceptance of any one of the numerous systems of belief regarding a supernatural power and the relation of mankind thereto." [4]

A family seeking to follow simultaneously the dictates of conscience and the compulsory education law may not now, for all practical purposes, share in the state's provision for the common welfare. In the concrete, the state has set up what amounts to a religious test. If public benefits are so administered that citizens must do violence to their conscience in order to share in them, then the benefits are discriminatory. They are not truly public because to them is attached a religious qualification. That portion of the public which prefers to follow the dictates of conscience fails to qualify (1) in general for the basic benefit of free education and (2) in most states for the bulk of the supplementary benefits given for the sake of the school child.

It is not the American way simply to dismiss this conscience as a private affair, a Catholic idiosyncrasy, and to let it go at that. Religious liberty and the constitutional prohibition of religious qualifications mean little unless these are related to the distinctive peculiarities of each type of conscience. As Dean Robert Henle of St. Louis University has pointed out,[3]

> our courts have shown a punctilious and precise concern to protect the consciences even of minorities commonly regarded as extremists. The court simply inquires what the conscience of the individual is; it does not judge that conscience as a conscience, but takes it into account as a fact and provides for it. (p. 244)

Nor can the question be loftily waived with a statement, like that of Justice Wiley B. Rutledge in his *Everson* (1947) dissent, that, "Like St. Paul's freedom, religious liberty with a great price must be bought. And for those who exercise it most fully, by insisting on religious education for their children mixed with secular, by the terms of our Constitution the price is greater than for others." This is preposterous. The last thing our founding fathers intended to do was to put a price tag on the religious liberty protected by the First Amendment that would put it beyond the reach of some citizens. The rights and freedoms guaranteed to American citizens in the Bill of Rights were intended to be common. The equal protection guarantee, said the Supreme Court, "requires that all persons . . . shall be treated alike, under like circumstances and conditions, both in the privileges conferred and in the liabilities imposed" (*Hayes v. Missouri*, 1887).

RELIGIOUS FREEDOM

In its simplest terms, this entire issue boils down to a question of the primacy of spiritual over temporal concerns. Maybe more of us should agree with Dr. Butts's assumption [1] that every American somehow owes a prior duty of loyalty to a "democratic" state-established school. But neither the history of Western civilization nor the tradition of our American courts offer support for this assumption.

Based upon their acknowledgement of the primacy of the spiritual order, the courts have made it clear that the government must leave parents free to send their children to schools of their choice. The corollary question is now before us: Does the First Amendment permit the government to respect that freedom further by arranging distribution of its various benefits so as to avoid discrimination against parents or students who make this choice? As far as auxiliary benefits are concerned, the courts have given an affirmative answer to this question, although they have not always applied it with consistency.

It is a matter of record that the same majority decision of the U. S.

Supreme Court in the *Everson* (1947) case that declared, "no tax in any amount, large or small, can be levied to support any religious activities or institutions," also solemnly warned, "We must be careful in protecting the citizens of New Jersey against state-established churches, to be sure that we do not inadvertently prohibit New Jersey from extending its general state law benefits to all its citizens without regard to their religious belief." The high court made it clear that fear of establishment must not lead to a restriction of constitutionally guaranteed freedom:

> Other language of the First Amendment commands that New Jersey cannot hamper its citizens in the free exercise of their own religion. Consequently, it cannot exclude individual Catholics, Lutherans, Mohammedans, Baptists, Jews, Methodists, Nonbelievers, Presbyterians or the members of any other faith, because of their faith, or lack of it, from receiving the benefits of public welfare legislation.

The purpose of the First Amendment is frustrated in that its protection of religious freedom does not extend to citizens who wish to send their children to religiously oriented schools. At present, these citizen-parents do not enjoy full freedom to direct the education of their offspring, but are forced to pay a price to implement the theoretical right that is theirs.

The usual rejoinder here is to repeat (1) that Catholics may share equally in the basic and supplemental benefits of publicly supported education by sending their children to the public schools, where they will be welcome, and (2) that Catholics have every right to establish religious schools but they cannot expect any public support because *that* would violate the American tradition of separation of church and state. Within the somber shadow of that wall there is no place for further discussion. So the mystical wall remains high, the public conscience is soothed, and each succeeding year the Catholic community feels itself more aggrieved. And yet the men who built the American Republic proclaimed the separation of church and state only as a means to an end. Separation was never conceived as an end in itself but as something instrumental and subordinate to the great end they envisioned of religious liberty.

Those who share Dr. Butts's concern for freedom's future might profitably consider the reflection of Fred Hechinger, Education Editor of the New York *Times:* [2]

The parents' right to choose the school they wish for their children is perhaps the only doctrine to be considered even more important than the creation and maintenance of a strong and universally available public-school system. The dangers that spring from the absence of such freedom are strikingly evident in all totalitarian societies in which the schools are not a matter of choice but of dictation.

If freedom is endangered, let me speak in all frankness, the peril lies in the kind of dogmatic liberalism that would make the public school the shrine of a secularist faith in democracy and, in so doing, take away or render inoperative the basic constitutional rights of parent and citizen.

CULTIVATION OF TALENT

My second reason for suggesting appropriate public recognition and support for church-related schools is that only in this way can the nation's youthful talent be fully realized.

Perhaps this argument can be best appreciated by a look at Title I of the National Defense Education Act of 1958, which states the philosophy of this important public law. In summary, it holds (1) that the security of the nation requires the fullest development of the mental resources and technical skills of its young men and women and (2) that we must increase our efforts to identify and educate more of the talent of the nation. To all this, Catholic parents and educators voice a hearty amen. But let us see how these basic assumptions are interpreted in the rest of the Act.

In Title II, there is provision for the cancellation of up to one-half of any loan, plus interest, at a yearly rate of 10 per cent for college students who will enter full-time teaching in a *public* elementary or secondary school. No "forgiveness" of debt is granted to interest future teachers in nonpublic schools, where the pressures and the needs are just as great, if not greater.

According to the terms of Title III, outright grants go to states for the acquisition of laboratory or other special equipment for instruction in science, mathematics, and modern foreign languages in *public* schools. Nonprofit, nonpublic schools may borrow money from the government for these same purposes. Under the same title, there is provision for a grant to states for the expansion or improvement of supervisory services in the fields of mathematics, science, and foreign languages, but exclusively in *public* elementary and secondary schools or junior colleges. But is it not conceivable that a fair proportion of the scientific "brains" the government sorely needs can be developed within Catholic schools?

Title V makes grants to assist public secondary schools in their counseling and guidance programs. But what happens to the program in Rhode Island, for instance, where 31 per cent of the elementary and secondary school population is enrolled in parochial schools?

While the NDEA does not distinguish between public and private institutions of higher learning, it clearly does on the secondary and elementary school level. Thus despite its many excellent provisions, the Act pinpoints the Catholic grievance. It is projected for the defense of the American people; it offers support for the improved training of the nation's school population. Yet simply because they are in religiously oriented schools, Catholic students and teachers are accorded second-class treatment for fear of non-Catholic protest that the benefits of the Act might incidentally accrue to Catholic institutions.

Let me read once more the assumptions underlying this Act in their *applied* meaning: First, the security of the nation requires the fullest development of the mental resources and technical skills of its young men and women *except* those had by the five million young people that are in Catholic schools. Second, we must increase our efforts to identify and educate more of the talent of the nation *except* in Milwaukee, Boston, Chicago, Philadelphia, Buffalo and New Orleans and other places, where one-third or more of the school enrollment is in Catholic schools.

Put this way, the whole thing sounds harshly discriminatory. It is. During these years, when the nation cannot afford to leave any talent undeveloped wherever available, have not Catholics the right to expect that government supported programs in counseling, testing, and guidance will include their children in parochial schools? If the federal government, in the interests of national defense and world leadership, is going to help local communities to identify, guide, and subsidize student talent, should it not do so in a rational, comprehensive manner?

IMMEDIATE OBJECTIVES

Several times I have used the phrase "appropriate" recognition and support. In this discussion, I have been arguing for the acceptance of a principle. However, the Catholic laity and clergy of the United

States are fully aware that direct basic support by the government to parochial schools is out of the question for perhaps several more generations. If for no other reason, the rancor and strife set off by organized Catholic efforts to obtain such aid would poison community relations for years to come, and Catholics themselves would be losers in the long run. But this is not an abjuration of the claim to support in principle, for this is basically a question of civil rights.

But what do Catholics want *now?* Fundamentally, they want a sympathetic hearing for their case, public recognition of their problem, and help in working out an equitable solution. There is wide consensus among clergy and laity that Catholic energies would be best spent on achieving fuller distribution of educational items immediately related to the child benefit principle, the legal dimensions of which have already been largely indicated by the courts.

Even back in 1949, Cardinal Spellman was emphasizing that the subject of the controversy over Federal aid was not basic institutional support (New York *Times,* August 6, 1949) but what the U. S. Supreme Court and the Supreme Courts of California, Kentucky, Louisiana, Massachusetts, Maryland, and New Jersey had solemnly approved. These items concerned health services, nonreligious textbooks, and bus transportation for all American school children.

Dr. Butts's worry over the future of public education is incredible. During the 'sixties, the population of the United States will rise from 180 million to 207 million, a gain of 15 per cent. School enrollment will increase by 25 per cent, with the high school population doubling. The 1959–60 public-school bill was an estimated $15.5 billion, an increase of nearly 10 per cent over the preceding year and a sum representing 3.8 per cent of the nation's total income. Ten years ago, our public-school bill took 2.7 per cent of the national income and 15 years ago, 1.6 per cent. Officials of the National Education Association say the figure will be $20 billion in 1965 and $30 billion in 1970. A massive breakthrough on the Federal aid front is in the offing. Let's be frank. The 'sixties are going to be a seller's dream market. Just what is the basis of Dr. Butts's concerns? Catholic citizens are under no illusion that their schools are going to reap any large share of public largesse in the decade ahead. Wider extension of bus service, a share in the provisions of the National Defense Education Act, and even modest income tax rebates for private-school tuition are by no stretch of the imagination going to put the public schools out of business.

The expansion of any rival independent system is, in some measure, made at the expense of the public schools. It can be granted that this situation somewhat affects the good of the present structure of public education. The well-being of American society, however, is neither identical nor coextensive with the good of the public schools. The common good of American society has been nobly served by the public schools, yes; but it would be a case of wagging the puppy by the tail to insist that society conform forever to a rigid pattern of public education. We must not forget that service to society is the function of all public institutions, including every type of school.

An awareness is growing that the sheer dimensions of the Catholic school system make its needs and interest more than the concern of the Catholic community. Having recognized the primacy of parental choice in education, the wider American public cannot be indifferent to the consequences of the exercise of this freedom. Neither Dr. Butts nor the citizens of Pittsburgh, for instance, can turn their backs completely on 42 per cent of that city's school population in Catholic schools. The international pressures and social realities of today are different from those of yesterday. In its own time, American society will translate its appreciation of the religious school into a corresponding pattern of appropriate support. The American people have approached other delicate problems of culture and freedom with honesty, fairness, and mutual sympathy. America's more-than-a-century-old school problem will one day be resolved in the same spirit.

REFERENCES

1. Butts, R. F. Public funds for parochial schools? No! *Teachers Coll. Rec.*, 1960, 62, 57–62.
2. Hechinger, F. New York *Times*, Feb. 7, 1960.
3. Henle, R. American principles and religious schools. *St. Louis Univer. Law J.*, 1955, 3, 237–251.
4. National Education Association—American Association of School Administrators, Educational Policies Commission. *Moral and spiritual value in the public schools.* Washington: The Commission, 1951.

DR. R. FREEMAN BUTTS

R. Freeman Butts, holder of the William F. Russell professorship at Teachers College, Columbia University, presented his views on public funds for parochial schools in a paper read at the annual convention of the American Association of School Administrators, held at Atlantic City, New Jersey, on February 15, 1960. This paper was adapted for presentation in the *Teachers College Record* as reprinted here.*

PUBLIC FUNDS FOR PAROCHIAL SCHOOLS? NO!

The fundamental issue posed by this debate is *not* whether certain welfare or auxiliary services for private and parochial school children should be paid out of public tax moneys. It is *not* simply a question of whether free bus rides, free textbooks, free lunches, or free testing, guidance, or health services should be provided equitably to parochial school children as well as to public school children. These questions may have been the center of public argument ten years ago, and they may be controversial political questions today, but they are not now and they never have been the fundamental issue.

The fundamental issue has to do with the role of the state *vis-a-vis* the churches in the education of the American people. Basically, we must decide how to reconcile the disparate and diverse individual freedoms of parents and churches with the common and general freedom of the whole people as expressed through their free government.

THE BASIC QUESTION

The public policy issue before us may be stated as a three-fold question: In the coming decades, should we as a free society use public tax money to strengthen the public schools in preference to private schools, or should we encourage private schools at the expense of public schools, or should we maintain approximately the present balance between public and private schools?

As we face the problem of public and private schools, we all know that the really controversial element in it for over a century has had to do with religion. As Americans sought to create a republican form of society to replace their colonial status, and as they built a public school system to be the main support for a free society, they had to face the religious problem.

During the century of political and religious conflict from 1830 to 1930, the public school idea was hammered out. As we know it and cherish it, that idea involves five basic principles: (1) Universal free education must be available for all in common public schools supported by taxation upon everyone. (2) Public schools should be maintained under the authority of the state and administered by local public

* Reprinted from *Teachers College Record*. 62: 57–62, by permission of the author and *Teachers College Record*.

authorities. (3) In order to protect freedom of conscience, the public schools should not engage in religious instruction. (4) In order to keep church separated from state, public funds cannot be given to religious schools. Finally, (5) the state can compel all children to attend some school, but children cannot be compelled to attend a public school. This idea of public education gave enormous strength, vitality, and unity to American society. It made possible, within a relatively short time, the creation of a democratic American nation out of diverse peoples.

As Seymour M. Lipset [2] points out, freedom and democracy have flourished most fully in those countries where church-state issues were solved fairly early and relatively amicably. In the same way, the relatively early solution of the problem of religion and education enabled America to build the first strong system of free public education in the world. The results in economic and technological progress, in political stability, and in strength of loyalty to the processes of a free society have been incalculable.

Now, the question is, "Shall we modify or possibly reverse this general pattern of public education?" An increasing number of voices in recent decades has begun to argue, to plead, to cajole, and to demand that we do so. One of the most dynamic forces in this process has been the Roman Catholic Church. I am sure that no one will debate this.

NONPUBLIC SCHOOL GROWTH

In recent years, Catholic schools have grown at a much more rapid rate than the public schools. In 1900, Catholic schools represented about five per cent of the total elementary and secondary school enrollments. For forty years this proportion rose only gradually; in 1940 it was still around six or seven per cent. But during the past twenty years, the rise has been spectacular. While public school enrollments increased 36 per cent, nonpublic enrollments increased 118 per cent. Today, about 14 per cent of all school children are in Catholic schools, perhaps as much as 16 per cent in all nonpublic schools.

The problem posed by the growth of separate religious schools supported by public funds is worldwide. State schools in Belgium and the Netherlands have already been reduced to the status of minority institutions, and rivalry, tension, and conflict have marked this state of affairs. The French Republic, in addition to all its other troubles, has just gone through one of its periodic crises over the issue of state support for Catholic schools. Last December, France reversed its fifty-year policy and decided to give subsidies to Catholic schools. In all likelihood, this is only the beginning of a debilitating internal strife. Poland continues to seethe over the question of Church and State in education. I saw the problem first-hand a few years ago in Australia, where the drive for state support of Protestant as well as Catholic schools threatened to hold back the development of government schools.

Last year I saw the educational plight of India, which inherited the policy of state support for separate "communal" schools based upon distinctions of language, religion, and "community" (sometimes a euphemism for class or caste). I heard Prime Minister Nehru say just a year ago that communal strife is India's number one internal problem, next to food and overpopulation. Struggle over control of schools triggered the revolt against the communist government in Kerala. One wonders if India can create a viable nation without establishing a common school system to overcome her age-old group divisions. And Africa is next.

DOCTRINE OF PRIVATE RIGHTS

On the other hand, the American idea of universal free public education has captured the imagination of many colonial peoples who would be free and strong—and quickly. Will it continue to do so if we ourselves begin to weaken or undermine it?

For one hundred years, the public school idea was on the march throughout America, but since 1930 or so it has been on the defensive. Piecemeal exceptions to the basic idea began to be made. Public funds were sought to give the same welfare benefits to parochial school children as were given to public school children: e.g., free textbooks (*Cochran* case, 1930), free bus rides (*Everson* case, 1947), and school lunches (federal funds to go directly to parochial schools even though state funds could not be so used). All we want, said the Catholic bishops in 1948, is cooperation between church and state in education. All we want, said Cardinal Spellman in 1949, is public aid for auxiliary services, including health and welfare services. The services will benefit the child, they said, not aid the school; therefore, they are quite within the constitutional and legal limitations of the public school idea.

But since 1950 the character of the campaign has changed radically. The argument for benefits to the child and for the right of parents to choose the school they desire has been extended to a full blown theory of private rights in education. In 1955 the Catholic bishops spoke of the *partnership* of private and public schools, each having equal rights to public aid because they both perform a public service.

Since that time we have heard more and more of the argument that the rights of parents in the education of their children are prior to the rights of the state. Similarly, the rights of the Church in education are presented as superior to those of the state. Therefore, the Catholic parent is obligated to follow the Church rather than the state on educational matters. These are not new arguments. They are contained in the Encyclical Letters of Pius XI in 1929, but they are now being made more directly and more bluntly than ever before. They add up to the contention that the role of the state in education is subordinate to that of church and family; the state's real function is simply to aid the church and family to obtain the kind of education they wish. Father McCluskey's own book [3] makes this point over and over. He never mentions explicitly the right of the state to establish and support public schools.

We hear the argument that the only real purpose of taxation for education is merely to subsidize parents and thus aid them to get the kind of education they wish for their children. So, the argument implies, the whole idea of a common public school system, managed and controlled by the public and supported by tax funds, is really unnecessary. Genuine freedom of choice can be achieved by dividing up the common pool of tax money among *all* parents to do with as they please. This *would* be perfectly constitutional because it would not aid religious schools as such. It would simply aid parents to exercise their fundamental freedom of educational choice.

What this means is that the earlier demand for indirect aid for peripheral welfare services in justice to children has become a demand for direct financial subsidy by government or for at least tax credit as a constitutional right of parents. The *principle* of liberty and of civil rights *requires* the state to subsidize parents by full government support for the education of their children, and if the state refuses such aid, it will be infringing their rights of freedom of conscience under the First Amendment. In other words, the state must subsidize parents to enable them to exercise the freedom to which they are entitled. Furthermore, if the state refuses such subsidy, it will also be discriminating against parents who exercise freedom of conscience by denying them equal protection of the laws under the Fourteenth Amendment.

As if these arguments of the last decade were not enough of a threat to the public school idea, we see this same principle of educational freedom for parents being applied to the problem of segregation in the South. Just as parents who want their children to go to religious schools should have their fair share of state aid, so parents who want their children to go to all-white schools should have *their* share of state aid.

IMPLICATIONS OF SUBSIDIES

When (1) the religious drive for subsidized private schooling is joined by (2) the segregationist drive for subsidized private schooling, by (3) the economy drive of taxpayer groups to defeat bond issues and to lower school taxes, and by (4) the reluctance of the Eisenhower administration to strengthen the public sector of the nation's well-being, it is no wonder that Congress is unable or unwilling to pass a full fledged federal aid bill for public education. The public school idea is clearly in peril. Voluntaryism or Privatism is in the saddle. If you accept the principle that the state should subsidize parents rather than maintain a common public school system, why not call upon the principle to justify parents' choices on economic, political, social status, or intellectual grounds as well as on religious or racial grounds?

I believe that the adoption of the subsidy principle would undermine if not destroy the public school system as we have known it for nearly 150 years. But, more important, I believe it would weaken the fabric of American society. I believe that it would reenforce the exclusiveness and the separateness that now tend to prevent communication and to increase suspicion among Catholic, Protestant, and Jew. Separateness need not automatically produce divisiveness, but it is likely to do so when sedulously cultivated for generation after generation.

Similarly, diversity and pluralism may be outcomes of a free society, but they do not necessarily promote freedom. It may be a mark of freedom to permit parents to choose the type of school they wish for their children, but unless that school makes its chief business the promotion of freedom among the children while they are there, the simple act of parental choice may not lead to further freedom of thought or of judgment in the society. A common school, on the other hand, need not necessarily produce a uniformity or conformity of outlook. In fact, it has a better chance to avoid doing this than a school already narrowed in its admission policy at the beginning.

Public schools run by the people in local districts under the authority of a free government are by no means the same as schools run by a centralized or totalitarian state. In America, we speak properly of "public" schools rather than of "state" schools or "government" schools as Europeans often do. Our schools are the direct responsibility of the people and not simply of a "state" that is somehow "out there." It is a disservice to speak of "the State" as always a Leviathan ready to swallow up the individual. It is by no means true, as Father Virgil C. Blum [1] says, that the only real threat to individual liberties is government. We are too familiar with the lonely crowd and the organization man to believe that.

GUIDE LINES

These, then, are the guides I propose to help us chart our course through the choppy straits between Scylla and Charybdis—the Scylla of voluntaryism with her girdle of subsidized private education on one side, and the Charybdis of totalitarianism and state monopoly of education on the other.

I believe, first, that the people of a free state through its free government have the right *and the obligation* to establish and maintain public schools devoted to the promotion of freedom. In a republican form of government, the people through their government have general authority over all education and the power to levy taxes upon everyone for support of public education. The republican form of government does not receive its sanction from religion or from churches but from the consent of the people themselves. They have the right and the duty to perpetuate themselves as a free people by a system of free public education which is the chief means by which a free society continually regenerates itself. Public education is therefore an integral responsibility of a free and republican form of government. It is a kind of fourth branch of government, as essential to freedom as are responsible executives, elected legislatures, and independent courts. In this sense, the rights of the free people in public education are prior to the rights of individual churches or of individual parents in private education. This is the individual's guarantee that he will have any educational rights to exercise at all.

My second belief is that the people of a free state cannot rightfully create a monopoly for public education by interfering with or destroying private schools, nor can they rightfully create a monopoly for private schools by undermining or destroying their public schools. The principle of freedom works both ways: On the one hand, properly approved private schools are free to exist, and parents are free to send their children to them. At the same time, public schools must be maintained by the state in order for a public education devoted to freedom to be available on a basis of equality for all. If the present balance between private and public schools were to be drastically modified, the delicate equilibria between the social values of unity and of diversity and between the freedom of the individual and the freedom of the people as a whole would be threatened.

Finally, the people of a free state should not use public tax funds to support private or religious schools either directly by grants to the schools or indirectly by subsidies to parents or children. Once subventions are begun for some purposes, claims will be extended until full support is achieved and the public schools themselves are weakened or undermined. Undermining free public schools is tantamount to undermining free government itself. Maintaining free public education is essential for maintaining republic government and free institutions. These are the reasons why everyone must pay taxes for public schools. Education is for the benefit of individuals, yes; but, even more, it is for the sustenance of the free society, which in turn creates and nourishes free individuals. The most fundamental reason for the people of a free state to support a public educational system is to ensure that the freedom of the mind of the whole people and of each generation will be perpetuated and will be enhanced. To do this job, the public schools must in turn have a genuine measure of autonomy resting upon the competent scholarship of teachers and of the educational profession.

The most distinctive mark of a free society is that it specifically delegates to its educational institutions the task of constant study and criticism of the free society itself. No other kind of society dares to do such a thing. No other kind of society with one hand prevents its government from endangering the liberties of the people and with the other entrusts the government with the obligation to guarantee the rights of the people against attack by powerful groups or individuals in the community. Just as a free government guarantees the freedom of the press, of association, and of religion, and the right of trial by jury, so must a free government guarantee the freedom of teaching and learning.

A free society knows that its surest foundation rests upon the liberal education of the people—a liberal education devoted to the pursuit of freedom, a liberal education available freely and equally to all, beginning with the earliest stages of the elementary school, extending to the highest reaches of the university, and limited only by considerations of talent. If the public common school lives up to its highest calling, it can perform this function for the vast majority of people better than any other type of school.

But if the public school is to be worthy of this task, it must reinvigorate and revitalize itself and put freedom in the foreground of its purposes. The profession devoted to public education cannot be defensive in outlook, narrow or limited in vision, weak in resolution, mealymouthed in argument, mushy in intellect, slipshod in training, arrogant in behavior, or selfish in motive. It must, rather, rededicate itself to the public service, discipline its arguments and behavior, toughen its preparation, broaden its horizons, and commit itself unswervingly to the interpenetration of scholarship and public policy as the foundation of freedom. The educational profession must be nothing less than a group of statesmanlike scholars devoted to preparing generations of scholarly statesmen among the whole people.

I believe that a genuinely free public education is the very foundation and chief regenerative agency of a free society. It is not simply another welfare benefit for individuals like unemployment insurance, old age pensions, or poor relief. I believe, therefore, that we should not change radically the present balance between private and public education. Private schools should be encouraged, and parents who so desire should be free to send their children to them; but not with public subsidy for religious purposes. We should go no further in public support of private or parochial schools.

Public funds must be devoted to the improvement of public schools so that they may better prepare young people for the obligations and privileges of freedom as well as for the pursuit of intellectual excellence and for personal development. If public schools make their first order of business the dual enhancement of the free society and the free person, then they will be worthy of their high mission.

REFERENCES

1. Blum, Virgil C., S. J. *Freedom of choice in education.* New York: Macmillan, 1958, p. 11.
2. Lipset, Seymour M. *Political man.* New York: Doubleday, 1960.
3. McCluskey, Neil, S. J. *Catholic viewpoint on education.* Garden City, New York, 1959.

Selected Readings

Blanshard, Paul, *Religion and the Schools: The Great Controversy*. Boston: Beacon Press, 1963.

Blum, Virgil. *Freedom of Choice in Education*. New York: Macmillan, 1958.

Boles, Donald. *The Bible, Religion and the Public Schools*. Ames, Iowa: Iowa State University Press, 1961.

Brickman, William W. and Stanley Lehrer, eds. *Religion, Government and Education*. New York: Society for the Advancement of Education, 1961.

Butts, R. Freeman. *The American Tradition in Religion and Education*. Boston: Beacon Press, 1950.

Drinan, Robert F. *Religion, the Court, and Public Policy*. New York: McGraw-Hill, 1963.

Kervin, Jerome G. *Catholic Viewpoint on Church and State*. New York: Hanover House, 1960.

McCluskey, Neil G. *Catholic Viewpoint on Education*. Garden City, New York: Doubleday, 1959.

O'Neill, James M. *Religion and Education under the Constitution*. New York: Harper, 1949.

Pfeffer, Leo. *Church, State and Freedom*. Boston: Beacon Press, 1953.

Tussman, Joseph, ed. *The Supreme Court on Church and State*. New York: Oxford University Press, 1962.

VI

THE KENNEDY-JOHNSON ADMINISTRATION

> Our progress as a nation can be no
> swifter than our progress in education
> . . . The human mind is our funda-
> mental resource.
>
> JOHN F. KENNEDY
>
> The nation that has the schools has
> the future.
>
> LYNDON B. JOHNSON

This chapter focuses on the four-year period from the beginning of John F. Kennedy's administration in 1961 to the election of Lyndon B. Johnson as President. This period is one of the most interesting, controversial, and productive of any in the long, convoluted history of American education. As Anthony J. Celebrezze, then Secretary of Health, Education, and Welfare, testified in 1963:

What we do or do not do to assist higher education, to expand the capacity of our institutions of higher education, to improve the quality of teacher education, to develop strength in specialized fields will have a direct and forceful impact on the quality of education at the elementary and secondary levels. And what we do or do not do to aid our public elementary and secondary schools to meet their problems of crowded classrooms, underpaid teachers, and changing curriculum needs is of direct consequence to the continued growth and strengthening of higher education [76].

There is some difficulty in writing of the recent situation, for one does not have the benefit of perspective in analyzing events that have occurred. In discussing the activity of the federal government relevant to the question of federal aid to education during this four-year period, we shall focus on three broad categories: (1) Major proposed bills involving education, (2) Major laws *directly* involving education, and (3) Major laws *indirectly* aiding education.

Proposed Bills

The purpose of this section is to present in some detail the two major educational laws proposed under the Kennedy administration. Each bill is set forth in detail because in many ways these bills, while not enacted *in toto*, did serve to set the stage for later enactments in the field of education.

In some instances, specific provisions of these bills were used in subsequent legislation. At other times, specific titles were enacted as part of a later bill. These bills provide the reader with an introduction to the educational philosophy of the Kennedy-Johnson administration, as well as giving him a background for comparing the bills which did succeed in Congress. The first bill to be discussed is Senate Bill 1021, the School Assistance Act of 1961. The second bill to be considered is the proposal presented by President Kennedy in January of 1963, the National Education Improvement Act.

SCHOOL ASSISTANCE ACT OF 1961
(S. 1021, H.R. 7300)

On February 20, 1961, President Kennedy proposed a $2.3 billion aid-to-education program, to extend over a three-year period, which would "set a new standard of excellence in education for all who are willing and able to pursue it." The Kennedy proposal embodied in the School Assistance Act of 1961, introduced by Senator Wayne Morse, specified that the state determine how this money would be spent—whether on school construction or teachers' salaries. The bill provided for: (1) an increase in teachers' salaries, (2) aid in building classrooms, and (3) special aid to underprivileged children in depressed areas. The five-year scholarship program (with an authorization of slightly over $26 million) would provide for 25,000 scholarships in the first year of operation, 37,000 for the next year, and 50,000 for each of the following three years. The bill also asked Congress to amend and expand the National Defense Education Act of 1958. Under this program, the states were expected to continue their own efforts and contributions. Furthermore, "in accordance with the clear prohibition of the Constitution no elementary or secondary school funds were allocated for constructing church schools or paying church school teachers' salaries."

Called a "modest program with ambitious goals," Kennedy's proposal fell between the recommendations of his Task Force (which suggested $9 billion to be spent over 4½ years) and those of the Committee for Economic Development (which recommended $600 million to be allocated only to those states in which there was a "clear and present need for federal financial assistance"). The Task Force, headed by Frederick L. Hovde, president of Purdue University, called for $30 per pupil in average daily attendance, plus an additional $20 per pupil in states where income was less than 70 per cent of the national average income. It was estimated that the first year cost of the program recommended by the Hovde Committee would be $1½ billion. The program proposed at this time by President Kennedy cost less by comparison, asking for an average of $15 per pupil in states such as Alaska, Connecticut, Delaware, Illinois, Massachusetts, New Jersey, Pennsylvania, and Rhode Island, and a high of $30 per pupil in Mississippi. The allocation formula in this bill was based on the personal income per child in average daily attendance, with the state figures compared to the national average.

This "most important piece of domestic legislation," in the words of Kennedy, was passed by the Senate (49-34) in May of 1961. It was also approved by the House Education and Labor Committee, but was then tabled by the House Rules Committee (8-7). When an attempt was made in August to present a compromise bill (H.R. 8890), the House refused to consider the bill (termed "hastily conceived" and "woefully inadequate") by a floor vote of 242 to 170.

Why did Kennedy's bill fail? A number of reasons are cited:

1. Many individuals, particularly Republicans, opposed the idea of federal aid to education.
2. Economy-minded Democrats opposed increased spending.
3. Leadership by Democrats was only lukewarm (John W. McCormick was the Senate majority leader and Sam Rayburn was the Speaker of the House).
4. Roman Catholics wanted some form of aid for their schools.

In his State of the Union Message of 1962, President Kennedy again asked Congress to pass his aid-to-education bill. At this time, however, he asked that three particular aspects of the bill be studied and given priority: (1) aid to higher education, (2) improvement of teaching standards, and (3) adult literacy. To aid higher education the administration proposed to remedy the impact of mushrooming enrollments with $180 million in grants and $121 million in loans. Although far less than the colleges desired, even this small sum would have a multiplier effect on college spending. The second priority program, a quality education program to improve teaching standards, was to cost $750 million over a five-year period. It would have provided grants to teacher education institutions and scholarships to teachers to help update their preparation in subject fields and methodology. The third priority item was an attack on adult illiteracy. It was estimated that functional illiterates (defined as "those adults with fewer than 5 years' schooling") numbered approximately 8 million persons in 1960, comprising a solid core of individuals who were unemployable. To alleviate this condition a 5-year program, costing $50 million, was proposed. It would have trained teachers and given aid to states with pronounced illiteracy rates.

All three of these priority items skirted the issue that many believed caused the demise of the 1961 bill; i.e., aid to parochial elementary and secondary schools. In Congress, however, very little happened. As John Lumley of the National Education Association commented: "If general federal support died an early death in the House during the first session of the 87th Congress, then it was stillborn in the second session of the 87th Congress." The following reasons were responsible for the bill's failure:

1. Friends of federal aid were not in control of the 87th Congress, especially in the House.
2. Opposition was strong, particularly that of the Republican leadership.
3. The lack of aid for segregated schools antagonized many members.
4. Support for private and parochial schools was still the subject of controversy.
5. The House Rules Committee exhibited an anti-education attitude.

THE NATIONAL EDUCATION IMPROVEMENT ACT OF 1963 (S. 580, H.R. 3000)

On January 29, 1963, President Kennedy submitted to Congress a special message on education in which he proposed "a comprehensive, balanced program to enlarge the federal government's investment in the education of its citizens." This proposal was embodied in an omnibus bill, commonly called the NEIA. In the words of Fred Hechinger, education writer for the *New York Times*, it covered the "academic waterfront." It was certainly one of the most complete bills ever introduced into Congress, including all aspects of education from fighting illiteracy to setting up graduate centers.

In introducing this imperative request for approximately $5.7 million over a 5-year period, Kennedy stated in part:

Our concern as a nation for the future of our children and the growing demands of modern education which federal financing is better able to assist—make it necessary to expand federal aid to education beyond the existing limited number of special programs. We can no longer afford the luxury of endless debate over all the complicated and sensitive questions raised by each new proposal on federal participation in education. To be sure, these are all hard problems—but this nation has not come to its present position of leadership by avoiding hard problems. We are at a point in history where we must face and resolve these problems.

The President further stated in his 4000-word special message: "We cannot afford to lose another year in mounting a national effort to eliminate a shortage of classrooms, to make teachers' salaries more competitive, and to lift the quality of instruction."

Just what was included in this program for education? Kennedy's omnibus bill included 24 points under 7 different titles. A brief summary of each title will provide dimensions to the scope of its coverage.

Title I: Expansion of Opportunities for Individuals in Higher Education. Included under this title were extending the NDEA student loan program; liberalizing the payment plan; raising the ceiling on total appropriations; establishing student loan insurance; and providing for graduate fellowships and a new work-study program for needy college students.

Title II: Expansion and Improvement of Higher Education. This title included a program to provide loans to public and private non-profit institutions for constructing academic facilities. It contained a program of grants to build community junior colleges and a program to aid technical education on the college level. College and university libraries were aided not only in construction, but also in the expansion of library facilities and materials. Grants would also encourage the development of graduate centers throughout the country and the expansion of facilities for teaching modern foreign languages.

Title III: Improvement of Educational Quality. This title called for institutes for advanced study for teachers, aid to teacher preparation programs, money to broaden the Cooperative Research Act in order to improve educational research and demonstration projects, and, finally, aid in the provision of statistical services.

Title IV: Strengthening Public Elementary and Secondary Education. This title proposed a four-year program to provide $1.5 billion to help states in undertaking urgent improvements in their public elementary and secondary schools. Aims expressed were: (1) increasing salaries, (2) constructing classrooms, and (3) initiating experimental and demonstration projects to meet particular educational needs. Under this title, too, were provisions to extend the life of NDEA (1958), which

88TH CONGRESS
1ST SESSION

S. 580

IN THE SENATE OF THE UNITED STATES

JANUARY 29 (legislative day, JANUARY 15), 1963

Mr. MORSE (for himself, Mr. McNAMARA, Mr. YARBOROUGH, Mr. CLARK, Mr. RANDOLPH, Mr. WILLIAMS of New Jersey, Mr. BURDICK, Mr. PELL, Mr. MANSFIELD, and Mr. HUMPHREY) introduced the following bill; which was read twice and referred to the Committee on Labor and Public Welfare

---

A BILL

To strengthen and improve educational quality and educational opportunities in the Nation.

1   *Be it enacted by the Senate and House of Representa-*

2   *tives of the United States of America in Congress assembled,*

3   That this Act, with the following table of contents, may be

4   cited as the "National Education Improvement Act of 1963".

TABLE OF CONTENTS

J. 85001–I——1

Shown here Figures 3 and 4 are facsimiles of pages 1 and 2 of Senate Bill 580, as presented by Senator Wayne Morse to the first session of the 88th Congress. Since few persons have an opportunity to see copies of these bills

2

TABLE OF CONTENTS—Continued

1 TITLE I—EXPANSION OF OPPORTUNITIES FOR

2 INDIVIDUALS IN HIGHER EDUCATION

3 PART A—STUDENT LOANS

4 APPROPRIATIONS AUTHORIZED

5 SEC. 101. The first sentence of section 201 of the Na-

6 tional Defense Education Act of 1958 (20 U.S.C. 421) is

7 amended by striking out "$90,000,000 each for the fiscal

8 year ending June 30, 1962, and for the two succeeding fiscal

9 years, and such sums for the fiscal year ending June 30,

10 1965, and each of the three succeeding fiscal years as may

11 be necessary to enable students who have received a loan

as they actually appear in print, these pages have been included to show the format of a bill: (1) date, (2) sponsors, (3) statement of the purpose, (4) title, (5) table of contents, and (6) a portion of the running text.

has contributed to the improvement of programs in guidance and counseling, science, mathematics, and foreign languages. Included also was the extension of the Impact Laws (1950), which were due to expire June 30, 1963.

Title V: Vocational and Special Education. Under this title, budget funds were provided to double the number of workers assisted by the Manpower Development and Training Act, and to expand the scope and level of vocational education as supported through the U.S. Office of Education. Also under Title V were provisions for the education and employment of unemployed youth.

Title VI: Continuing Education. Included in this title were federal grants to states for expanding extension courses and a program to assist states in offering basic adult education. The purpose of this title was chiefly to eliminate illiteracy. It also provided a two-year program of grants for the construction and operation of urban and rural libraries.

Title VII: General Provisions. Listed here were provisions for the administration of the bill.

President Kennedy, in concluding his message to Congress regarding NEIA, stated:

Fundamentally, education is and must always be a local responsibility, for it thrives best when nurtured in the grass roots of our democracy. But in our present era of economic expansion, population growth, and technological advance, state, local, and private efforts are insufficient. These efforts must be reinforced by national support, if American education is to yield a maximum of individual development and national well-being.

The program here proposed is reasonable and yet far-reaching. It offers federal assistance without federal control. It provides for economic growth, manpower development, and progress toward our educational and humanitarian objectives. It encourages the increase of the knowledge, skills, attitudes, and critical intelligence necessary for the preservation of our society. It will help keep America strong and safe and free. I strongly recommend it to the Congress for high priority action.

It was soon evident, however, that the National Education Improvement Act of 1963, proposed in January, could not be moved in the House. Several separate bills were therefore extracted from the omnibus bill, and were subsequently passed. Included were the following three bills which are discussed in the next section:

Vocational Education Act of 1963 (P.L. 88–210)

Higher Education Facilities Act of 1963 (P.L. 88–204)

Health Professions Educational Assistance Act (P.L. 88–129).

Why did Kennedy's omnibus bill fail? The reasons were much the same as those for the failure of his previous attempts at passing general federal aid:

1. The "omnibus" character of the program was so vast as to be overwhelming.
2. Lack of aid for private and parochial schools.
3. Traditional Congressional reluctance to become involved in education *per se*.
4. Wide coverage provided many vulnerabilities for attack.
5. Control of education by House Rules Committee.
6. Poor legislative management of the bill.

It is interesting to speculate whether Senate Bill 580 will be the last of the line of omnibus bills in education to be presented to Congress. Viewing the historical development of federal aid to education, it is soon perceived that it has been the more focused, specific types of aid that have been consistently enacted.

Major Laws Directly Involving Education

VOCATIONAL EDUCATION ACT OF 1963 (P.L. 88–210)

The Vocational EducationAct (the Perkins-Morse Bill), signed by President Johnson on December 18, 1963, aims "to strengthen and improve the quality of vocational education and to expand the vocational education opportunities in the nation. . . ." This act authorizes a permanent program, with appropriations for vocational education amounting to $60 million for the first year, $118.5 million for the second year, and $225 million for each subsequent fiscal year. One of the special features of this act is the requirement that 10 per cent of each year's appropriation be reserved for grants made by the Commissioner of Education. These grants are for research and demonstration projects in vocational education. Funds are to be allocated among the respective states on the basis of population and per capita income.

This law represents an attempt to "retool" vocational education in order to teach modern skills; it is the first major revamping of vocational education since the Smith-Hughes Act of 1917. The effect of the Vocational Education Act will be a quadrupling of aid in this area by 1967; never before has as much money been spent in this area of education. The major revisions will have the following results:

1. Vocational programs will be vastly expanded in terms of facilities, staff, and classroom space.
2. The curriculum will be updated to meet the newer job needs in such fields as computer programming and other highly technical occupations.
3. An effort will be made to upgrade the whole concept of vocational education.
4. An attempt will be made to pioneer new programs, one of which is the vocational boarding school. Five of these residential schools will be built in city slum areas; each will accommodate students ages 15 to 21. Another experimental plan will be work-study programs which will try to solve the high school dropout problem by providing subsistence pay and part time work while students attend school.

The hope of this sweeping legislation is to help wage war on poverty, as well as to assist youth in acquiring high level skills that will be needed in the future. Stated President Johnson on signing the Vocational Education Act:

This bill . . . is dramatic evidence of our commitment to education as the key to our social and economic and technological and moral progress . . .

Modern demands upon labor and industry require new skills and an upgrading of old skills, require more education and greater knowledge. It has been said that we need over 100,000 technicians a year just to meet our needs in the engineering field alone but all our present programs combined, we are told, turn out a maximum not of 100,000 a year but only 20,000 technicians a year. We believe that this new law will help close this gap . . .

AMENDMENTS TO NATIONAL DEFENSE EDUCATION ACT— 1963, 1964

In 1963, under the second part of the Vocational Education Act, the NDEA of 1958 was extended for one more year. Amendments to the law were as follows:

1. The amount of money available for student loans was increased from $90 million to $125 million in 1964, and to $135 million in 1965. Ceilings for individual colleges were raised from $250,000 to $800,000.
2. Student loans were extended to include attendance at foreign universities, and repayment features were extended to include teaching in Armed Forces schools.
3. Unneeded allotments were to be reallocated to states in need of additional funds.
4. Guidance, counseling, and testing programs were expanded. Also expanded were institutes for training teachers of pupils for whom English is a second language.

In 1964, the National Defense Education Act was again amended; this time it was extended (P.L. 88–665) to June 30, 1968, with a broadened program which included teachers of "English, reading, history, and geography," teachers of "disadvantaged youth, librarians, and educational media specialists." The new amendments provide a liberalization of loans for college and university students. Funds are increased from $135 million to $163 million during the fiscal year 1965. They are to be further increased to $179 million in 1966, and to $190 million in 1967 and 1968. The number of fellowships has also been increased from 1500 a year to a total of 7500 in 1967–68. Loans and grants to states for the purchase of equipment have been extended to materials used in the teaching of English, reading, history, geography, and civics.

HIGHER EDUCATION FACILITIES ACT OF 1963
(P.L. 88–204)

The Higher Education Facilities Act of 1963 (the Morse-Green Bill) was signed by President Johnson on December 16, 1963. Its purpose is "to assist the nation's institutions of higher education to construct needed classrooms, laboratories, and libraries in order to accommodate mounting student enrollments and to meet demands for skilled technicians and for advanced graduate education."

Termed "a bricks and mortar act," this law appropriates $1.2 billion to be spent over a period of five years. On signing this bill President Johnson commented:

A great former President of the Republic of my State said: "The cultivated man is the guardian genius of democracy. It is the only dictator that free men recognize and the only ruler that free men desire." So this new law is the most significant education bill passed by the Congress in the history of the Republic. In fact, this session of the Congress will go down in history as the "Education Congress of 1963". . . .

The major provisions of the Higher Education Facilities Act include:

1. Grants to all four-year colleges, junior colleges, and technical institute to construct libraries and buildings for instruction in science, language, and mathematics.
2. Loans totaling $120 million for all types of classroom construction. They can extend 50 years at an interest rate of 3⅝ per cent.
3. Fifty million dollars in grants to communities for construction of junior colleges.
4. Funds for establishment of graduate centers—$25 million increased to $60 million.

Preference is to be given to institutions which have increasing enrollments, and institutions are required to match federal funds on a two-to-one basis. In this way, up to $3 billion could be genrated for school construction throughout the country.

One of the most controversial elements of this bill is its inclusion of all of the some two thousand institutions of higher education within its scope; hence church-supported and private schools, as well as public institutions, are eligible for aid. There has consistently been less concern about assisting private colleges chiefly because attendance at this level is voluntary. The only restriction is that no government monies may be expended for any facilities intended for religious use, sectarian instruction, or religious worship. The bill thus avoided the "rocks and shoals" of the religious question.

Why did this education bill pass when others failed? A number of points can be cited to account for its popularity:

1. It was associated with the Vocational Education Bill; thus Congress was able to provide a little something for everyone.
2. The question of need was well demonstrated; Congress was convinced.
3. There is a strong precedent for federal aid to higher education beginning with the Morrill Act in 1862.
4. The provision of aid for both private and public schools pleased religious groups.
5. Willingness to negotiate differences; the Senate bill called for $2.67 billion, compared to the House bill which amounted to $1.5 billion.
6. An attempt to attach aid to elementary and secondary schools was rejected; the bill retained its specific focus.

Major Laws Indirectly Aiding Education

Two major acts, the Economic Opportunity Act of 1964 and the Civil Rights Act of 1964, although not education laws *per se*, will have effects in the area of education. A number of minor laws which also have educational implications are noted in the following discussion.

ECONOMIC OPPORTUNITY ACT OF 1964
(S. 2642, H.R. 11377)

Addressing Congress on March 16, 1964, President Johnson presented his War on Poverty measure. He stated in part:

We are citizens of the richest and most fortunate nation in the history of the world. . . .

With the growth of our country has come opportunity for our people—opportunity to educate our children, to use our energies in productive work, to increase our leisure—opportunity for almost every American for hope that through work and talent he could create a better life for himself and his family. . . .

There are millions of Americans—one-fifth of our people—who have not shared in the abundance which has been granted to most of us, and on whom the gates of opportunity have been closed.

What does this poverty mean to those who endure it?

It means a daily struggle to secure the necessities for even a meager existence. It means that the abundance, the comforts, the opportunities they see all around them are beyond their grasp.

Worst of all, it means hopelessness for the young. . . .

Technically called the Economic Opportunity Act of 1964, the War on Poverty Bill passed the House of Representatives on August 8, 1964, by a vote of 226 to 184. Voting for final passage in the House were 204 Democrats and 22 Republicans; opposing the bill were 144 Republicans and 40 Democrats. The Senate, on August 11, 1964, passed by voice vote and sent to the White House the impressive $947.5 million poverty bill which provides "exits from poverty," primarily through the doors of education. The educational implications of this bill are found in the first two titles.

Title I, "Youth Programs," establishes the Job Corps, which will provide job training for 40,000 young men and women in camps or residential centers, with enrollment reaching a possible total of 100,000. Provided for this program is $412.5 million to help train youth, to enable them to finish high school, and to increase their general employability with a work-study program. Provided, too, are part-time jobs so that needy students may continue their education.

Title II, "Urban and Rural Community Action Programs," allocates $340 million for the first year of operation. Under this program the federal government will pay up to 90 per cent of the cost of projects in such fields as job training, vocational rehabilitation, and health and welfare. Also provided are programs to ensure literacy training and basic education for adults. For the first year, it is intended to concentrate the majority of funds on projects related to education.

Work experience programs, costing in the neighborhood of $150 million, will include demonstration projects designed to stimulate state programs to provide work and work experience for unemployed individuals and needy persons. A volunteer program, to be called VISTA, Volunteers in Service to America, a type of domestic Peace Corps, will be established. These volunteers will serve in poverty-stricken areas throughout the country—on Indian reservations, in mental hospitals, in migratory farm camps. VISTA is one of the most popular features of the Economic Opportunity Act, due partly to the success of the Peace Corps. It is estimated that $10 million will be spent in administering and setting this program into operation.

College work-study programs will provide approximately $500 a year to students for work in and around the campus to aid the economically deprived and to expand opportunities for campus employment. There are other programs included in this act, but these are the ones most directly involved with education. The provisions of this act emphasize education as the first line of attack on poverty. It is hoped that this legislation will boost the living standards of the forgotten fifth of our people and will offer, to quote President Johnson, "an opportunity and not an opiate . . . It will help our people find their footing for a long climb toward a better way of life."

THE CIVIL RIGHTS ACT OF 1964
(S. 1731, S. 1750, H.R. 7152)

Encouraging and easing the course of desegregation in public schools is the main object of the Civil Rights Act of 1964. Several titles of this act directly involved the Commissioner of Education and education itself as a means. Title IV, for example, empowers the Attorney General to initiate civil action against local school boards which deny equal rights to any young people. It provides that "no person in the United States shall on the grounds of race, color, or national origins, be excluded from participation in or denied the benefits of, or be subject to discrimination in any program or activity receiving federal financial assistance." There is, however, a waiting period and a provision for hearing and judicial review before action is taken, since the emphasis is on voluntary compliance to the act.

Under Title IX the Commissioner of Education is required to conduct a study to determine whether equal opportunity to education is being denied because of race, color, religion, or national origins. The findings of this study are to go directly to the President. This law also provides assistance to educational officials who request it to facilitate programs of desegregation. Help might consist of technical assistance in carrying out programs of desegregation, or of information and individuals who might help in an advisory capacity. Title IX also gives aid to colleges and universities for institutes to deal with the desegregation problem.

The Civil Rights Act, like the Economic Opportunity Act, utilizes education as a means to achieve its objectives. In the Economic Opportunity Act education is a weapon against poverty; in the Civil Rights Act it is the means of ensuring freedom and equal opportunity in our society.

OTHER LEGISLATION RELEVANT TO EDUCATION

The following acts were also passed by the 88th Congress and involve education in a subsidiary form.

Manpower Development and Training Act Amendments (P.L. 88–214). This act underwent several changes in Congress. Its emphasis is on combating teenage joblessness and providing training programs for those persons whose lack of education hampers their ability to obtain employment. The amendments aim at increasing the monies available and extending the coverage of the provisions.

Library Services and Construction Act (P.L. 88–269). This $135 million program allows for three-year development of the country's public libraries. This act amends the Library Service Act of 1956.

Health Professions Educational Assistance Act of 1963 (P.L. 88–129). This $236.4 million act provides funds for construction of medical and dental schools and aid for students attending such universities or centers.

Nurse Training Act of 1964 (P.L. 88–581). These provisions establish a program for construction and rehabilitation of nurseries and schools, and for student loan programs similar to those under NDEA.

Mental Retardation Facilities and Community Mental Health Center Construction Act of 1963 (P.L. 88–164). Authorizing the spending of $329 million, this law is considered a tremendous step toward a new era in the country's treatment of the mentally ill.

Juvenile Delinquency and Youth Offenses Control Act Amendment of 1964 (P.L. 88–368). This law extends and expands the 1961 Juvenile and Youth Offenses Control Act. It authorizes several new programs, including a special study of compulsory school attendance and child labor laws to determine what effects they have on juvenile delinquency. It also authorizes an anti-delinquency project in the Washington, D.C., area.

The National Commission on Technology and Automation and Economic Progress (P.L. 88–444). This law provides for the creation of a fourteen-member presidential commission to study the impact of technological change and automation on employment, production, and communities themselves.

It is instructive and interesting to note the far ranging nature of the laws that utilize education, schools, and the processes of teaching to aid in the solution of social problems.

The extent to which the federal government is involved in education is shown by the table following: "Federal Funds for Education and Related Activities: Estimated Obligations for Fiscal Years 1963 and 1964" (71, p. 134). In spite of the lack of official commitment to financial aid to education, the federal government has obviously become increasingly involved.

Federal funds for education and related activities: Estimated obligations for fiscal years 1963 and 1964 [1]

[Amounts in thousands]

Type of support, level, and program area	1963	1964
1	2	3

Part I. Federal funds supporting education in educational institutions excluding funds for services rendered to Federal Government

A. GRANTS, TOTAL	$2,008,605	$2,384,556
ELEMENTARY-SECONDARY EDUCATION	608,693	679,050
School Assistance in Federally Affected Areas....	332,200	382,871
National Defense Education Act (titles III, V, and X)	69,872	71,121
Indian education	60,876	64,186
Public lands revenue for schools	44,550	48,513
Education for dependents of military personnel overseas	45,289	45,289
Vocational education	26,323	27,053
School assistance in special areas	17,684	27,203
Teaching and teacher training grants, Educational Exchange Program	6,800	7,400
Science education, National Science Foundation..	3,901	4,043
Other	1,198	1,371
HIGHER EDUCATION	1,175,955	1,404,780
Basic research and research facilities in U.S. educational institutions proper	648,361	810,930
Basic research	(478,600)	(610,700)
Research facilities	(169,761)	(200,230)
Training grants	237,935	267,695
Fellowships	120,146	145,585
Special institutional support	38,695	56,419
Veterans education	68,445	52,732
Traineeships	22,861	23,612
Special training programs	10,071	10,606
Training State and local personnel	6,261	7,890
Other	23,180	29,311

[1] Based on Federal agency responses to Office of Education survey of Federal education and related activities. Included are (1) funds, commodities, or services to educational institutions and agencies and (2) funds for support of education and training to educational institutions, agencies, or individuals. Research data are from *Federal Funds for Science XII*, National Science Foundation.

Federal funds for education and related activities: Estimated
obligations for fiscal years 1963 and 1964 [1]—Continued

[Amounts in thousands]

Type of support, level, and program area	1963	1964
1	2	3
ADULT EDUCATION	111,705	192,611
Veterans education	29,007	25,082
Vocational and technical training	74,719	154,114
Training State and local personnel	1,432	5,390
Indian education	6,165	7,736
Other	382	289
NOT CLASSIFIED BY LEVEL	112,252	108,115
Value of surplus property transferred	112,252	108,115
B. LOANS, TOTAL	481,851	482,193
ELEMENTARY-SECONDARY EDUCATION	616	750
Private school loans (NDEA, title III)	616	750
HIGHER EDUCATION	481,235	481,443
Student loan program, NDEA	90,692	90,900
College housing loans	390,543	390,543

Part II. Other Federal funds for education and related activities

Research and Development	$1,154,600	$1,350,200
Research and development in educational institutions proper and research centers, exclusive of basic research in U.S. educational institutions proper	1,154,600	1,350,200
Related School Services	386,708	384,637
School lunch program	379,258	377,187
Job placement for high school seniors	6,900	6,900
Bus transportation, military dependents	550	550
Training of Federal Personnel	83,196	86,131
Military academies	51,327	53,262
Training in non-Federal facilities	31,869	32,869
Library Services	24,020	26,920
Library of Congress	12,073	13,364
Library Services Act grants	7,406	7,444
National Library of Medicine	3,321	4,080
National Library of Agriculture	1,096	1,876
AEC library services, Oak Ridge	124	155

Federal funds for education and related activities: Estimated
obligations for fiscal years 1963 and 1964 ¹—*Continued*

[Amounts in thousands]

Type of support, level, and program area	1963	1964
1	2	3
International Education	63,000	63,800
AID cooperative projects	54,000	54,000
Grants for observation and advisory servcies, Educational Exchange Program	9,000	9,800
Other	77,523	86,381
Cooperative agricultural extension service	63,008	67,108
Apprenticeship and training programs	4,667	4,815
Education in Federal correctional institutions ...	2,518	2,885
Mine safety training	1,400	1,400
Civil defense education	5,930	10,173

ENACTMENTS BY THE 88TH CONGRESS CONCERNING EDUCATION AND TRAINING 1963–1964 (81).

Bills Reported from the Committee on Labor and Public Welfare:
1. War Orphans' Educational Assistance Act (approval of courses)
2. Health Professions Educational Assistance Act of 1963
3. Mental Retardation Facilities and Community Mental Health Centers Construction Act of 1963
4. The Higher Education Facilities Act of 1963
5. The Vocational Education Act of 1963 (provisions affecting education and training)
6. National Defense Education Act (amendments and extension, 1963)
7. School Assistance to Federally Affected Areas (extension, 1963)
8. Manpower Development and Training Act Amendments (1963)
9. The Library Services and Construction Act (1964)
10. Educational Assistance for Veterans' Children (1964)
11. Extensions of the Juvenile Delinquency and Youth Offenses Control Act of 1961 (1964)

12. Economic Opportunity Act of 1964 (educational and training aspects)
13. Graduate Public Health Training Amendments of 1964
14. National Arts and Cultural Development Act of 1964
15. Nurse Training Act of 1964
16. Loans to students of optometry
17. National Defense Education Act (amendments and extension, 1964)
18. School Assistance to Federally Affected Areas (amendment and extension, 1964)

Bills Reported from Other Committees of the Senate:
1. Universal Military Training and Service Extension (1963)
2. Labor, Health, Education, and Welfare Appropriations (1964)
3. Department of Defense Appropriations (1964)
4. Peace Corps Act Amendments (1963)
5. Foreign Assistance Act of 1963
6. The Clean Air Act (training provisions, 1963)
7. Independent Offices Appropriations (1964)
8. Indian Vocational Training Amendments (1963)
9. Departments of State, Justice, and Commerce, the Judiciary and Related Agencies Appropriations (1964)
10. Preparation of High School and College Debate Materials (1963)
11. Appointments to the U. S. Military, Naval, and Air Force Academies (1964)
12. Civil Rights Act of 1964 (education and training)
13. Establishment of Water Resources Research Centers at Land-Grant Colleges and State Universities (1964)
14. Housing Act of 1964 (new training programs)
15. Labor, Health, Education, and Welfare Appropriations (1965)
16. Supplemental Appropriations for Fiscal 1965
17. Foreign Assistance Act of 1964 (education and training)
18. Reserve Officers' Training Corps Program

Representative Statements

Presented in this section are statements relevant to education which were made during the Kennedy-Johnson administration. Included are selections which mark the development of education during this four-year period, which was characterized by tremendous activity in educational legislation.

1. Report from the Task Force Committee: January 6, 1961.
2. Education Message: February 20, 1961.
3. Education Message: February 6, 1962.
4. Education Message: January 29, 1963.
5. Remarks to a Joint Session of Congress.: November 27, 1963.
6. Excerpts from State of the Union Message: January 14, 1964.

REPORT FROM THE TASK FORCE COMMITTEE

On January 6, 1961, the Task Force Committee on Education submitted its report to President Kennedy. A summary of this committee's influential recommendations follows:

The national interest demands a first-rate system of schools and that every child have full opportunity to benefit from that system. Present standards and facilities must be improved. Millions of children, particularly in certain rural areas and in the great cities, are deprived of an opportunity to develop talents that are needed both for society and for their own lives. The Task Force Committee concludes that first priority should be given to a vigorous program to lift the schools to a new level of excellence.

State and local governments alone cannot provide the funds needed. Federal support is required. The Task Force Committee recommends that action be taken in three closely related areas: a general program of support for all public schools to reach the new level; a special program for States in economic distress in providing for schools; and a special program for city schools.

(1) The Task Force Committee recommends that the President support legislation to provide $30 per annum per pupil, based on average daily attendance in public schools. The funds should be sent to the States for transmission to local boards of education on the basis of average daily attendance in their public schools. The boards of educa-

tion should be authorized to use the funds for construction, salaries, or other purposes related to the improvement of education. The program should require State and local governments to maintain or increase their support of education. The annual cost is estimated at $1.2 billion.

(2) The Task Force Committee recommends that the President support legislation designed to provide $20 per child for States with personal income per student in average daily attendance in public schools that is below 70 percent of the national average. The legislation should include provision to assure maintenance of State and local effort, and funds should be available for construction, salaries, or other purposes related to the improvement of education in the public schools, as the State may determine. It is estimated that roughly one-quarter of the States might benefit from this legislation (mostly in the South), that approximately 7 million children would be helped toward full educational opportunity, and that the annual cost would be $140 million.

(3) The Task Force Committee recommends that the President support legislation designed to provide an amount equivalent to $20 per child in average daily attendance in the public schools of the great cities (over 300,000 population) which are facing unique and grave educational problems. The legislation should authorize the U.S. Commissioner of Education to make grants to such cities based upon plans proposed by their boards of education or by boards together with other boards of education within their area, for support of research and experimental programs in the special problems of these urban schools, for the planning and construction of facilities, for the acquisition of land sites, for the improvement of programs of community service by the schools, and for the strengthening of guidance and job placement programs for pupils over 16 years of age. Eligibility for such grants should be based on a formula which includes density of population, nature of housing, and percent of students finishing high school. Provisions to assure maintenance of local effort should be included, as well as coordination with Federal and local housing agencies. It is estimated that the education of approximately 6 million children can be improved at a cost of $120 million annually . . .

RECOMMENDATIONS FOR PRESIDENTIAL ADMINISTRATIVE ACTION

The Task Force Committee recommends immediate action by the President with respect to four important matters listed below in order of priority. The Committee believes the taking of these actions will demonstrate in a positive way that the President not only gives top priority to the development of the Nation's educational system, but also stands ready to give his full backing to the establishment of helpful administrative policies and regulations in all Federal agencies charged with the spending of Federal funds flowing to the colleges and universities in support of education, research, and public service.

(1) The Task Force Committee recommends that the President take immediate action to establish a President's Advisory Committee on Education.

Such a move will demonstrate that the President believes that education is one of the truly fundamental and important requirements for the preservation and development of the American society and will place the field of education on a level with that now enjoyed by Presidential advisory groups in both science and economics.

(2) The Task Force Committee recommends that the President specifically request all Federal agencies, including the Federal Council for Science and Technology, the National Science Foundation, the Atomic Energy Commission, the Department of Defense, and the Department of Health, Education, and Welfare, to take all possible steps within existing statutory and legislative authorizations to support and implement the recommendations of the President's Science Advisory Committee issued under date of November 15, 1960, in a report entitled "Scientific Progress, the Universities, and the Federal Government."

This excellent report recommends objectives, policies, and actions which will strengthen American science and technology the benefits from which will serve to increase not only national defense, but also national industrial and economic growth.

The active implementation of these recommendations will be enthusiastically received by all institutions of higher learning in the country now concerned and faced with the problems of financing, staffing, and equipping an expanded capacity for graduate training and basic research.

(3) The Task Force Committee recommends that the President take action—presumably through the Secretary of the Treasury—to request the Internal Revenue Service to rescind Ruling 60-370, dated December 2, 1960.

The rescission of this ruling (which ruling has been vigorously opposed by all educational institutions, both public and private) will demonstrate that the new administration is anxious to do all in its power to stimulate private giving in support and our educational institutions.

(4) The Task Force Committee recommends that the President request the Director of the Bureau of the Budget to proceed with immediate revision of Bureau of the Budget Circular A–21, issued September 10, 1958, the intent of which is "to provide to educational institutions recognition of their full allocated costs of research under generally accepted cost accounting principles."

The revision of this directive will settle one of the most annoying problems in the field of university-Government relationships that has plagued our institutions of higher education for the past 10 years.

Specific recommendations on the changes desired were submitted to the Bureau of the Budget in September 1960 by a special committee on sponsored research of the American Council on Education, and to the Department of Defense and the three services.

EDUCATION MESSAGE: FEBRUARY 20, 1961

Following is the entire text of John F. Kennedy's Education Message as delivered before Congress in 1961:

To the Congress of the United States:

Our progress as a nation can be no swifter than our progress in education. Our requirements for world leadership, our hopes for economic growth, and the demands of citizenship itself in an era such as this all require the maximum development of every young American's capacity.

The human mind is our fundamental resource. A balanced Federal program must go well beyond incentives for investment in plant and equipment. It must include equally determined measures to invest in human beings—both in their basic education and training and in their more advanced preparation for professional work. Without such measures, the Federal Government will not be carrying out its responsibilities for expanding the base of our economic and military strength.

Our progress in education over the last generation has been substantial. We are educating a greater proportion of our youth to a higher degree of competency than any other country on earth. One-fourth of our total population is enrolled in our schools and colleges. This year $26 billion will be spent on education alone.

But the needs of the next generation—the needs of the next decade and the next school year—will not be met at this level of effort. More effort will be required—on the part of students, teachers, schools, colleges, and all 50 States—and on the part of the Federal Government.

Education must remain a matter of State and local control, and higher education a matter of individual choice. But education is increasingly expensive. Too many State and local governments lack the resources to assure an adequate education for every child. Too many classrooms are overcrowded. Too many teachers are underpaid. Too many talented individuals cannot afford the benefits of higher education. Too many academic institutions cannot afford the cost of, or find room for, the growing numbers of students seeking admission in the sixties.

Our twin goals must be: A new standard of excellence in education —and the availability of such excellence to all who are willing and able to pursue it.

I. ASSISTANCE TO PUBLIC ELEMENTARY AND SECONDARY SCHOOLS

A successful educational system requires the proper balance, in terms of both quality and quantity, of three elements: students, teachers, and facilities. The quality of the students depends in large measure on both the quality and the relative quantity of teachers and facilities.

Throughout the 1960's there will be no lack in the quantity of students. An average net gain of nearly 1 million pupils a year during the next 10 years will overburden a school system already strained by well over a half million pupils in curtailed or half day sessions, a school system financed largely by a property tax incapable of bearing such an increased load in most communities.

But providing the quality and quantity of teachers and facilities to meet this demand will be major problems. Even today, there are some 90,000 teachers who fall short of full certification standards. Tens of thousands of others must attempt to cope with classes of unwieldy size because there are insufficient teachers available.

We cannot obtain more and better teachers—and our children should have the best—unless steps are taken to increase teachers' salaries. At present salary levels, the classroom cannot compete in financial rewards with other professional work that requires similar academic background.

It is equally clear that we do not have enough classrooms. In order to meet current needs and accommodate increasing enrollments, if every child is to have the opportunity of a full-day education in an adequate classroom, a total of 600,000 classrooms must be constructed during the next 10 years.

These problems are common to all States. They are particularly severe in those States which lack the financial resources to provide a better education, regardless of their own efforts. Additional difficulties, too often overlooked, are encountered in areas of special educational need, where economic or social circumstances impose special burdens and opportunities on the public school. These areas of special educational need include our depressed areas of chronic unemployment and the slum neighborhoods of our larger cities, where underprivileged children are overcrowded into substandard housing. A recent survey of a very large elementary school in one of our major cities, for example, found 91 percent of the children coming to class with poor diets, 87 percent in need of dental care, 21 percent in need of visual correction, and 19 percent with speech disorders. In some depressed areas roughly one-third of the children must rely on surplus foods for their basic sustenance. Older pupils in these schools lack proper recreational and job guidance. The proportion of dropouts, delinquency, and classroom disorders in such areas is alarmingly high.

I recommend to the Congress a 3-year program of general Federal assistance for public elementary and secondary classroom construction and teachers' salaries.

Based essentially on the bill which passed the Senate last year (S. 8), although beginning at a more modest level of expenditures, this program would assure every State of no less than $15 for every public school student in average daily attendance, with the total amount appropriated ($666 million being authorized in the first year, rising to $866 million over a 3-year period) distributed according to the equalization formula contained in the last year's Senate bill, and already familiar to the Congress by virtue of its similarity to the formulas contained in the Hill-Burton Hospital Construction and other acts. Ten percent of the funds allocated to each State in the first year, and an equal amount thereafter, is to be used to help meet the unique problems of each State's "areas of special educational need"—depressed areas, slum neighborhoods, and others.

This is a modest program with ambitious goals. The sums involved are relatively small when we think in terms of more than 36 million public school children, and the billions of dollars necessary to educate them properly. Nevertheless, a limited beginning now—consistent with our obligations in other areas of responsibility—will encourage all

States to expand their facilities to meet the increasing demand and enrich the quality of education offered, and gradually assist our relatively low-income States in the elevation of their educational standards to a national level.

The bill which will follow this message has been carefully drawn to eliminate disproportionately large or small inequities, and to make the maximum use of a limited number of dollars. In accordance with the clear prohibition of the Constitution, no elementary or secondary school funds are allocated for constructing church schools or paying church school teachers' salaries; and thus nonpublic school children are rightfully not counted in determining the funds each State will receive for its public schools. Each State will be expected to maintain its own effort or contribution; and every State whose effort is below the national average will be expected to increase that proportion of its income which is devoted to public elementary and secondary education.

This investment will pay rich dividends in the years ahead—in increased economic growth, in enlightened citizens, in national excellence. For some 40 years, the Congress has wrestled with this problem and searched for a workable solution. I believe that we now have such a solution; and that this Congress in this~year will make a landmark contribution to American education.

II. CONSTRUCTION OF COLLEGE AND UNIVERSITY FACILITIES

Our colleges and universities represent our ultimate educational resource. In these institutions are produced the leaders and other trained persons whom we need to carry forward our highly developed civilization. If the colleges and universities fail to do their job, there is no substitute to fulfill their responsibility. The threat of opposing military and ideological forces in the world lends urgency to their task. But that task would exist in any case.

The burden of increased enrollments—imposed upon our elementary and secondary schools already in the fifties—will fall heavily upon our colleges and universities during the sixties. By the autumn of 1966, an estimated 1 million more students will be in attendance at institutions of higher learning than enrolled last fall—for a total more than twice as high as the total college enrollment of 1950. Our colleges, already hard pressed to meet rising enrollments since 1950 during a period of rising costs, will be in critical straits merely to provide the necessary facilities, much less the cost of quality education.

The country as a whole is already spending nearly $1 billion a year on academic and residential facilities for higher education—some 20 percent of the total spent for higher education. Even with increased contributions from State, local, and private sources, a gap of $2.9 billion between aggregate needs and expenditures is anticipated by 1965, and a gap of $5.2 billion by 1970.

The national interest requires an educational system on the college level sufficiently financed and equipped to provide every student with adequate physical facilities to meet his instructional, research, and residential needs.

I therefore recommend legislation which will—

(1) *Extend the current college housing loan program with a 5-year $250 million a year program designed to meet the Federal Government's appropriate share of residential housing for students and faculty. As a start, additional lending authority is necessary to speed action during fiscal 1961 on approvable loan applications already at hand.*

(2) *Establish a new, though similar, long-term, low-interest rate loan program for academic facilities, authorizing $300 million in loans each year for 5 years to assist in the construction of classrooms, laboratories, libraries, and related structures—sufficient to enable public and private higher institutions to accommodate the expanding enrollments they anticipate over the next 5 years; and also to assist in the renovation, rehabilitation, and modernization of such facilities. . . .*

EDUCATION MESSAGE: FEBRUARY 6, 1962

In 1962, President Kennedy again recommended the expansion and improvement of educational opportunities in his Education Message to Congress:

No task before our Nation is more important than expanding and improving the educational opportunities of all our people. The concept that every American deserves the opportunity to attain the highest level of education of which he is capable is not new to this administration—it is a traditional ideal of democracy. But it is time that we moved toward the fulfillment of this ideal with more vigor and less delay.

For education is both the foundation and the unifying force of our democratic way of life—it is the mainspring of our economic and social progress—it is the highest expression of achievement in our society, ennobling and enriching human life. In short, it is at the same time the most profitable investment society can make and the richest reward it can confer.

Today, more than at any other time in our history, we need to develop our intellectual resources to the fullest. But the facts of the matter are that many thousands of our young people are not educated to their maximum capacity—and they are not, therefore, making the maximum contribution of which they are capable to themselves, their families, their communities and the Nation. Their talents lie wasted—their lives are frequently pale and blighted—and their contribution to our economy and culture are lamentably below the levels of their potential skills, knowledge, and creative ability. Educational failures breed delinquency, despair, and dependence. They increase the costs of unemployment and public welfare. They cut our potential national economic output by billions. They deny the benefits of our society to large segments of our people. They undermine our capability as a nation to discharge world obligations. All this we cannot afford—better schools we can afford.

To be sure, Americans are still the best educated and best trained people in the world. But our educational system has failed to keep pace with the problems and needs of our complex technological society. Too many are illiterate or untrained, and thus either unemployed or underemployed. Too many receive an education diminished in quality in thousands of districts which cannot or do not support modern and adequate facilities, well-paid and well-trained teachers, or even a sufficiently long school year.

Too many—an estimated 1 million a year—leave school before completing high school—the bare minimum for a fair start in modern-day life. Too many high school graduates with talent—numbering in the hundreds of thousands—fail to go on to college; and 40 percent of those who enter college drop out before graduation. And too few, finally, are going on to the graduate studies that modern society requires in increasing number. The total number of graduates receiving doctorate degrees has increased only about one-third in 10 years; in 1960 they numbered less than 10,000, including only 3,000 in mathematics, physical sciences, and engineering.

An educational system which is inadequate today will be worse tomorrow, unless we act now to improve it. We must provide facilities for 14 million more elementary, secondary school, and college students by 1970, an increase of 30 percent. College enrollments alone will nearly double, requiring approximately twice as many facilities to serve nearly 7 million students by 1970. We must find the means of financing a 75-percent increase in the total cost of education—another $20 billion a year for expansion and improvement—particularly in facilities and instruction which must be of the highest quality if our Nation is to achieve its highest goals.

THE ROLE OF THE FEDERAL GOVERNMENT

The control and operation of education in America must remain the responsibility of State and local governments and private institutions. This tradition assures our educational system of the freedom, the diversity, and the vitality necessary to serve our free society fully. But the Congress has long recognized the responsibility of the Nation as a whole—that additional resources, meaningful encouragement, and vigorous leadership must be added to the total effort by the Federal Government if we are to meet the task before us. For education in this country is the right—the necessity—and the responsibility—of all. Its advancement is essential to national objectives and dependent on the greater financial resources available at the national level.

Let us put to rest the unfounded fears that "Federal money means Federal control." From the Northwest Ordinance of 1787, originally conceived by Thomas Jefferson, through the Morrill Act of 1862, establishing the still-important and still-independent land-grant college system, to the National Defense Education Act of 1958, the Congress has repeatedly recognized its responsibility to strengthen our educational system without weakening local responsibility. Since the end of the Korean war, Federal funds for constructing and operating schools in districts affected by Federal installations have gone directly to over 5,500 districts without any sign or complaint of interference or dictation from Washington. In the last decade, over $5 billion of Federal funds have been channeled to aid higher education without in any way undermining local administration.

While the coordination of existing Federal programs must be improved, we cannot meanwhile defer action on meeting our current pressing needs. Every year of further delay means a further loss of the opportunity for quality instruction to students who will never get that opportunity back. I therefore renew my urgent request of last year to the Congress for early action on those measures necessary to help this Nation achieve the twin goals of education: a new standard of educational excellence—and the availability of such excellence to all who are willing and able to pursue it.

I. ASSISTANCE TO ELEMENTARY AND SECONDARY EDUCATION

Elementary and secondary schools are the foundation of our educational system. There is little value in our efforts to broaden and improve our higher education, or increase our supply of such skills as science and engineering, without a greater effort for excellence at this basic level of education. With our mobile population and demanding needs, this is not a matter of local or State action alone—this is a national concern.

Since my message on education of last year, our crucial needs at this level have intensified and our deficiencies have grown more critical. We cannot afford to lose another year in mounting a national effort to eliminate the shortage of classrooms, to make teachers' salaries competitive, and to lift the quality of instruction.

Classrooms

To meet current needs and accommodate increasing enrollments—increasing by nearly 1 million elementary and secondary pupils a year in the 1960's—and to provide every child with the opportunity to receive a full-day education in an adequate classroom, a total of 600,000 classrooms must be constructed during this decade. The States report an immediate shortage today of more than 127,000 classrooms and a rate of construction which, combined with heavily increasing enrollments, is not likely to fill their needs for 10 years. Already over half a million pupils are in curtailed or half-day sessions. Unless the present rate of construction is accelerated and Federal resources made available to supplement State and local resources that are already strained in many areas few families and communities in the Nation will be free from the ill effects of overcrowded or inadequate facilities in our public schools.

Teachers' salaries

Teachers' salaries, though improving, are still not high enough to attract and retain in this demanding profession all the capable teachers we need. We entrust to our teachers our most valuable possession—our children—for a very large share of their waking hours during the most formative years of their life. We make certain that those to whom we entrust our financial assets are individuals of the highest competence and character—we dare not do less for the trustees of our children's minds.

Yet in no other sector of our national economy do we find such a glaring discrepancy between the importance of one's work to society and the financial reward society offers. Can any able and industrious student, unless unusually motivated, be expected to elect a career that pays more poorly than almost any other craft, trade, or profession? Until this situation can be dramatically improved—unless the States and localities can be assisted and stimulated in bringing about salary levels which will make the teaching profession competitive with other professions which require the same length of training and ability—we cannot hope to succeed in our efforts to improve the quality of our children's instruction and to meet the need for more teachers.

These are problems of national proportion. Last year I sent to the Congress a proposal to meet the urgent needs of the Nation's elementary and secondary schools. A bill (S. 1021) embodying this proposal passed the Senate last year; and similar legislation (H.R. 7300) was favorably reported to the House by its Committee on Education and Labor. It offered the minimum amount required by our needs and— in terms of across-the-board aid—the maximum scope permitted by our Constitution. It is imperative that such a proposal carrying out these objectives be enacted this session. I again urge the Congress to enact legislation providing Federal aid for public elementary and secondary classroom construction and teachers' salaries.

As noted earlier, Federal aid for construction and operation of many public schools has been provided since 1950 to those local school districts in which enrollments are affected by Federal installations. Such burdens which may remain from the impact of Federal activities on local school districts will be eased by my proposal for assistance to all school districts for construction and teachers' salaries, thus permitting modification and continuation of this special assistance program as proposed in last year's bill.

A fundamental overhauling and modernization of our traditional vocational education programs is also increasingly needed. Pursuant to my message on education last February, a panel of consultants to the Secretary of Health, Education, and Welfare is studying national needs in this area. They have been asked to develop recommendations by the close of this year for improving and redirecting the Federal Government's role in this program.

Improvement of educational quality

Strengthening financial support for education by general Federal aid will not, however, be sufficient. Specific measures directed at selected problems are also needed to improve the quality of education. And the key to educational quality is the teaching profession. About 1 out of every 5 of the nearly 1,600,000 teachers in our elementary and secondary schools fails to meet full certification standards for teaching or has not completed 4 years of college work. Our immediate concern should be to afford them every possible opportunity to improve their professional skills and their command of the subjects they teach.

In all of the principal areas of academic instruction—English, mathematics, physical and biological sciences, foreign languages, history, geography, and the social sciences—significant advances are being made, both in pushing back the frontiers' of knowledge and in the methods of transmitting that knowledge. To keep our teachers up to date on such advances, special institutes are offered in some of these areas by many colleges and universities, financed in part by the National Science Foundation and the Office of Education. Many elementary and secondary schoolteachers would profit from a full year of full-time study in their subject-matter fields. Very few can afford to do so. Yet the benefits of such a year could be shared by outstanding teachers with others in their schools and school systems as well as with countless students. We should begin to make such opportunities available to the elementary and secondary schoolteachers of this country and thereby accord to this profession the support, prestige, and recognition it deserves.

Another need is for higher standards of teacher education, course content, and instructional methods. The colleges and universities that train our teachers need financial help to examine and further strengthen their programs. Increased research and demonstration efforts must be directed toward improving the learning and teaching of subject matter and developing new and improved learning aids. Excellent but limited work in educational research and development has been undertaken by projects supported by the National Science Foundation, the Office of Education, and private groups. This must be increased—introducing and demonstrating to far more schools than at present up-to-date educational methods using the newest instructional materials and equipment, and providing the most effective in-service training and staff utilization.

Finally, in many urban as well as rural areas of the country, our school systems are confronted with unusually severe educational problems which require the development of new approaches—the problems of gifted children, deprived children, children with language problems, and children with problems that contribute to the high dropout rate, to name but a few.

To help meet all of these needs for better educational quality and development, and to provide a proper Federal role of assistance and leadership, I recommend that the Congress enact a program designed to help improve the excellence of American education by authorizing—

(1) The award each year of up to 2,500 scholarships to outstanding elementary and secondary school teachers for a year of full-time study;

(2) The establishment of institutes at colleges and universities for elementary and secondary school teachers of those subjects in which improved instruction is needed;

(3) Grants to institutions of higher education to pay part of the cost of special projects designed to strengthen teacher preparation programs through better curriculums and teaching methods;

(4) Amendment of the Cooperative Research Act to permit support of extensive, multipurpose educational research, development, demonstration, and evaluation projects; and

(5) Grants for local public school systems to conduct demonstration or experimental projects of limited duration to improve the quality of instruction or meet special educational problems in elementary and secondary schools. . . .

EDUCATION MESSAGE: JANUARY 29, 1963

Outlined by President Kennedy in his Education Message of 1963 are the goals for American education to be achieved through federal aid:

Education is the keystone in the arch of freedom and progress. Nothing has contributed more to the enlargement of this Nation's strength and opportunities than our traditional system of free, universal elementary and secondary education, coupled with widespread availability of college education.

For the individual, the doors to the schoolhouse, to the library, and to the college lead to the richest treasures of our open society: to the power of knowledge; to the training and skills necessary for productive employment; to the wisdom, the ideals, and the culture which enrich life; and to the creative, self-disciplined understanding of society needed for good citizenship in today's changing and challenging world. For the Nation, increasing the quality and availability of education is vital to both our national security and our domestic well-being. A free nation can rise no higher than the standard of excellence set in its schools and colleges. Ignorance and illiteracy, unskilled workers and school dropouts—these and other failures of our educational system breed failures in our social and economic system: delinquency, unemployment, chronic dependence, a waste of human resources, a loss of productive power and purchasing power, and an increase in tax-supported benefits. The loss of only 1 year's income due to unemployment is more than the total cost of 12 years of education through high school. Failure to improve educational performance is thus not only poor social policy, it is poor economics.

At the turn of the century, only 10 percent of our adults had a high school or college education. Today such an education has become a requirement for an increasing number of jobs. Yet, nearly 40 percent of our youths are dropping out before graduating from high school; only 43 percent of our adults have completed high school; only 8 percent of our adults have completed college; and only 16 percent of our young people are presently completing college. As my Science Advisory Committee has reported, one of our most serious manpower shortages is the lack of Ph.D's in engineering, science, and mathematics; only about one-half of 1 percent of our school-age generation is achieving Ph.D. degrees in all fields.

This Nation is committed to greater investment in economic growth; and recent research has shown that one of the most beneficial of all such investments is education, accounting for some 40 percent of the Nation's growth and productivity in recent years. It is an investment which yields a substantial return in the higher wages and purchasing power of trained workers, in the new products and techniques which come from skilled minds and in the constant expansion of this Nation's storehouse of useful knowledge.

In the new age of science and space, improved education is essential to give new meaning to our national purpose and power. In the last 20 years, mankind has acquired more scientific information than in all of previous history. Ninety percent of all the scientists that ever lived are alive and working today. Vast stretches of the unknown are being explored every day for military, medical, commercial, and other reasons. And finally, the twisting course of the cold war requires a citizenry that understands our principles and problems. It requires skilled manpower and brain power to match the power of totalitarian discipline. It requires a scientific effort which demonstrates the superiority of freedom. And it requires an electorate in every State with sufficiently broad horizons and sufficient maturity of judgment to guide this Nation safely through whatever lies ahead.

In short, from every point of view, education is of paramount concern to the national interest as well as to each individual. Today we need a new standard of excellence in education, matched by the fullest possible access to educational opportunities, enabling each citizen to develop his talents to the maximum possible extent.

Our concern as a nation for the future of our children—and the growing demands of modern education which Federal financing is better able to assist—make it necessary to expand Federal aid to education beyond the existing limited number of special programs. We can no longer afford the luxury of endless debate over all the complicated and sensitive questions raised by each new proposal on Federal participation in education. To be sure, these are all hard problems—but this Nation has not come to its present position of leadership by avoiding hard problems. We are at a point in history when we must face and resolve these problems.

State and local governments and private institutions, responsive to individual and local circumstances, have admirably served larger national purposes as well. They have written a remarkable record of freedom of thought and independence of judgment; and they have, in recent years, devoted sharply increased resources to education. Total national outlays for education nearly trebled during the 1940's and more than doubled during the 1950's, reaching a level of nearly $25 billion in 1960. As a proportion of national income, this represented a rise from little more than 4 percent in 1940 to nearly 6 percent in 1960, an increase of over 40 percent in total effort.

But all this has not been enough. And the Federal Government— despite increasing recognition of education as a nationwide challenge, and despite the increased financial difficulties encountered by States, communities, and private institutions in carrying this burden—has clearly not met its responsibilities in education. It has not offered sufficient help to our present educational system to meet its inadequacies and overcome its obstacles.

I do not say that the Federal Government should take over responsibility for education. That is neither desirable nor feasible. Instead, its participation should be selective, stimulative, and, where possible, transitional.

A century of experience with land-grant colleges has demonstrated that Federal financial participation can assist educational progress and growth without Federal control. In the last decade, experience with the National Science Foundation, with the National Defense Education Act, and with programs for assisting federally affected school districts has demonstrated that Federal support can benefit education without leading to Federal control. The proper Federal role is to identify national education goals and to help local, State, and private authorities build the necessary roads to reach those goals. Federal aid will enable our schools, colleges, and universities to be more stable financially and therefore more independent.

These goals include the following:

First, we must improve the quality of instruction provided in all of our schools and colleges. We must stimulate interest in learning in order to reduce the alarming number of students who now drop out of school or who do not continue into higher levels of education. This requires more and better teachers—teachers who can be attracted to and retained in schools and colleges only if pay levels reflect more adequately the value of the services they render. It also requires that our teachers and instructors be equipped with the best possible teaching materials and curriculums. They must have at their command methods of instruction proven by thorough scientific research into the learning process and by careful experimentation.

Second, our educational system faces a major problem of quantity—of coping with the needs of our expanding population and of the rising educational expectations for our children which all of us share as parents. Nearly 50 million people were enrolled in our schools and colleges in 1962—an increase of more than 50 percent since 1950. By 1970, college enrollment will nearly double, and secondary schools will increase enrollment by 50 percent—categories in which the cost of education, including facilities, is several times higher than in elementary schools.

Third, we must give special attention to increasing the opportunities and incentives for all Americans to develop their talents to the utmost —to complete their education and to continue their self-development throughout life. This means preventing school dropouts, improving and expanding special educational services, and providing better education in slum, distressed, and rural areas where the educational attainment of students is far below par. It means increased opportunities for those students both willing and intellectually able to advance their education at the college and graduate levels. It means increased attention to vocational and technical education, which have long been underdeveloped in both effectiveness and scope to the detriment of our workers and our technological progress.

In support of these three basic goals, I am proposing today a comprehensive, balanced program to enlarge the Federal Government's investment in the education of its citizens—a program aimed at increasing the educational opportunities of potentially every American citizen, regardless of age, race, religion, income, and educational achievement.

This program has been shaped to meet our goals on the basis of three fundamental guidelines:

A. An appraisal of the entire range of educational problems. Viewing educational opportunity as a continuous lifelong process, starting with preschool training and extending through elementary and secondary schools, graduate education, college, vocational education, job training and retraining, adult education, and such general community educational resources as the public library;

B. A selective application of Federal aid aimed at strengthening, not weakening, the independence of existing school systems and aimed at meeting our most urgent education problems and objectives, including quality improvement; teacher training; special problems of slum, depressed, and rural areas; needy students; manpower shortage areas, such as science and engineering; and shortages of educational facilities; and

C. More effective implementation of existing laws, as reflected in my recent budget recommendations.

To enable the full range of educational needs to be considered as a whole, I am transmitting to the Congress with this message a single comprehensive education bill, the National Education Improvement Act of 1963. For education cannot easily or wisely be divided into separate parts. Each part is linked to the other. The colleges depend on the work of the schools; the schools depend on the colleges for teachers; vocational and technical education is not separate from general education. This bill recalls the posture of Jefferson:

"Nobody can doubt my zeal for the general instruction of the people.

I never have proposed a sacrifice of the primary to the ultimate grade of instructions. Let us keep our eye steadily on the whole system."

In order that its full relation to economic growth, to the new age of science, to the national security, and to human and institutional freedom may be analyzed in proper perspective, this bill should be considered as a whole, as a combination of elements designed to solve problems that have no single solution.

This is not a partisan measure—and it neither includes nor rejects all the features which have long been sought by the various educational groups and organizations. It is, instead, an attempt to launch a prudent and balanced program drawing upon the efforts of many past Congresses and the proposals of many Members of both Houses and both political parties. It is solely an educational program, without trying to solve all other difficult domestic problems. It is clearly realistic in terms of its cost and it is clearly essential to the growth and security of this country. . . .

REMARKS TO A JOINT SESSION OF CONGRESS: NOVEMBER 27, 1963

Addressing Congress immediately following the death of John F. Kennedy, Lyndon B. Johnson called for action in all areas, including education:

. . . .

The greatest leader of our time has been struck down by the foulest deed of our time. Today John Fitzgerald Kennedy lives on in the immortal words and works that he left behind. He lives on in the mind and memories of mankind. He lives on in the hearts of his countrymen.

No words are sad enough to express our sense of loss. No words are strong enough to express our determination to continue the forward thrust of America that he began.

The dream of conquering the vastness of space—the dream of partnership across the Atlantic—and across the Pacific as well—the dream of a Peace Corps in less developed nations—the dream of education for all of our children—the dream of jobs for all who seek them and need them—the dream of care for our elderly—the dream of an all-out attack on mental illness—and above all, the dream of equal rights for all Americans, whatever their race or color—these and other American dreams have been vitalized by his drive and by his dedication.

And now the ideas and ideals which he so nobly represented must and will be translated into effective action. . . .

. . .

And let all know we will extend no special privilege and impose no persecution. We will carry on the fight against poverty and misery, disease and ignorance, in other lands and in our own. . . .

. . .

In short, this is no time for delay. It is time for action—strong, forward-looking action on the pending education bills to help bring the light of learning to every home and hamlet in America—strong, forward-looking action on youth employment opportunities; strong, forward-looking action on the pending foreign aid bill, making clear that we are not forfeiting our responsibilities to this hemisphere or to the world, nor erasing Executive flexibility in the conduct of our foreign affairs—and strong, prompt, and forward-looking action on the remaining appropriations bills. . . .

STATE OF THE UNION MESSAGE: JANUARY 14, 1964

President Johnson presented his first State of the Union Message to Congress in 1964, stressing assistance to the nation's poor by improving their educational opportunities:

. . .

Let this session of Congress be known as the session which did more for civil rights than the last hundred sessions combined; as the session which enacted the most far-reaching tax cut of our time; as the session which declared all-out war on human poverty and unemployment in these United States; as the session which finally recognized the health needs of all our older citizens; as the session which reformed our tangled transportation and transit policies; as the session which achieved the most effective, efficient foreign aid program ever; and as the session which helped to build more homes, and more schools, and more libraries, and more hospitals than any single session of Congress in the history of our Republic. All this and more can and must be done. It can be done by this summer.

. . .

For my part, I pledge a progressive administration which is efficient, and honest, and frugal.

The budget to be submitted to the Congress shortly is in full accord with this pledge. It will cut our deficit in half, from $10 billion to $4.9 billion. It will be, in proportion to our national output, the smallest budget since 1951. It will call for a substantial reduction in Federal employment, a feat accomplished only once before in the last 10 years. While maintaining the full strength of our combat defenses, it will call for the lowest number of civilian personnel in the Department of Defense since 1950.

It will call for total expenditures of $97.9 billion—compared to $98.4 for the current year, a reduction of more than $500 million. It will call for new obligational authority of $103.8 billion—a reduction of more than $4 billion below last year's request of $107.9 billion.

But it is not a standstill budget—for America cannot afford to stand still. Our population is growing. Our economy is more complex. Our people's needs are expanding. But by closing down obsolete installations, by curtailing less urgent programs, by cutting back where cutting back seems to be wise, by insisting on a dollar's worth for a dollar spent, I am able to recommend in this reduced budget the most Federal support in history for education, for health, for retraining the unemployed, and for helping the economically and the physically handicapped.

This budget, and this year's legislative program, are designed to help each and every American citizen fulfill his basic hopes: His hopes for a fair chance to make good, his hopes for fairplay from the law, his hopes for a full-time job on full-time pay, his hopes for a decent home for his family in a decent community, his hopes for a good school for his children with good teachers, and his hopes for security when faced with sickness or unemployment or old age.

.   .   .

This administration today here and now declares unconditional war on poverty in America. I urge this Congress and all Americans to join with me in that effort.

.   .   .

The program I shall propose will emphasize this cooperative approach to help that one-fifth of all American families with incomes too small to even meet their basic needs.

Our chief weapons in a more pinpointed attack will be better schools, and better health, and better homes, and better training, and better job opportunities to help more Americans—especially young Americans—escape from squalor and misery and unemployment rolls where other citizens help to carry them. Very often a lack of jobs and money is not the cause of poverty but the symptom.

The cause may lie deeper—in our failure to give our fellow citizens a fair chance to develop their own capacities—in a lack of education and training, in a lack of medical care and housing, in a lack of decent communities in which to live and bring up their children.

But whatever the cause, our joint Federal-local effort must pursue poverty, pursue it wherever it exists, in city slums and small towns, in sharecropper shacks or in migrant worker camps, on Indian reservations, among whites as well as Negroes, among the young as well as the aged, in the boomtowns and in the depressed areas.

Our aim is not only to relieve the symptoms of poverty but to cure it; and, above all, to prevent it. No single piece of legislation, however, is going to suffice. We will launch a special effort in the chronically distressed areas of Appalachia. We must expand our small but our successful area redevelopment program. We must enact youth employment legislation to put jobless, aimless, hopeless youngsters to work on useful projects. We must distribute more food to the needy through a broader food stamp program. We must create a National Service Corps to help the economically handicapped of our own country as the Peace Corps now helps those abroad. We must modernize our unemployment insurance and establish a high-level Commission on Automation. If we have the brainpower to invent these machines, we have the brainpower to make certain that they are a boon and not a bane to humanity. We must extend the coverage of our minimum wage laws to more than 2 million workers now lacking this basic protection of purchasing power. We must, by including special school aid funds as part of our education program, improve the quality of teaching and training and counseling in our hardest hit areas. We must build more libraries in every area, and more hospitals and nursing homes under the Hill-Burton Act, and train more nurses to staff them. We must provide hospital insurance for our older citizens, financed by every worker and his employer under social security contributing no more than $1 a month during the employee's working career to protect him in his old age in a dignified manner, without cost to the Treasury, against the devastating hardship of prolonged or repeated illness. We must, as part of a revised housing and urban renewal program, give more help to those displaced by slum clearance, provide more housing for our poor and our elderly, and seek as our ultimate goal in our free enterprise system a decent home for every American family. We must help obtain more modern mass transit within our communities as well as low-cost transportation between them. Above all, we must release $11 billion of tax reduction into the private spending stream to create new jobs and new markets in every area of this land.

These programs are obviously not for the poor or the underprivileged alone. Every American will benefit by the extension of social security to cover the hospital costs of their aged parents. Every American community will benefit from the construction or modernization of schools, libraries, hospitals, and nursing homes; from the training of more nurses; and from the improvement of urban renewal and public transit. And every individual American taxpayer and every corporate taxpayer will benefit from the earliest possible passage of the pending tax bill—from both the new investment it will bring and the new jobs that it will create.

.   .   .

Let me make one principle of this administration abundantly clear: housing, and in every field—must be open to Americans of every color. As far as the writ of Federal law will run, we must abolish not some but all racial discrimination.

For this is not merely an economic issue—or a social, political, or international issue. It is a moral issue; and it must be met by the passage this session of the bill now pending in the House.

All members of the public should have equal access to facilities open to the public. All members of the public should be equally eligible for Federal benefits that are financed by the public. All members of the public should have an equal chance to vote for public officials, and to send their children to good public schools, and to contribute their talents to the public good.

VII

CONTEMPORARY DEVELOPMENTS

> I think it is time now, I think it is
> past time, for a new, adventurous,
> imaginative, courageous breakthrough,
> for a new revolution in education in
> America.
>
> LYNDON B. JOHNSON

This final chapter will examine the contemporary relationship of education and the federal government and attempt to ascertain what the future holds for this aspect of education. President Johnson's 1965 push for federal assistance to education will be discussed, as will selected approaches to the solution of problems inherent in federal aid to education.

The Contemporary Scene

On January 12, 1965, President Lyndon B. Johnson presented to the 89th Congress his proposals for aid to education. In summary, these proposals included:

1. Aid to poverty-impacted public schools to cost about $1 billion annually, beginning in the fiscal year 1966.
2. A series of grants for the purchase of books and library materials for student use in both public and private elementary and secondary schools.
3. The establishment of "supplemental educational centers" to be shared by students of both public and private institutions.
4. Regional educational laboratories to train teachers and to develop new teaching systems along the lines of the NDEA institutes.

5. Monies to assist state departments of education to help them administer this new program.
6. A college scholarship program to help those students of the greatest need and greatest promise, including up to 140,000 students in the first year, with a total cost of $260 million.
7. Expansion of college work-study programs.
8. Payment by the government of a set percentage of interest payments on federally guaranteed loans to college students.
9. Legislation to "strengthen less developed colleges," including purchase of library materials and faculty exchanges.
10. Support for university-based community extension and continuing education programs.

ELEMENTARY AND SECONDARY EDUCATION ACT OF 1965
(S. 370, H.R. 2362)

The first five objectives listed by President Johnson were almost immediately encompassed in a single education bill, the Elementary and Secondary Education Act of 1965, introduced by Morse in the Senate (S. 370) and Perkins in the House (H.R. 2362). A summary of the provisions of this act (Public Law 89–10), which was passed with relative rapidity by both the House and Senate, presents the broad scope of the first general aid to be voted for elementary and secondary schools. In the words of President Johnson, it is an act designed to "strengthen and improve educational quality and educational opportunities in the Nation's elementary and secondary schools."

Title I: "Federal Assistance for Local Educational Agencies for the Education of Children of Low-Income Families" extends Impact Law 874 for three years. It specifies school construction and the development of special programs to aid educationally deprived children. To qualify, school districts must have at least 100 students, or 3 per cent of the student body coming from families with incomes of less than $2000 per year. It is estimated that more than 90 per cent of the total school districts in the country are eligible under these criteria, the aim of which is to improve the education of educationally deprived students. Payments will be made up to one-half the average per pupil expenditure in any state multiplied by the number of deprived children aged five to seventeen. The first year cost of this program of assistance is funded at $1.06 billion. The following phrasing indicates that the act envisages a degree of co-operation between public and private schools: ". . . for the benefit of all children within the area served, including those who participate in shared services of other special educational projects."

Title II: "School Library Resources, Textbooks, and Other Instructional Materials" includes the purchase of all printed and published instructional materials for "student use" whether in public or private institutions, although title to materials is to be vested only in a public agency. This five-year expenditure, estimated at $100 million for the first year, is to be distributed on the basis of the total number of school children enrolled in school.

Title III: "Supplementary Educational Centers and Services" provides for the establishment of model schools, pilot programs, and community centers. The aim is to supplement the offerings of local school systems in a wide variety of educational areas—continuing adult education, guidance and counseling, remedial instruction, special educational services, enriched academic programs, and health. The first-year allotment is set at $100 million.

Title IV: "Educational Research and Training; Amendments to the Cooperative Research Act of 1954" amends P.L. 83–531, which stressed the improvement of research in education and the dissemination of information to teachers and teacher training institutions. Regional educational laboratories are to be established; they will be sponsored by universities working closely with state departments of education. This program, funded at $45 million, is aimed at the development of research in education and the publicizing of the results. It emphasizes the training of teachers in the use of newly developed materials.

Title V: "Strengthening State Departments of Education" is a five-year program aimed at improving educational planning, research, and the competency of personnel. At a first year cost of $10 million, the program could be used to meet needs specific to the individual state agency. It also encourages the interchange of staff among educational agencies to facilitate co-operative educational activities aimed at improving education in general.

CRITIQUE

On April 9, the Elementary and Secondary Education Act of 1965 was passed in the Senate by an overwhelming vote of 73 to 18. The act was passed, furthermore, in the same form as that which had earlier been passed by the House of Representatives.

Signed immediately by the President because he "did not want a single day's delay in placing this landmark legislation on the statute books of this country," this comprehensive law is a major achievement of the Johnson administration. As he signed the measure in the one-room school he attended as a child, President Johnson stated:

By this Act we bridge the gap between helplessness and hope for more than five million educationally deprived children. As a son of a tenant farmer, I know that education is the only valid passport from poverty. As a former teacher—and I hope a future one—I have great expectations of what this law will mean for our young people.

Those for whom federal aid to education has been a major concern were rightfully impressed by the relative ease with which this bill was enacted into law. How can one explain the success of this bill when numerous others have been rejected just as firmly?

President Johnson, in his Education Message to Congress, conceived what James Reston termed "a masterpiece of evasive action." The bills presented clearly indicate a thorough study and analysis of many previous education bills, particularly those bills which actually were enacted into Law. To illustrate this observation, let us examine the Elementary and Secondary Education Act of 1965 in the light of other education legislation.

First, the term *impact* was used, "Impact on Poverty." Few would deny that among the most successful laws in educational legislation are those designated as the Federal Impact Laws (P.L. 815 and P.L. 874). These two bills, passed in 1950, at the height of the Korean War, have been extended and expanded, and continue in force at the present. Even one of the strongest opponents of federal aid to education, Barry Goldwater, favored these laws. Thus the use of the word *impact*, which for congressmen has a favorable connotation, demonstrates a shrewd knowledge of political psychology.

Secondly, programs which are very specific in nature are those which have found favor in the past. Programs which aid one area or one particular type of educational program have generally had less trouble passing Congress than have those of a very general nature; e.g., President Kennedy's omnibus bill. In spite of frequently voiced fears of federal control, the types of bills passed have usually entailed more control than would those granting flat sums.

It has also been found that in recent years the legislation which has been more successful contained the expressed aim of improvement of instruction, particularly the improvement of instruction in specific prestige subjects; e.g., mathematics, foreign languages, and science. The pace-setter was the National Defense Education Act, which was expanded in 1964 to include almost all subject areas, specifying improvement not only in the aforementioned subjects but also in English, reading, history and geography.

Most education bills have historically involved emergency or wartime measures. It is strange, but apparently true, that we can only pass a federal aid bill which has implications of war. In this time of apparent peace, therefore, we have a federal aid bill proposed as a "War Against Poverty." Here again, the National Defense Education Act can be cited as an example of a bill passed to combat the Cold War.

Finally, the President's 1965 proposals held something for every segment of society. The poor, the rich, the private school, elementary, secondary, and higher education—all are named as recipients of assistance. The major portion of the act, Title I, involves 90 per cent of the country's school districts.

In summary it might be said that the President and his educational advisers read the history of educational legislation very carefully and learned significant lessons. Johnson gathered ideas from varied sources. J. Kenneth Galbraith, for example, suggested that a teaching corps, a "Prosperity Corps," be formed to go into backward areas such as Appalachia to upgrade the education systems of the poor. It was he who suggested that federal aid be focused on the poorest districts. This was also the recommendation of the Council for Economic Development, which early in 1963 presented a formula providing aid for the 18 states having the greatest need.

Aware that, for the first time, the Catholics have a plurality in the 89th Congress, with 107 Catholic members compared to 88 Methodists, educational advisers have carefully made provisions for aid to private and parochial schools. It is clearly specified, however, that no aid is to be used for religious purposes—either instruction or worship.

Critics of Johnson's proposals maintain that the program is actually too limited and represents only a fringe attack. The point is made, for example, that with 75 million school children between the ages of five and seventeen, $1½ billion will scarcely be noticed. The problem of poverty itself is so extensive, so gigantic, that a remedy would, of necessity, have to involve a change in the entire society.

Finally, supporters of the Johnson administration point out the political power and skill of Lyndon B. Johnson himself. His experience in the Senate and his intimate acquaintance with many strong political leaders have undoubtedly assisted the passage of this law. The skill, too, of those who sponsored the bill in both House and Senate was also instrumental in securing its smooth passage into law.

Federal Aid to Education: A Forecast

Before we consider the future possibilities of federal involvement in education, it is interesting to note what has been accomplished since the eighteenth century, for it has been said that "the future is but an extension of the past." Following is a chronological summary of federal legislation since 1777.

SUMMARY OF FEDERAL AID LEGISLATION: 1777–1965

1777 Initiation of direct administration of education programs—the instruction of military personnel, including schooling in mathematics.

1785 Commencement of aid to territories for education by endowment of schools with public lands.

1787 Commencement of endowment of public institutions of higher education with public lands—Northwest Ordinance: "Schools and the means of education shall forever be encouraged."

1802 Establishment of the first federal institution of higher education—Military Academy at West Point.

1804 District of Columbia—federal provision for education begins.

1862 The First Morrill Act—initiated federal policy of aid to states for agricultural and industrial education through land grants for colleges.

1867 Federal Department of Education established by Congress; later the Office of Education.

1874 Introduction of the principle of federal-state matching of funds for education.

1887 Hatch Act—encouraged scientific investigation in agriculture.

1890 The Second Morrill Act—introduction of federal grants of money for college instruction in specified areas of learning.

1914 Smith-Lever Act—matching of funds for agricultural and and home economics instruction.

1917 The Smith-Hughes Act—began policy of promoting vocational education below college level through assistance with teachers' salaries.

1918 Rehabilitation training for disabled veterans.

1919 Federal surplus property available to educational institutions.

1920 The National Defense Act of 1920—direct relationship between the federal government and educational institutions.

1920 Smith-Bankhead Act—federal-state cooperation in vocational rehabilitation; education for people disabled in industry.

1933 Federal Emergency Relief Administration—supported educational programs.

1935 National Youth Administration—employment for college students.

1935 Bankhead-Jones Act—increased support for land-grant colleges.

1936 Promotion of Inter-American Cultural Relations Convention—international educational exchanges.

1936 George-Deen Act—extended the Smith-Hughes Act.

1937 National Cancer Institute Act—provided fellowship grants.

1937 Civilian Conservation Corps—provided vocational education.

1941 Lanham Act—provided educational assistance for schools in communities affected by the federal government's activities.

1943 Vocational Rehabilitation Act—aid for disabled veterans.

1944 The Servicemen's Readjustment Act—G.I. Bill, educational aid for veterans.

1944 Surplus Property Act—government surplus given to educational institutions.

1946 George-Barden Act—extended Smith-Hughes Act by increasing appropriation.

1946 National School Lunch—gave funds and food to public and non-public schools; school milk program added in 1954.

1948 Smith-Mundt Act—program of international educational exchanges.

1949 Federal Property and Administrative Services Act—surplus property disposal for educational, health, and civil defense purposes.

1950 The National Science Foundation Act—promoted progress in science through scholarships and fellowships in fields of science.

1950 The Housing Act—low interest rates for loans to institutions of higher learning for building of housing facilities.

1950   Federal Impact Laws (P.L. 815 and P.L. 874)—extended the Lanham Act of 1941; provided assistance to communities affected by activities of the federal government for construction and operation of schools.

1952   National Science Foundation—fellowship program.

1956   Library Services Act—grants for improvement of library facilities.

1958   United States and Union of Soviet Socialist Republics agree to exchange study groups in educational and cultural fields.

1958   The National Defense Education Act—provided for graduate fellowships in education—science, mathematics, foreign languages, counseling and guidance, educational technology.

1958   Fogarty-McGovern Act—federal grants to train teachers of mentally retarded children.

1961   Area Redevelopment Act—training of persons in redevelopment areas.

1961   Peace Corps Act—supplied teachers and technicians to underdeveloped nations.

1961   Juvenile Delinquency and Youth Offenses Control—study of problem.

1962   Manpower Development and Training Act—up-to-date training for the unemployable.

1963   Health Professions Educational Assistance Act—construction of facilities and student loans.

1963   Mental Retardation Facilities and Community Mental Health Centers Construction Act—training of teachers and demonstration projects.

1963   Higher Education Facilities Act of 1963—grants to all colleges, public and private, for improvement of facilities.

1963   Amendments to the Manpower Development and Training Act—expansion of provisions of law, 1962.

1963   Vocational Education Act of 1963—construction of vocational schools with expanded offerings; extended Impact Laws (1950) and NDEA (1958).

1964   Economic Opportunity Act of 1964—war on poverty through retraining and remedial education and other opportunities.

1964   The Civil Rights Act of 1964—desegregation of the schools enforced and assisted.

1964   Juvenile Delinquency and Youth Offenses Control Act Amendment—new programs and special studies.

1964   The National Commission on Technology and Automation and Economic Progress—commission to study impact of technological change.

1964   Amendments to National Defense Education Act—extended and expanded to include areas of English, reading, history and geography.

1965   Elementary and Secondary Education Act—federal grants to states for allocation to school districts with low income families.

1965   National Foundation for the Arts and Humanities—foundation to support humanities and the arts through grants.

1965   Higher Education Act of 1965—aid to colleges, students, and teachers.

Whatever other predictions are made regarding the future of federal aid to education, this much is certain: The importance of education to the nation has clearly been recognized, and attention will continue to focus on education for all the people and on the general improvement of the quality of that education. The years ahead promise to be the most exciting and challenging in all educational history as we Americans follow the precedents which have been established, for we have the record before us of an American educational system which has moved from provincial beginnings toward a high degree of centralization and federal involvement.

FEDERAL INVOLVEMENT

Despite opposition, the involvement of the federal government will continue at a rapidly increasing rate at all levels of education. One reason for this increased involvement is that the number of individuals directly concerned with education will continue to grow. At the present time, approximately one-fouth of the nation is directly involved in education; this number will soon encompass fully one-third of the national population as enrollments at all levels of education increase. College enrollments alone, for example, are expected to increase 50 per cent before the end of this decade. With increased enrollments, will come increased spending in education. The cost of education will rise until the educational budget rivals that of the Defense Department. In 1965, educational expenditures were estimated at $30 billion. President Johnson's budget for the fiscal year 1965–66 called for a 75 per cent increase in spending through the U.S. Office of Education.

The basis for the *Great Society* is clearly education. Peter F. Drucker, writing in *Harper's* in 1965, stated: "Education is about to take over from the Welfare State as a basic commitment of the American people. One might call this new phenomenon the Knowledge State. Education is bound to become a focus of political life and political conflict" (20, p. 42). The administration has obviously placed increased emphasis on domestic affairs, with a definite focus on education.

Not only are we concerned with the sheer quantity of the educational enterprise, but we are also becoming increasingly involved in improving the quality of education—the teaching, the curriculum, and the methodology. Patterned after the very successful National Science Foundation is the National Foundation of the Arts and Humanities, which also attempts to improve the quality of education. The expansion of NDEA in 1964 encompassed broad areas of the curriculum, emphasizing teacher education as well as content and new media. The Elementary and Secondary Education Act of 1965 also stressed research and development in education. It is clear, therefore, that the federal government intends to increase its direct involvement in the general improvement of the nation's education.

Assistance to education by the federal government will continue to be of a pragmatic nature following the course established by previous Congresses, for there has been a close correlation between the federal government's involvement in education and both foreign and domestic crises. Education has been used to solve society's problems, and it will be called upon again to solve the problems posed by automation and leisure.

CO-ORDINATION OF EDUCATION

Although control of education will continue to be a local matter, the evident national concern for education will result in the use of co-operative groups and boards to view the larger picture of education. Educational organization will follow the lines recommended by James B. Conant in his book, *Shaping Educational Policy* (14).

In recognition of the federal government's increased concern with education is H.R. 25, introduced by Edith Green of Oregon. This bill proposes the establishment of a permanent National Advisory Council on Education. Either this bill or a similar proposal will find acceptance, for with the agreement that education is a matter of national consideration will come the realization that there is a need for some type of advisory board to perform the following functions:

1. Advise the President on educational matters.
2. Analyze the development of national education.
3. Propose needed legislation.
4. Develop a system of priorities in education.

EXPANSION OF THE U.S. OFFICE OF EDUCATION

A development that is almost certain to take place in the near future is the expansion of the role of the Office of Education. The budget allocated for this office has already increased so that it is bigger than that for the departments of Commerce, Interior, Justice, or Labor. Increased federal aid to education will inevitably entail a larger staff and greater responsibilities for this office.

Monies spent on education will tend to be more strongly focused in this office. In 1965, the Office of Education controlled approximately one-third of all federal money spent on education, while the other two-thirds of funds for education were administered by the Department of Agriculture, the National Aeronautics and Space Administration, the International Science Foundation, and

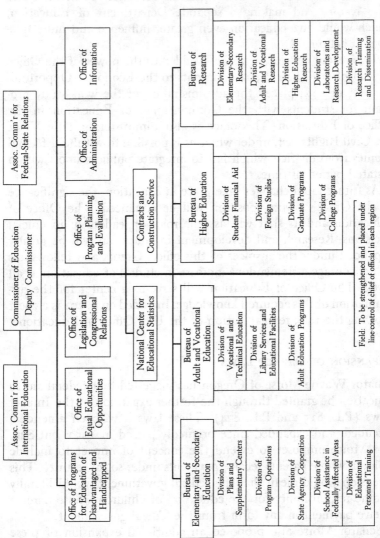

Field: To be strengthened and placed under line control of chief of official in each region

From: U.S. Dept. of Health, Education and Welfare. Office of Education. Legislative Notes, July 19, 1965.

forty-two other agencies. More power and prestige will come to the Office of Education as federal spending increases. There are those who recommend making a separate Department of Education, which would give education even greater influence and more freedom of action.

Two recent developments have added to the power of the Office of Education. The 1965 amendments to the Economic Opportunities Act of 1964 placed the administration of the work-study program for students with the Commissioner of Education in the Office of Education. This office is also administering Title VI of the Civil Rights Act, under which it is possible to withhold federal monies from districts which fail to integrate public schools within a stated period of time.

As future rapid changes take place in education, the significance of the Office's pivotal position will be enhanced. The Office of Education and its staff will assume roles of leadership in crucial decisions. Research and development in education will be greatly expanded under the auspices of this office. Grants and fellowships will encourage a tremendous increase in studies of education at all levels. The Office of Education will serve as a center for the dissemination of this acquired knowledge. Included on p. 201 is a chart showing the 1965 reorganization of the U.S. Office of Education.

EXPANSION OF IMPACT LAWS

Senator Wayne Morse of Oregon has suggested that federal aid to education be granted through the further expansion of the Impact Laws (P.L. 815 and P.L. 874). These laws have been amended, extended, and expanded since originally passed in 1950, but Senator Morse proposes to extend the concept of impact to include children whose parents receive payments under social security. This extension would mean that the federal government would literally assume responsibility for the education of children whose parents receive payment in any form from the federal government.

Senator Morse also proposed an additional expansion of these laws, presented to the 88th Congress as S. 2725, after the 1964 Alaskan earthquake disaster. This bill proposed the provision of financial assistance under the Impact Laws in construction and operation of public elementary and secondary schools in areas affected by major disasters. Stated the Senator: ". . . as a result of the earthquake and tidal wave, perhaps we should explore the utility of an automatic standby authority which would release Federal funds for the replacement of schools damaged by such acts of God."

INTERNATIONAL EDUCATION

The forecast in this area of education includes a great increase in the involvement of the United States government in improving education in underdeveloped countries around the world. An increased number of AID (Agency for International Development) contracts will be made with colleges and universities to provide teachers who will assist in establishing training institutions to enable countries to help themselves. The Peace Corps program will continue to expand as greater use is made of enthusiastic, talented Americans, young and old.

International scholarships and student exchanges will encourage an exchange of information. Specialists in comparative education will continue to cross national borders as close international co-operation is developed in and through education.

CHURCH, STATE, AND EDUCATION

Although major strides have been made toward the reconciliation of Church, State, and education, this issue still remains a problem area in legislation. It will continue to receive attention in all three branches of the federal government. Outlined here are possible approaches to the problem which are being, and will be, explored as ways to break through the traditional impasse.

Tuition Payments. One of the proposed solutions is an arrangement whereby each state gives parents a specific amount of money per school-age child. The parents may spend it on any type of education or schooling deemed desirable. One of the more vocal proponents of this approach is Milton Friedman, an economist at the University of Chicago. The tuition payment is also favored by southern segregationalists, as well as by a Catholic lay group named Citizens for Educational Freedom.

Tax Deductions. This system calls for income tax deductions to be allowed for at least a portion of private school tuition at the elementary and secondary levels. Some writers have contended that tax deductions might be allowed as contributions to religious activities, considering tuition as a contribution to a religious organization. Since contributions are already tax deductible, this practice would merely expand the existing deduction to include tuition payments for education.

Other spokesmen have suggested that parents of college-age youngsters be allowed tax deductions. Former Senators Goldwater and Humphrey are two persons favoring the plan which gives parents income tax deductions on a sliding scale. Parents of college students would be allowed to deduct for example, 100 per cent of the first $100 spent for tuition each year, 30 per cent of the next $400, and 20 per cent of the next $500.

In the plan proposed by Abraham Ribicoff, Senator from Connecticut and former Secretary of Health, Education, and Welfare, parents would be allowed to subtract up to $325 of college costs annually.

Still another plan is that of Richard Goode, an economist for the Brookings Institution, who suggested that the tax benefit go to the student himself. Under this plan, direct expenses of college—tuition, books, etc.—would be deductible over a period of ten to twenty years. One of the effects of this plan might be the encouragement of student-borrowing for college expenses.

Direct Aid. Two plans for direct aid have been proposed. One plan calls for the federal government's giving direct aid to the states, with each state deciding on the allocation of the money. Beardsley Ruml, nationally known tax expert, was one advocate of this position. The chief advantage of this plan is that it would involve the states in educational decision-making, while the federal government would not enter this field. Another effect of this type of direct aid, however, would be to decrease the likelihood of aid for private and parochial schools because of the frequently strict interpretation of state constitutions by state judiciary. (See Chapter V.)

Dr. William S. Vincent, professor of education at Columbia University's Teachers College, has proposed what he called a "shared cost plan" whereby direct aid would go to local school districts. The local board of education would receive funds directly, "which it then may disburse as it does other funds for which it is accountable." Thus the local school board might allocate monies to private and parochial schools also in its area. This plan would give the local school board some power over this part of the educational sector which they do not have at the present time. It might make for a closer relationship between public and private schools, although some difficulties might arise. Dr. Vincent believes that this plan is the only way to solve the problem of federal aid to education.

Fringe Benefits. Some writers feel that if we could arrive at firmer definitions of fringe benefits, perhaps on the basis of the child benefit theory, it would be possible to aid the child as well as the parent without aiding the religious institutions *per se.* Three criteria help to clarify what benefits are possible under the Constitution: (1) no religious organization or school would acquire new property because of state action; (2) no religious use can be made of monies provided by the state, and (3) the state would keep complete control over the administration and distribution of state benefits.

Fringe benefits might continue in terms of teacher education, transportation, health and welfare, school lunches, and federal construction of science, mathematics, and foreign language laboratories. It is felt that by this method it might be possible to differentiate between religious and secular aspects of education in religious schools.

Shared Time. One of the most interesting of the ideas proposed is that of "shared time." Since this is one of the more provocative of the newer developments, we shall examine it in detail. Much of the information for this discussion is derived from a committee print, prepared at the request of Senator Morse, entitled: "Proposed Federal Promotion of Shared Time Education" (85).

What is "shared time"? There are several definitions of this term. The research department of the National Education Association, for example, terms it: "An arrangement whereby non-public schools send their pupils to public schools for instruction in one or more subjects during the regular school day." The research department of the American Federation of Teachers defines this program as: "An educational system sanctioned by law which permits parents to enroll their children in both public and non-public schools at the same time." The Superintendent of Schools in Englewood, New Jersey, Dr. Harry L. Stearns, defines shared time as: "The sharing of the school time of children between state-supported schools, which provide a general education in a denominationally neutral context, and church-supported schools, which proceed with a specific denominational religious emphasis."

In summary, then, shared time means an arrangement for students enrolled in non-public elementary and secondary schools to attend public school for instruction in specific subject areas. In some ways, while not usually discussed in the same context, shared time resembles "released time" in reverse; i.e., instead of public schools' releasing students to attend religious classes in non-public schools, students of non-public schools are now to be released to receive instruction in purely secular subjects in the public schools.

One of the pioneer programs involving shared time was conducted by a Pittsburgh public high school and a Roman Catholic high school in that city. The Catholic students spent one-half of the school day in the Catholic school studying religion, the social sciences, and English, while the other half of the day was spent in the public school studying science, mathematics, foreign languages, physical education, and vocational subjects.

The concept of shared time is not a new idea, for in some areas of the country this type of program has been in operation for more than forty years. As the importance of education has received national emphasis and debate involving the role of the federal government has increased, so have attempts at solving the problems of federal aid to education received greater attention. Shared time, therefore, is gaining national importance as a possible answer to the problem which has impeded the passage of general federal aid to education; i.e., shall aid be extended to private and parochial schools? Many writers view this program as a workable plan which would lessen the bitterness and divisiveness which have been an integral part of the arguments over federal funds for schools. Writings on this topic, moreover, indicate a great willingness to co-operate. As one writer stated: "It is worth a try." Monsignor O'Neill C. D'Amour, Associate Secretary of the School Superintendents Department of the National Catholic Education Association, wrote: "I am convinced that Catholics will look upon the shared time proposal with sympathy."

In an article written for the general public (*Good Housekeeping*, February, 1963), Arthur Flemming, President of the University of Oregon and former Secretary of Health, Education, and Welfare, discussed the recent opinions and actions of Catholic and Protestant leaders as indicating a greater willingness to come to grips with the question of shared time.

There are, of course, those who are not strongly in favor of this type of shared program. Some school administrators, for example, exhibit an unwillingness to become involved with shared time. In many cases, however, this reluctance has been chiefly a question of adequate financial arrangements.

There are many arguments and ideas which have been advanced in favor of shared time arrangements. Outlined here are a few of the salient points made:

1. Is there a better solution? It is a compromise that is worth trying.
2. It is a constitutional means of extending federal aid to students of non-public schools.
3. Federal contributions could be based on the number of class hours spent in public schools by all children either as full-time or part-time enrollees.
4. Shared time arrangements could easily be financed through amendment to the NDEA.
5. Through this method, the public schools would serve all children; the argument of double taxation would have less basis, for Catholic children would receive benefits from tax-supported schools, too.

6. Children would have a broader social experience as would parents and school staffs. The co-operative system would be a true experience in democracy which would tend to eliminate antagonistic feelings.
7. Shared time would reduce pressures to include religious observances during school hours in public schools; Bible reading cases would have less significance.

Those who view the other side of the question have doubts about the feasibility and advisability of the shared time program. Outlined here are arguments which are unfavorable to the proposal:

1. Shared time is not a way out of the federal aid dilemma; one problem is merely substituted for another.
2. Administrative problems involved in extension of shared time programs are prohibitive—transportation, scheduling, length of school day and year, overtaxing of facilities.
3. This assistance to students of non-public schools actually results in federal aid to the religious schools by easing their financial burden and permitting them to expand religious offerings; shared time would, therefore, be unconstitutional.
4. Many state laws would not permit shared time programs, and new legislation would be necessary. This would result in bitterness and tension.
5. The public school will be weakened, becoming a supplementary school which teaches only those subjects which sectarian schools consider less important.
6. The division of the curricular offering would eliminate possibilities for close integration of subjects taught. Undesirable pressures would result in both schools as disputes arise over *how* and *what* is taught.
7. Public school facilities would require vast expansion in classroom space and teaching staff. Taxes would have to be increased to cover these expenses.
8. Religious schools, on the other hand, would no longer require teachers in many subject areas. This would result in dislocation of many teachers at the secondary level, thus causing dissatisfaction.

9. Students will become even more aware of grouping by denomination. Serious antagonism, bitterness, and competition could result. The dominant group might also pressure others into conformity with their beliefs.

10. Shared time would not be practical in the elementary school where children are in one classroom all day. Moving children results in loss of time and is disruptive for the young child. Do we have the right to gamble with the lives of our children?

PROBING THE FUTURE

Is there profit to be gained from extending our viewpoints beyond the immediate horizon for education? What, for example, will be the relationship of education and the federal government at the turn of the next century? What assistance will the federal government offer education? How and when will the federal government apply funds to support the educative process?

There seems, to this author, to be a great need for looking ahead with education for the next decade, but, in spite of uncertainties and inherent difficulties, there appears to be an even greater reason for reaching out in time to those years which lie still farther beyond us. Education, of all our basic institutions, must be forward-looking, for the child born today will spend his adulthood in the twenty-first century. Schools are not preparing citizens for today, but for tomorrow, an age which lies around a far distant corner, an age which many decision-makers of today will never see.

Perhaps what we need to perform this visionary task is a National Educational Brain Trust composed of this country's most creative, far-sighted individuals who will propel education into the future. Forming such a group would direct attention on the far horizons of education, rather than on the pedestrian precedents of the past to which eyes have too often turned. Composed of innovators in all fields, this "trust" could perhaps assist the nation in making the quantum leaps in education which seem necessary if we are to maintain intellectual leadership in the twenty-first century.

It is this writer's contention that federal involvement in education now exists; it will continue; and it will expand. The realistic student of this issue, which is no longer a question for political debate, will analyze the present relationship in terms of specific needs and specific programs. Efforts should be directed, therefore, toward determining the most effective utilization of this partnership. Research and study are needed to focus thought on this burgeoning field of interdisciplinary concern as we attempt both to understand the complexity of the relationship and to realize its full potential. An institute for study of these areas of involvement is clearly needed to probe the legal, social, political, and educational implications of this relationship.

Is it not inevitable that a comparatively intimate relationship will develop between the federal government and education despite the persistent opposition of those who have opposed governmental *interference?* With the present emphasis firmly on quality education has come direct involvement of the federal government with the educative process, and at the present time we find the federal government actively participating in the retraining of thousands of teachers, the funding of research and demonstration projects, the preparation of instructional materials, and the development of new educational media.

What will be the long-range effect of the federal government's expanded participation in education? The effect of federal involvement will probably be in terms of the encouragement, facilitation, and guidance of development in education as American schools strive to meet the changing foci of society. The need to educate students for the future and the stress on excellence in education will put new demands on teachers. Recognition of innovation in education will be encouraged and rewarded, and scholarly contributions by the teacher operating on the classroom frontier will be stimulated. These efforts will result in the upgrading of the teaching profession and the general improvement of the quality of education.

In the future, education will emphasize the teaching of ideas and abstract processes rather than facts which are quickly outdated. Processes of thinking, abilities to adjust to change, skills in assimilating information and in perceiving relationships will be among the teachings of the New School. As the nation realizes the importance of the educational process itself, federal monies will be spent directly on the solution of educational problems. With education recognized as more than a means for solving social problems, the problems specific to education will be studied. The following ten areas will be among the first to receive concerted attention:

1. Educating for diversity.
2. Providing for a science of education.
3. Extending education downward, upward, outward.
4. Determining the content of the curriculum.
5. Recruiting the most able persons as teachers.
6. Teaching every citizen to read.
7. Providing for the culturally deprived.
8. Equalizing educational opportunities.
9. Promoting the creativity of every individual.
10. Developing effective materials, methods, and media.

We are now at a threshhold in education. Looking back, we can clearly see that we have solved some problems, and that we have reached compromises in others. At this important juncture we can also perceive unlimited opportunities in education as we move into a new era of increased co-operation between the State and the School. The role of the federal government in education promises to be increasingly active, influential, and inspiring.

Representative Statements

Included in this section are two statements made by President Johnson in 1965.

STATE OF THE UNION MESSAGE

President Lyndon B. Johnson, elected in 1964, addressed Congress on January 4, 1965. Following is that portion of his State of the Union Message which is directly pertinent to education:

. . . Our third goal is to improve the quality of American life.

We begin with learning.

Every child must have the best education that this nation can provide.

Thomas Jefferson said no nation can be both ignorant and free. Today no nation can be both ignorant and great.

In addition to our existing programs, I will recommend a new program for schools and students with a first year authorization of one billion, 500 million dollars.

It will help at every stage along the road to learning.

For the pre-school years we will help needy children become aware of the excitement of learning.

For the primary and secondary school years we will aid public schools serving low income families and assist students in both public and private schools.

For the college years we will provide scholarships to high school students of the greatest promise and greatest need and guaranteed low interest loans to students continuing their college studies.

New laboratories and centers will help our schools lift their standards of excellence and explore new methods of teaching. These centers will provide special training for those who need and those who deserve special treatment.

Greatness requires not only an educated people but a healthy people.

Our goal is to match the achievements of our medicine to the afflictions of our people.

We already carry on a large program for research and health.

In addition, regional medical centers can provide the most advanced diagnosis and treatment for heart disease, cancer, stroke, and other major diseases.

New support for medical and dental education will provide the trained men to apply our knowledge.

Community centers can help the mentally ill and improve health care for school-age children from poor families, including services for the mentally retarded. . . .

EDUCATION MESSAGE

On January 12, 1965, President Johnson addressed a joint session of Congress to present his proposals for education. Here, given in its entirety, is the message which recommended "an educational system restudied, reinforced, and revitalized":

To the Congress of the United States:

In 1787, the Continental Congress declared in the Northwest Ordinance:

Schools and the means of education shall forever be encouraged.

America is strong and prosperous and free because for 178 years we have honored that commitment.

In the United States today—

One-quarter of all Americans are in the Nation's classrooms.

High school attendance has grown eighteenfold since the turn of the century—six times as fast as the population.

College enrollment has advanced eightyfold. Americans today support a fourth of the world's institutions of higher learning and a third of its professors and college students.

In the life of the individual, education is always an unfinished task. And in the life of this Nation, the advancement of education is a continuing challenge.

There is a darker side to education in America:

One student out of every three now in the fifth grade will drop out before finishing high school—if the present rate continues.

Almost a million young people will continue to quit school each year—if our schools fail to stimulate their desire to learn.

Over 100,000 of our brightest high school graduates each year will not to go college—and many others will leave college—if the opportunity for higher education is not expanded.

The cost of this neglect runs high—both for the youth and the Nation:

Unemployment of young people with an eighth grade education or less is four times the national average.

Jobs filled by high school graduates rose by 40 percent in the last 10 years. Jobs for those with less schooling decreased by nearly 10 percent.

We can measure the cost in even starker terms. We now spend about $450 a year per child in our public schools. But we spend $1,800 a year to keep a delinquent youth in a detention home, $2,500 a year for a family on relief, $3,500 a year for a criminal in State prison.

The growing numbers of young people reaching school age demand that we move swiftly even to stand still.

Attendance in elementary and secondary schools will increase by 4 million in the next 5 years; 400,000 new classrooms will be needed to meet this growth. But almost one-half million of the Nation's existing classrooms are already more than 30 years old.

The post-World War II boom in babies has now reached college age. And by 1970, our colleges must be prepared to add 50 percent more enrollment to their presently overcrowded facilities.

In the past, Congress has supported an increasing commitment to education in America. Last year, I signed historic measures passed by the 88th Congress to provide—

Facilities badly needed by universities, colleges, and community colleges;

Major new resources for vocational training;

More loans and fellowships for students enrolled in higher education; and

enlarged and improved training for physicians, dentists, and nurses.

I propose that the 89th Congress join me in extending the commitment still further. I propose that we declare a national goal of

FULL EDUCATIONAL OPPORTUNITY

Every child must be encouraged to get as much education as he has the ability to take.

We want this not only for his sake—but for the Nation's sake.

Nothing matters more to the future of our country: not our military preparedness, for armed might is worthless if we lack the brainpower to build a world of peace; not our productive economy, for we cannot sustain growth without trained manpower; not our democratic system of government, for freedom is fragile if citizens are ignorant.

We must demand that our schools increase not only the quantity but the quality of America's education. For we recognize that nuclear age problems cannot be solved with horse-and-buggy learning. The three R's of our school system must be supported by the three T's—teachers who are superior, techniques of instruction that are modern, and thinking about education which places it first in all our plans and hopes.

Specifically, four major tasks confront us—

to bring better education to millions of disadvantaged youth who need it most;

to put the best educational equipment and ideas and innovations within reach of all students;

to advance the technology of teaching and the training of teachers; and to provide incentives for those who wish to learn at every stage along the road to learning.

Our program must match the magnitude of these tasks. The budget on education which I request for fiscal year 1966 will contain a total of $4.1 billion. This includes $1.1 billion to finance programs established by the 88th Congress. I will submit a request for $1.5 billion in new obligational authority to finance the programs described in this message. This expenditure is a small price to pay for developing our Nation's most priceless resource.

In all that we do, we mean to strengthen our State and community education systems. Federal assistance does not mean Federal control—as past programs have proven. The late Senator Robert Taft declared:

> Education is primarily a State function—but in the field of education, as in the fields of health, relief, and medical care, the Federal Government has a secondary obligation to see that there is a basic floor under those essential services for all adults and children in the United States.

In this spirit, I urge that we now push ahead with the No. 1 business of the American people—the education of our youth in preschools, elementary and secondary schools, and in the colleges and universities.

I. PRESCHOOL PROGRAMS

My budget will include up to $150 million for preschool projects under the community action program of the Economic Opportunity Act.

Education must begin with the very young. The child from the urban or rural slum frequently misses his chance even before he begins school. Tests show that he is usually a year behind in academic attainment by the time he reaches the third grade—and up to 3 years behind if he reaches the eighth grade. By then the handicap has grown too great for many children. Their horizons have narrowed; their prospects for lifetimes of failure have hardened. A large percentage of our young people whose family incomes are less than $2,000 do not go beyond the eighth grade.

Preschool programs have demonstrated marked success in overcoming this initial handicap:

In New York City, children from slum neighborhoods who attended nursery school have performed better when tested in the third and fourth grades than those who did not attend.

In Baltimore, children with language and cultural handicaps are being helped greatly by a preschool program. According to preliminary reports, two-thirds of them are in the top 50 percent of their kindergarten and first grade classes on a citywide measure; one-sixth of them are in the top quarter.

But today, almost half of our school districts conduct no kindergarten classes. Public nursery schools are found in only about 100 of our 26,000 school districts. We must expand our preschool program in order to reach disadvantaged children early.

Action on a wide front will begin this summer through a special "head-start" program for children who are scheduled to begin school next fall. In addition, funds for low-income schools, regional education laboratories, and supplementary educational centers and services (recommended below) will be devoted to these vital preschool programs.

II. ELEMENTARY AND SECONDARY SCHOOLS

Elementary and secondary schools are the foundation of our education system:

Forty-eight million students are now in our grade and high schools.

Seventy-one percent of the Nation's expenditures for education are spent on elementary and secondary schooling.

If these schools are to do their job properly; they need help and they need it now. I propose that we give first priority to a program of:

A. To Low-Income School Districts

I recommend that legislation be enacted to authorize a major program of assistance to public elementary and secondary schools serving children of low-income families. My budget for fiscal year 1966 will request $1 billion for this new program.

One hundred years ago, a man with 6 or 7 years of schooling stood well above the average. His chances to get ahead were as good as the next man's. But today, lack of formal education is likely to mean low wages, frequent unemployment, and a home in an urban or rural slum.

Poverty has many roots, but the taproot is ignorance:

Poverty is the lot of two-thirds of the families in which the family head has had 8 years or less of schooling.

20 percent of the youth aged 18 to 24 with an eighth-grade education or less are unemployed—four times the national average.

Just as ignorance breeds poverty, poverty all too often breeds ignorance in the next generation:

Nearly half the youths rejected by selective service for educational deficiency have fathers who are unemployed or else working in unskilled and low income jobs.

Fathers of more than one-half of the draft rejectees did not complete the eighth grade.

The burden on the Nation's schools is not evenly distributed. Low-income families are heavily concentrated in particular urban neighborhoods or rural areas. Faced with the largest educational needs, many of these school districts have inadequate financial resources. This imbalance has been increased by the movement of high income families from the center of cities to the suburbs—and their replacement by low-income families from rural areas:

The five States with the lowest incomes spend only an average of $276 per pupil, less than half the average of the five highest income States.

Despite a massive effort, our big cities generally spend only about two-thirds as much per pupil as their adjacent suburbs.

In our 15 largest cities, 60 percent of the 10th-grade students from poverty neighborhoods drop out before finishing high school.

This is a national problem. Federal action is needed to assist the States and localities in bringing the full benefits of education to children of low-income families.

Assistance will be provided—

on the basis of census data showing the distribution of low-income families among the counties or school districts within States.

through payments made to States for distribution to school districts.

with the assurance that the funds will be used for improving the quality of education in schools serving low-income areas.

on the condition that Federal funds will not be used to reduce State and local fiscal efforts.

for the benefit of all children within the area served, including those who participate in shared services or other special educational projects.

B. School Library Resources and Instructional Materials

I recommend legislation to authorize Federal grants to States to assist in the purchase of books for school libraries and for student use, to be made available to children in public and private nonprofit elementary and secondary schools.

Thomas Carlyle once said: "All that mankind has done, thought, gained, or been: it is lying as in magic preservation in the pages of books." Yet our school libraries are limping along:

Almost 70 percent of the public elementary schools have no libraries; 84 percent lack librarians to teach children the value of learning through good books.

Many schools have an average of less than one-half book per child.

To meet the accepted standards for library materials would require a fourfold increase in current expenditures in our major cities.

The explosion of knowledge and the rapid revision of curriculums in the schools has created new demands for school textbooks. The obsolete text can suffocate the learning process. Yet the cost of purchasing textbooks at increasing prices puts a major obstacle in the path of education—an obstacle that can and must be eliminated.

C. Supplementary Educational Centers and Services

I recommend a program of Federal grants for supplementary education centers and services within the community.

We think of schools as places where youth learns, but our schools also need to learn.

The educational gap we face is one of *quality* as well as *quantity.*

Exciting experiments in education are underway, supported by the National Science Foundation, by the Office of Education, and other Government agencies, and by private philanthropic foundations. Many of our children have studied the "new" math. There are highly effective ways of teaching high school physics, biology, chemistry, and foreign languages.

We need to take full advantage of these and other innovations. Specialists can spark the interest of disadvantaged students. Remedial reading courses open up new vistas for slow learners. Gifted students can be brought along at a faster pace.

Yet such special educational services are not available in many communities. A limited local tax base cannot stand the expense. Most individual schools are not large enough to justify the services.

The supplementary center can provide such services as—

special courses in science, foreign languages, literature, music, and art.

programs for the physically handicapped and mentally retarded.

instruction in the sciences and humanities during the summer for economically and culturally deprived children.

special assistance after regular school hours.

common facilities that can be maintained more efficiently for a group of schools than for a single school—laboratories, libraries, auditoriums, and theaters.

a system by which gifted persons can teach part time to provide scarce talents.

a means of introducing into the school system new courses, instructional materials, and teaching practices.

a way of tapping the community's extracurricular resources for the benefit of students—museums, concert and lecture programs, and industrial laboratories.

Within each community, public and private nonprofit schools and agencies will cooperate to devise the plan and administer the program for these supplementary centers. Their services should be adapted to meet the pressing needs of each locality.

D. Regional Education Laboratories

I recommend the establishment under the Cooperative Research Act of regional educational laboratories which will undertake research, train teachers, and implement tested research findings.

I further recommend amendments to the act to—

broaden the types of research organizations now eligible for educational projects.

train educational research personnel.

provide grants for research, development of new curriculums, dissemination of information, and implementation of educational innovations.

support construction of research facilities and the purchase of research equipment.

Under auspices of the National Science Foundation, educators have worked with scientists—including Nobel laureates—to develop courses which capture the excitement of contemporary science. They have prepared totally new instructional materials—laboratory equipment, textbooks, teachers' guides, films, supplementary reading, and examinations. After testing, they are made available to public and private schools.

We need to extend our research and development to history, literature, and economics; to art and music; to reading, writing, and speaking; to occupational, vocational, and technical education. We need to extend it to all stages of learning—preschool, elementary and secondary schools, college and graduate training.

Regional laboratories for education offer great promise. They draw equally upon educators and the practitioners in all fields of learning—mathematics, scientists, social scientists, linguists, musicians, artists, and writers. They help both to improve curriculums and to train teachers.

E. Strengthening State Educational Agencies

I recommend a program of grants to State educational agencies.

State leadership becomes increasingly important as we seek to improve the quality of elementary and secondary education.

We should assist the States by strengthening State departments of education in their efforts to—

Provide consultative and technical assistance for local school districts and local school leadership.

Formulate long-range plans.

Expand educational research and development.

Improve local and State information about education.

Identify emerging educational problems.

Provide for the training of State and local education personnel.

Conduct periodic evaluation of educational programs.

Promote teacher improvement courses.

. . .

These new programs will substantially augment community resources in the war against poverty. As provided by sections 611 and 612 of the Economic Opportunity Act of 1964, I will see that the new efforts are kept in step with our other antipoverty efforts.

In those localities where the community has undertaken a community action program under the Economic Opportunity Act, the community agency should participate in the planning of these new educational programs and in their coordination with ongoing and developing antipoverty efforts.

. . .

Enactment of these proposals for elementary and secondary education is of utmost urgency. I urge early and favorable consideration by the Congress.

III. HIGHER EDUCATION

Higher education is no longer a luxury, but a necessity.

Programs enacted by Congress in the past have contributed greatly to strengthening our colleges and universities. These will be carried forward under my 1966 budget, which includes—

An additional $179 million to assist construction of college classrooms, libraries, and laboratories.

An additional $25 million for 4,500 more graduate fellowships to overcome college teaching shortages.

An additional $110 million to further basic research in the universities, to provide science fellowships, and to promote science education.

But we need to do more:

To extend the opportunity for higher education more broadly among lower and middle income families.

To help small and less well developed colleges improve their programs.

To enrich the library resources of colleges and universities.

To draw upon the unique and invaluable resources of our great universities to deal with national problems of poverty and community development.

A. Assistance to Students

1. *Scholarships.—*

I recommend a program of scholarships for needy and qualified high school graduates to enable them to enter and to continue in college.

Loans authorized by the National Defense Education Act currently assist nearly 300,000 college students. Still the following conditions exist:

Each year an estimated 100,000 young people of demonstrated ability fail to go on to college because of lack of money. Many thousands more from low-income families must borrow heavily to meet college costs.

Only one out of three young people from *low*-income families attend college compared with four out of five from *high*-income families.

For many young people from poor families loans are not enough to open the way to higher education.

Under this program, a special effort will be made to identify needy students of promise early in their high school careers. The scholarship will serve as a building block, to be augmented by work-study and other support, so that the needy student can chart his own course in higher studies.

My 1966 budget provides sufficient funds for grants to help up to 140,000 students in the first year.

2. *Expansion of work-study opportunity and guaranteed low-interest loans.—*

I recommend—

That the existing college work-study program be made available to more students and that authority for the program be transferred to the Department of Health, Education, and Welfare.

That a part of the cost of interest payments on guaranteed private loans to college students be paid by the Federal Government.

Going to college is increasingly expensive. A student must pay nearly $2,400 a year in a private college and about $1,600 in a public college. These costs may rise by one-third over the next decade.

Two aids should be extended to meet the heavy costs of college education. First, the existing work-study program should be expanded for students from low-income families and extended to students from middle-income families. Under this program the Federal Government pays 90 percent of the wages earned by students on useful projects. This will enable a student to earn on the average of $450 during a school year, and up to $500 more during the summer.

Second, many families cannot cover all of college expenses on an out-of-pocket basis. We should assure greater availability of private credit on reasonable terms and conditions: This can best be done by paying part of interest cost of guaranteed loans made by private lenders—a more effective, fairer, and far less costly way of providing assistance than the various tax credit devices which have been proposed.

B. Aid to Smaller Colleges

I recommend that legislation be enacted to strengthen less developed colleges.

Many of our smaller colleges are battling for survival. About 10 percent lack proper accreditation, and others face constantly the threat of losing accreditation. Many are isolated from the main currents of academic life.

Private sources and States alone cannot carry the whole burden of doing what must be done for these important units in our total educational system. Federal aid is essential.

Universities should be encouraged to enter into cooperative relationships to help less developed colleges, including such assistance as—

A program of faculty exchanges.

Special programs to enable faculty members of small colleges to renew and extend knowledge of their fields.

A national fellowship program to encourage highly qualified young graduate students and instructors in large universities to augment the teaching resources of small colleges.

The development of joint programs to make more efficient use of available facilities and faculty.

In union there is strength. This is the basic premise of my recommendation.

C. More Support for College Library Resources

I recommend enactment of legislation for purchase of books and library materials to strengthen college teaching and research.

Fifty percent of our 4-year institutions and 82 percent of our 2-year institutions fall below accepted professional standards in the number of volumes possessed.

As student enrollment mounts, we must look not only to the physical growth of our colleges and universities. They must be developed as true centers of intellectual activity. To construct a library building is meaningless unless there are books to bring life to the library.

D. University-Community Extension Program

I recommend a program of grants to support university extension concentrating on problems of the community.

Institutions of higher learning are being called on ever more frequently for public service—for defense research, foreign development, and countless other programs. They have performed magnificently. We must now call upon them to meet new needs.

Once 90 percent of our population earned its living from the land. A wise Congress enacted the Morrill Act of 1862 and the Hatch Act of 1887 which helped the State universities help the American people. With the aid of the land-grant colleges, American agriculture produced overwhelming abundance.

Today, 70 percent of our people live in urban communities. They are confronted by problems of poverty, residential blight, polluted air and water, inadequate mass transportation and health services, strained human relations, and overburdened municipal services.

Our great universities have the skills and knowledge to match these mountainous problems. They can offer expert guidance in community planning; research and development in pressing educational problems; economic and job market studies; continuing education of the community's professional and business leadership; and programs for the disadvantaged.

The role of the university must extend far beyond the ordinary extension-type operation. Its research findings and talents must be made available to the community. Faculty must be called upon for consulting activities. Pilot projects, seminars, conferences, TV programs, and task forces drawing on many departments of the university —all should be brought into play.

This is a demanding assignment for the universities, and many are not now ready for it. The time has come for us to help the university to face problems of the city as it once faced problems of the farm.

E. Special Manpower Needs

We must also ask the colleges and universities to help overcome certain acute deficiencies in trained manpower. At least 100,000 more professional librarians are needed for service in public libraries and in schools and colleges. We need 140,000 more teachers for handicapped children.

I recommend:

Grants to institutions of higher education for training of school, college, and community librarians and related services.

Extension and expansion of grants for training teachers and handicapped children.

CONCLUSION

In 1838, Mirabeau B. Lamar, the second President of the Republic of Texas and the father of Texas education, declared: "The cultivated mind is the guardian genius of democracy. It is the only dictator that freeman acknowledges. It is the only security that freeman desires."

Throughout the history of our Nation, the United States has recognized this truth. But during the periods when the country has been most astir with creative activity, when it most keenly sensed the sturdiness of the old reaching out for the vigor of the new, it has given special attention to its educational system.

This was true in the expansive 1820's and 1830's, when the American people acted decisively to build a public school system for the lower grades. It was no less true at the vigorous turn of the 20th century, when high schools were developed for the millions. Again, during the questing 1930's, fresh ideas stirred the traditions of the ruler and blackboard.

We are now embarked on another venture to put the American dream to work in meeting the new demands of a new day. Once again we must start where men who would improve their society have always known they must begin—with an educational system restudied, rein-forced, and revitalized.

LYNDON B. JOHNSON.

THE WHITE HOUSE, *January 12, 1965.*

NATIONAL FOUNDATION ON THE ARTS AND THE HUMANITIES ACT OF 1965

Included here is a summary of S. 1483 as it was cleared for the President after having been passed by both the House and Senate in September, 1965.

S. 1483 would establish a National Foundation on the Arts and the Humanities, for the purpose of developing and promoting a national policy of support for the humanities and the arts.

Its organization is shown in the following chart:

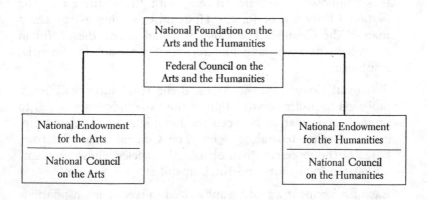

The National Endowment for the Arts would provide matching grants to nonprofit organizations, to state and other public organizations, and to individuals engaged in the creative and per-forming arts for artistic activity, including construction of neces-sary facilities. Special grants would be earmarked for states to support state organizations which have a parallel function. A $25,000 grant to states having no arts council would be authorized for the purpose of establishing arts councils.

The National Council on the Arts, established in 1964, would be transferred to the National Endowment for the Arts. The chairman of the Council would be the chairman of the National Endowment. The Council, composed of private citizens, would advise the chairman on policies and programs and review applications for financial assistance.

The National Endowment for the Humanities would provide nonmatching grants and loans for research, award fellowships and grants to institutions or individuals for training, support publication of scholarly works, provide for the interchange of information, and foster understanding and appreciation of the humanities.

S. 1483 would also establish a National Council on the Humanities composed of private citizens, with the chairman of the National Endowment for the Humanities serving as the chairman of the Council. The Council would advise the chairman on policies and programs and review applications for financial assistance.

A Federal Council on the Arts and the Humanities will be established to insure coordination of the two Endowments and to promote coordination between the Foundation and related programs of other federal agencies. The Council would be composed of the representatives of federal agencies whose programs are related to the arts and the humanities.

Each Endowment would be authorized to receive appropriations of $5 million for fiscal year 1966 and for each of 2 succeeding fiscal years.

Additional sums would be authorized to match total amounts donated to each endowment.

For fiscal year 1966, and for each of 2 succeeding years, the Office of Education would be authorized to receive $500,000 for payments to state and local educational agencies, and for loans to private elementary and secondary schools, for the acquisition of equipment and minor remodeling related to the arts and humanities; and $500,000 to be used for training institutes to strengthen the teaching of the humanities and the arts in elementary and secondary schools.

Maximum appropriations authorized for each of the first 3 fiscal years under this bill would be $21 million per annum.

DISCUSSION QUESTIONS

1. Why has general aid to education failed in passing Congress?
2. What distinction, if any, do you see between the terms "federal support" and "federal aid"?
3. What solutions are the most likely to succeed in the Church and State impasse?
4. What title would you have given the last chapter of this book?
5. Discuss the quotation: "The child is not the mere creature of the state."
6. List five predictions regarding the role the federal government may assume vis-à-vis education.
7. What title would you give this book?
8. What do you consider the ideal role for the federal government in education?
9. What are some of the unresolved questions or issues relevant to federal aid to education?
10. Is it possible to equalize educational opportunity?
11. If we were to have a national board of education, how should it be organized and what should be its purpose?
12. Do you see any value in aiding specific subject areas rather than giving flat grants of unspecified aid?
13. Compare the Education Messages of John F. Kennedy and Lyndon B. Johnson.
14. Do you believe federal aid to education will increase in the future?
15. Have the arguments regarding federal aid to education changed over the years? How?
16. Which arguments have changed more—those favoring or those opposing federal aid to education?
17. Is the question of aid to private and parochial schools one of constitutionality or public policy?
18. Why is federal aid to education considered only during periods of national stress?
19. Which federal aid measures do you consider the most significant? Why?

20. Which arguments on either side have the most validity? Why?
21. Do you agree with the following statement: "It is no longer a question of whether there should be aid or not."?
22. Have Supreme Court decisions relevant to aid for private and parochial schools affected decision-making in this area?
23. What types of court cases can you imagine being brought before the Supreme Court in the future?
24. Do you think the Supreme Court is serving as a National School Board?
25. Should we have a national system of education? What would be the advantages?

BIBLIOGRAPHY

1. Allen, Hollis P. *The Federal Government and Education*. New York: McGraw-Hill, 1950.
2. American Assembly. *The Federal Government and Higher Education*. Englewood Cliffs, New Jersey: Prentice-Hall, 1960.
3. Babbidge, Homer D., Jr. and Robert M. Rosenzweig. *The Federal Interest in Higher Education*. New York: McGraw-Hill, 1962.
4. Benson, Charles S. *The Economics of Public Education*. Boston: Houghton Mifflin, 1961.
5. Blanshard, Paul. *Religion and the Schools: The Great Controversy*. Boston: Beacon Press, 1963.
6. Blum, Virgil C. *Freedom of Choice in Education*. New York: Macmillan, 1958.
7. Boles, Donald. *The Bible, Religion, and the Public Schools*. Ames, Iowa: Iowa State University Press, 1961.
8. Brickman, William W. "College and University, 1862–1962." *School and Society*. 90:213–4.
9. Brickman, William W. and Stanley Lehrer, eds. *Religion, Government, and Education*. New York: Society for the Advancement of Education, 1961.
10. Buehler, Ezra C. *Federal Aid for Education*. New York: Noble, 1934.
11. Butts, R. Freeman. *The American Tradition in Religion and Education*. Boston: Beacon Press, 1950.
12. Butts, R. Freeman. "Public Funds for Parochial Schools? *No!*" *Teachers College Record*. 62:57–62.
13. Chamber of Commerce of the U. S. *Statement of the Chamber of Commerce of the U. S. on H.W. 3000*. Unpublished report. March 8, 1963.
14. Committee for Economic Development. *Paying for Better Public Schools*. New York: Commission for Economic Development, 1960.

15. Conant, James B. *Shaping Educational Policy*. New York: Mc-Graw-Hill, 1964.
16. Congressional Quarterly. *Federal Aid to Education*. Washington, D. C.: Government Printing Office, 1961.
17. Cubberley, Ellwood P. *Public Education in the United States*. Boston: Houghton Mifflin, 1947.
18. Cubberley, Ellwood P. *State School Administration*. Boston: Houghton Mifflin, 1927.
19. Drinan, Robert F. *Religion, the Court and Public Policy*. New York: McGraw-Hill, 1963.
20. Drucker, Peter F. "American Directions: A Forecast." *Harper's*, February 1965.
21. Educational Policies Commission. *National Policy and the Financing of the Public Schools*. Washington, D. C.: The Commission, 1959.
22. Ehlers, Henry and Gordon C. Lee. *Crucial Issues in Education*. New York: Holt, Rinehart, & Winston, 1964.
23. Fellman, David, ed. *The Supreme Court and Education*. New York: Teachers College, Columbia University Bureau of Publications, 1960.
24. Freeman, Roger A. *Federal Aid to Education, Boon or Bane?* Washington, D. C.: American Enterprise Association, 1955.
25. Freeman, Roger A. *School Needs in the Decade Ahead*. Washington, D.C.: Institute for Social Science Research, 1958.
26. Friedmann, Milton. "The Role of Government in Education." in: Solo, Robert A., ed. *Economics and the Public Interest*. New Brunswick, New Jersey: Rutgers University Press, 1955.
27. Frost, S. E., Jr. *American Education*. Garden City, New York: Doubleday, 1962.
28. Goldwater, Barry. "Historic and Current Federal Role in Education." *Congressional Record*: Speech, Sept. 23, 1961.
29. Gruber, Frederick C., ed. *Education and the State*. Philadelphia: University of Pennsylvania Press, 1960.
30. Hamilton, Robert R. *Selected Legal Problems in Providing Federal Aid for Education*. Washington, D.C.: Government Printing Office, 1938.
31. Harris, Seymour E. *How Shall We Pay for Education?* New York: Harper, 1948.
32. Harris, Seymour E. *More Resources for Education*. New York: Harper, 1960.

33. Humphrey, Hubert. "The Federal Government's Role in Support of Education." *Phi Delta Kappan*, 41:297.

34. Johns, R. L. and E. L. Morphet. *Financing the Public Schools.* Englewood Cliffs, New Jersey: Prentice-Hall, 1960.

35. Kerwin, Jerome G. *Catholic Viewpoint on Church and State.* New York: Hanover House, 1960.

36. Knight, Douglas M., ed. *The Federal Government and Higher Education.* Englewood Cliffs, New Jersey: Prentice-Hall, 1960.

37. LaNoue, George R. *Public Funds for Parochial Schools?* New York: National Council of the Churches of Christ in the U.S.A., 1963.

38. LaNoue, George R. "Religious Schools and 'Secular' Subjects." *Harvard Educational Review.* 32:255-291. Summer, 1962.

39. Lee, Gordon C. *The Struggle for Federal Aid.* New York: Teachers College, Columbia University Bureau of Publications, 1949.

40. Lipset, Seymour M. *Political Man.* New York: Doubleday, 1960.

41. Massachusetts (Colony). *Records of the Governor and Company of the Massachusetts Bay in New England.* Boston: William White, 1893.

42. McCluskey, Neil G. *Catholic Viewpoint in Education.* Garden City, New York: Doubleday, 1959.

43. McCluskey, Neil G. "Public Funds for Parochial Schools? *Yes!*" *Teachers College Record.* 62:49-56.

44. Morse, Wayne E. "Federal Support for Education: Now and in the Future." Speech, April 5, 1964.

45. Mort, Paul R. *Federal Support for Public Education.* New York: Teachers College, Columbia University Bureau of Publications, 1936.

46. Munger, Frank J. and Richard F. Fenno, Jr. *National Politics and Federal Aid to Education.* Syracuse, New York: Syracuse University Press, 1962.

47. National Advisory Commission on Education. *Federal Relation to Education.* Washington, D.C.: The Commission, 1930.

48. National Citizens Commission for the Public Schools. *How Do We Pay For Our Schools?* New York: The Commission, 1954.

49. National Education Association. *Federal Support of Education. Questions and Answers.* Washington, D.C.: The Association, n.d.

50. National Education Association. "The Folklore of Local Control." *National Education Association Journal.* December, 1961, p. 43.

51. National Education Association. *Handbook: Federal Aid for Education*. Washington, D.C.: The Association, 1944.
52. National Education Association. *Research Bulletin*. Washington, D.C.: The Association. 36:4:99–100.
53. National Education Association. "Statistics." Mimeographed release, December, 1961.
54. National Education Association. "Testimony in Elementary and Secondary Act of 1965." Mimeographed release, January 1965.
55. National Education Association. Division of Federal Relations. *Washington Outlook on Education*. Washington, D.C.: The Association. XI:5:1, July 15, 1964.
56. National Education Association. Legislative Commission. *Federal Legislative Policy*. Washington, D.C.: The Association, n.d.
57. O'Neill, James M. *Religion and Education under the Constitution*. New York: Harper, 1949.
58. Padover, Saul K. *The Complete Jefferson*. New York: Duell, Sloan and Pearce, 1943.
59. Pfeffer, Leo. *Church, State and Freedom*. Boston: Beacon Press, 1953.
60. Pierce, Truman M. *Federal, State, and Local Government in Education*. Washington, D.C.: Center for Applied Research in Education Institute, 1964.
61. Quattlebaum, Charles A. *Federal Aid to Elementary and Secondary Education*. Chicago: Public Administration Service, 1948.
62. Rivlin, Alice M. *The Role of the Federal Government in Financing Higher Education*. Washington, D.C.: Brookings Institution, 1961.
63. Ross, Earle D. "Contributions of Land-Grant Colleges and Universities to Higher Education." *School and Society*. 90:232. May 5, 1962.
64. Ruml, Beardsley. *Financing the Public Schools*. New York: National Citizens Commission for the Public Schools, 1954.
65. *Saturday Review*. "The Magnitude of the American Educational Establishment." *Saturday Review*. November 21, 1964.
66. Serdner, F. J. *Federal Support for Education; The Situation Today*, 1959. Washington, D.C.: Public Affairs Institute, 1959.
67. Tussman, Joseph, ed. *The Supreme Court on Church and State*. New York: Oxford University Press, 1962.
68. United States Commissioner of Education. *Eleventh Annual Re-*

port: Administration of Public Laws 874 and 815. Washington, D.C.: Government Printing Office, 1962.

69. United States Commission on Intergovernmental Relations. "A Report to the President." Washington, D.C.: U. S. Government Printing Office, 1955.

70. United States Commission on Intergovernmental Relations. *Twenty-five Federal Grant-in-Aid Programs.* Washington, D.C.: U. S. Government Printing Office, 1955.

71. United States Department of Health, Education, and Welfare. Office of Education. *Digest of Educational Statistics.* Washington, D.C.: U. S. Government Printing Office, 1964.

72. United States Department of Health, Education, and Welfare. Office of Education. *Health, Education, and Welfare Trends.* Washington, D.C.: U. S. Government Printing Office, 1963.

73. United States Department of Health, Education, and Welfare. Office of Education. *Interesting Statistics.* Washington, D.C.: Press Release, August 31, 1964.

74. United States Department of Health, Education, and Welfare. Office of Education. *Milestones in Education.* Washington, D.C.: U. S. Government Printing Office, 1964.

75. United States Department of Health, Education, and Welfare. Office of Education. "National Defense Act." *School Life.* 46:12.

76. United States Department of Health, Education, and Welfare. Office of Education. *1963: Year of Legislative Achievements.* Washington, D.C.: U. S. Government Printing Office, 1963.

77. United States Government. *Public Laws 815 and 874.* Washington, D.C.: U. S. Government Printing Office, 1959.

78. United States House of Representatives. Committee on Education and Labor. *The Federal Government and Education.* Washington, D.C.: U. S. Government Printing Office, 1961.

79. United States Senate. Committee on Labor and Public Welfare. *Constitutionality of Federal Aid to Education in Its Various Aspects.* Washington, D.C.: U. S. Government Printing Office, 1961.

80. United States Senate. Committee on Labor and Public Welfare. *Education Legislation 1963.* Washington, D.C.: U. S. Government Printing Office, 1963.

81. United States Senate. Committee on Labor and Public Welfare. *Enactments by the 88th Congress Concerning Education and Training.* Washington, D.C.: U. S. Government Printing Office, 1964.

82. United States Senate. Committee on Labor and Public Welfare. *Federal Legislation Concerning Education and Training.* Washington, D.C.: U. S. Government Printing Office, 1962.
83. United States Senate. Committee on Labor and Public Welfare. *National Education Improvement Act of 1963.* Washington, D.C.: U. S. Government Printing Office, 1963.
84. United States Senate. Committee on Labor and Public Welfare. *Proposed Federal Aid for Education: A Collection of Pro and Con Excerpts and a Bibliography.* Washington, D.C.: U. S. Government Printing Office, 1961.
85. United States Senate. Committee on Labor and Public Welfare. *Proposed Federal Promotion of "Shared Time" Education.* Washington, D. C.: U. S. Government Printing Office, 1963.
86. United States Senate. Committee on Labor and Public Welfare. *The War on Poverty: The Economic Opportunity Act of 1964.* Washington, D.C.: U. S. Government Printing Office, 1964.
87. United States Supreme Court. *Supreme Court of the U.S.: Opinion 1963.* Washington, D.C.: U. S. Government Printing Office, 1963.

INDEX

237